W9-BOA-810

WITHDRAWN

POSITIVELY AMERICAN

POSITIVELY

AMERICAN

WINNING BACK THE MIDDLE-CLASS
MAJORITY ONE FAMILY AT A TIME

POLO PUBLIC LIBRARY DISTRICT
302 W. MASON ST.
POLO, IL 61064

SENATOR CHUCK SCHUMER
with Daniel Squadron

RODALE

Notice

Mention of specific companies, organizations, or authorities in this book does not imply endorsement by the author or publisher, nor does mention of specific companies, organizations, or authorities imply that they endorse this book, its author, or the publisher.

Internet addresses and telephone numbers given in this book were accurate at the time it went to press.

© 2007 by Charles E. Schumer

All rights reserved..No part of this publication may be reproduced or transmitted in any form or by any means, electronic or mechanical, including photocopying, recording, or any other information storage and retrieval system, without the written permission of the publisher.

Rodale books may be purchased for business or promotional use or for special sales. For information, please write to:

Special Markets Department, Rodale Inc., 733 Third Avenue, New York, NY 10017

Printed in the United States of America

Rodale Inc. makes every effort to use acid-free ⊖, recycled paper ♻.

Book design by Christina Gaugler

Library of Congress Cataloging-in-Publication Data is on file with the publisher

ISBN-13 978–1–59486–572–5   hardcover
ISBN-10 1–59486–572–8   hardcover

Distributed to the trade by Holtzbrinck Publishers

2   4   6   8   10   9   7   5   3   1   hardcover

LIVE YOUR WHOLE LIFE™

We inspire and enable people to improve their lives and the world around them

For more of our products visit **rodalestore.com** or call 800-848-4735

This book is for my parents,
Abe and Selma Schumer,
to whom I owe everything
and with whom I originally met the Baileys

THE 50% SOLUTION

INCREASE READING AND MATH SCORES BY 50%

☆ Triple federal education spending to an average of $2,800 per student.

☆ Assess schools on one consistent federal standard.

☆ After four years, make increased federal dollars dependent on achievement and fund schools that are subpar only if they enact prescribed requirements and programs.

☆ Offer federal salary stipends directly to highly qualified math and science teachers.

REDUCE PROPERTY TAXES THAT FUND EDUCATION BY 50%

☆ Encourage localities to cut property taxes that fund education by 50% over ten years by freezing them now.

☆ If unforeseen circumstances arise, restore the highest-income tax bracket to mid-1990s levels before taking away the property tax reduction.

INCREASE THE NUMBER OF COLLEGE GRADUATES BY 50%

☆ Make up to $15,000 of tuition per child per year tax deductible for families making less than $150,000 a year.

☆ Give colleges and universities incentives to keep tuition hikes at or below the rate of inflation.

☆ Restore Pell Grants and federal loans to late-1990s levels, and peg future increases to the average cost of college, so *everyone* has a chance.

REDUCE ILLEGAL IMMIGRATION BY AT LEAST 50% AND INCREASE LEGAL IMMIGRATION BY UP TO 50%

☆ Establish real enforcement measures against employers that hire illegal immigrants.

☆ Create a biometric employment card.

☆ Offer a fair path to earned citizenship for those who are here.

☆ Increase the number of green cards granted a year to make up for the reduction in illegal immigration.

☆ Rationalize legal immigration to fill high-needs jobs, retain those who are educated here, increase geographic, economic and educational diversity and promote family reunification.

REDUCE OUR DEPENDENCE ON FOREIGN OIL BY 50%

☆ Short-term: Increase conservation *and* fossil fuel-production.

Double CAFE standards.

Drill in most of the eastern Gulf of Mexico.

Encourage exploration on certain leased federal lands.

Make existing power generation more efficient.

Expand Energy Star to include construction. Make it a requirement for all federal projects.

☆ Long-term: End dependence on fossil fuels.

Give $10 billion a year and broad powers to a new agency to design a fossil fuel–free solution within three years and implement it over the following seven.

REDUCE CANCER MORTALITY BY 50%

☆ Guarantee early-detection screenings for high-risk cancers for all Americans by requiring insurers to cover screenings and providing federal government coverage for the uninsured.

(continued)

☆ Fully fund all National Cancer Institute–approved research grants.

☆ Increase research funding for new genetically based "personalized medicine."

☆ Build world-class cancer centers in the nation's top fifty population centers.

☆ Fight smoking by encouraging reduced insurance rates for nonsmokers and increasing insurance coverage of smoking cessation programs.

☆ Create a new C-DOTS program to help cancer centers electronically share information nationwide.

REDUCE CHILDHOOD OBESITY BY 50%

☆ Add a Surgeon General's warning to junk-food marketing and packaging.

☆ Tax fast-food advertising to fund a national ad campaign to combat childhood obesity.

☆ Require chain restaurants to list caloric information on menus.

☆ Teach good health in school.

☆ Make school food and school vending machines lean and healthy.

☆ Get junk food out of the food stamp program.

☆ Help localities and schools encourage kids to exercise.

REDUCE ABORTIONS BY 50%

☆ Ensure real and age-appropriate sex education in public schools, including education on abstinence and contraception.

☆ Make contraceptives more available.

☆ Increase funding for federal family planning programs (Title X).

☆ Create a national media campaign to reduce unwanted pregnancies.

CUT CHILDREN'S ACCESS TO INTERNET PORNOGRAPHY BY AT LEAST 50%

☆ Hold credit card and other payment processing companies accountable for secure age verification for adult Web sites.

☆ Impose a 25% tax on pornographic sites to fund real enforcement of age verification and CAN-SPAM.

☆ Create a Schumer Box for all cell phone and electronic media player contracts.

REDUCE TAX EVASION AND AVOIDANCE BY 50%

☆ Restore enforcement levels for high earners and corporations.

☆ Withhold 10% of dividend and capital gains income.

☆ Increase compliance among sole proprietors and the self-employed.

☆ Crack down on illegal corporate tax shelters.

☆ Require corporations to report profits consistently.

INCREASE OUR ABILITY TO FIGHT TERRORISM BY 50%

☆ Strengthen international alliances.

☆ Expand Special Forces.

☆ Increase "humint" capacity.

☆ Create an effective international force to stabilize hot spots.

☆ Secure ports, borders and skies and prevent, bio-, nuclear and chemical terrorism.

CONTENTS

TO THE READER

AS THE TITLE suggests, this book is about creating a positive message—and delivering results—for middle-class Americans. The first section introduces a middle-class family, albeit an imagined composite, that has been by my side throughout my political life, and describes why they are so important to me, to the Democratic Party and to the country. The second section presents eleven goals, to be achieved within ten years, that are inspired by this family and would make their lives better. I believe these ideas could form the basis of a platform that will create a lasting Democratic majority in 2008 and beyond.

A couple of brief points of clarification before I begin.

The first is critical. This book is not about the Democratic Party turning away from its longstanding base of constituents; it is about expanding the party to include new ones. Under Karl Rove and George Bush, the Republican Party's strategy has been to excite the base and convince a few independents to join up—they want to govern at 51%. The goal of this book is different. I would like the base of the Democratic Party to expand so we can govern at 60% or 65%. The goals in Part 2 are not a repudiation of the issues that Democrats have advocated for a generation, they are in addition to them. I believe that we must expand Democratic goals *and* continue to fight for issues like affirmative action, a fair minimum wage and the viability of Social Security, Medicare and Medicaid. As you read, please always keep one thought in the front of your mind: The Democratic Party should not focus on the middle class exclusively, but it must include them.

Second, I'm not trying to move the Democratic Party to the left, right or center. Some of the thoughts and goals in the book could be called quite liberal; some are undeniably conservative. I believe that most, if not all, could be welcomed by both the moderate and liberal wings of the Democratic Party. This isn't triangulation; it's a straight line, heading in one direction—toward the middle class and those struggling to make it there (as my old protégé Congressman Anthony Weiner has put it so well).

Finally, I don't carry a tape recorder everywhere I go. Nor do I keep a diary. I never have. In putting the book together, I relied heavily on my memory and, in isolated instances, took slight literary license to more fully describe a story. As a result, this is by no means a journalistic enterprise. Still, I have reconstructed the timing and specifics of events as well I can; many apologies to any who feel that my recollection and theirs are not in accord.

Chuck Schumer

Chuck Schumer
Brooklyn, November 2006

PART 1

MEET THE BAILEYS

CHAPTER 1

VICTORY?

ELECTION DAY IS TORTURE. You've finished crafting the message, cutting the ads, knocking on doors and reading the polls. Everything that you can do is done. But everything that really matters is yet to happen.

It's all over, as they say, but the voting.

On election night 2006, I was in a suite on the eleventh floor of the Hyatt Regency Washington on Capitol Hill with a small group of staff, friends and family. While we waited, I paced the room and picked at cold calamari and oversized cookies. Having nothing to do brings out the worst in me—I get antsy, irritable and hungry.

I was not on any ballot this year. But the election was as personally important to me as any I'd ever lived through. I was the senator in charge of the Democratic Senatorial Campaign Committee (DSCC), the political organization responsible for all the Democratic Senate races. Two years earlier, I had taken the job because I worried that if we lost three more Senate seats, beyond the forty-five that we held, there would be no check on the Bush administration's policies, which were doing so much damage to the country I love. For two years, I had been obsessed with preparing for this election. I had recruited candidates. I had raised money. I had approved senior staffs. And I had become friends with many of the Senate hopefuls whose fates were being decided on that night.

Now, waiting for the first returns—the polls had closed in Virginia and Ohio less than an hour earlier—I knew that Democrats were, amazingly enough, on the edge of actually taking back the Senate majority. To do it, we had to pick up six of eight vulnerable Republican seats and hold on to every Democratic seat, including six tough ones. Supposedly, during a card game on Air Force One a few weeks before election day, President Bush had said that for Democrats to take back the Senate, "Schumer would need to pull an inside straight."

I was still waiting to see the cards.

For the four hundredth time that day, I called J. B. Poersch, executive director of the DSCC, for an update on the exit polls—voter information gathered on behalf of the networks and craved by campaign staffs, which are ravenous for any morsel of data.

"How's it look?" I asked as he picked up before it even rang.

"Mostly good."

"How about the big four?" These were four close states—Missouri, Montana, Tennessee and Virginia—where we would need three wins.

"Missouri's okay. Montana's tighter." In Missouri, we had Claire McCaskill, the popular state treasurer who had almost won the governorship two years earlier. In Montana, Jon Tester, a lifelong farmer with a quarter-inch crew cut and a keg for a belly, was our candidate. Both were trying to unseat Republican incumbents.

"Tennessee?"

"Not so good."

"Virginia?"

"The first precincts are reporting."

"And?"

"I don't know."

Suddenly, every BlackBerry in the room was buzzing.

"Chuck!" three aides yelled at once. "They're calling Ohio for Brown!"

Phil Singer, the DSCC's communications director—and the best in the business—came running into the room. "They're calling Ohio—"

"I know."

A staffer handed me a cell phone. "Sherrod Brown," she mouthed.

"Call you back, J.B." I said, pulling one phone from my right ear and putting another to my left. "Sherrod! You ran a great race! See you in the Senate." Sherrod Brown had beaten incumbent Mike DeWine by running an energetic populist campaign in Ohio—a state that, two years after making the difference for Bush, had turned bluer than a clear sky.

One down. Five to go.

Again, the room erupted in BlackBerry buzz.

"Chuck," everyone yelled, "they're calling . . . " Voices were lost in a jumble.

"Pennsylvania for Casey!" screamed half the room.

"And New Jersey for Menendez!" screamed the other half.

Bob Casey, pro-life and pro-gun, had unified the Pennsylvania Democratic Party and trounced the ultra-conservative Senator Rick Santorum. Bob Menendez, who had been appointed to his seat by New Jersey Governor Jon Corzine less than a year earlier, had overcome a barrage of nasty attacks to notch a solid win. They represented one pickup, in Pennsylvania, and one save, in New Jersey.

A minute later, two cell phones were thrust at me. "Bob!" I cheered. "Congratulations!"

Two down, four to go.

On the other side of the hotel room, an aide was monitoring Virginia's official returns on the Web between writing lines for that night's speech. I leaned over his shoulder. "How's Virginia?"

"Webb's down eight thousand. But less than half of precincts are in."

I looked at my watch—a little past eight. It was going to be a long night. The last time I had lived through an election night this long was during my first campaign, for the New York State Assembly, when I was twenty-three years old.

In 1974, I graduated from Harvard Law School. After the ceremony, as my parents drove me back to Brooklyn, I broke the news to them: I wasn't going to accept the job as an associate at the prestigious Manhattan law firm of Paul, Weiss, Rifkind, Wharton and Garrison for $400 a week—which, to us at least, seemed an enormous sum. Instead, I was going to run for the Assembly, right in the district where I grew up.

The Forty-Fifth Assembly District covered a row of middle-class neighborhoods extending from the Atlantic Ocean straight up into southern Brooklyn—Brighton Beach, Sheepshead Bay, Midwood and Kings Highway, where I was raised. My parents didn't want me to run. They had struggled to send me to college and hoped more than anything that I would earn a "comfortable living." My mother kept telling me to give up the silly dream of being a politician and accept my fate as a corporate lawyer—something secure and respectable.

I would have none of it. My mind was set on elective office. After seven years at Harvard, I wanted to come home to Brooklyn and go into public service. There was no point in arguing; I was sure I wanted to serve my neighborhood as an elected official. I may only have been twenty-three years old, but the seeds that led to my decision had been planted many years earlier.

In 1964, when I was fourteen, I had to get a summer job. I ran a mimeograph machine for a Madison High School teacher who had come up with a new idea for a small business: He would prepare students for the SATs. The teacher's name was Stanley Kaplan and the company was Kaplan, Inc. Less than twenty years after I graduated from Madison, he became a multimillionaire when he sold his business to the Washington Post Company. God bless America!

By nine each morning during that summer, I would be at Kaplan's place, in a windowless three-foot-by-three-foot room that reeked of ink and ozone, running the mimeo machines. Around 9:05, I'd be going gangbusters; at 9:10, I'd check my watch. I'd check again at 9:15, 9:20, 9:30—by a quarter of ten I'd be sure it was four in the afternoon.

By ten, I'd be out of my mind with boredom, thinking of all my friends at the beach, playing basketball and trying to pick up girls. I didn't know how I would survive until the end of the day, much less for the whole summer. All day, every day, from ten o'clock until the end of work, I swore to myself that I would never choose a career where I'd be bored.

After Madison, I got into Harvard (in part because of those endless hours spent staring at SAT prep material spinning around the mimeo drum). In those days very few people from places like Madison went to Harvard. Sixty percent of the freshman class were from private schools, most of the rest were from wealthy suburban school districts. I was scared—how would I fit in? The one Madison guy who had gone to Harvard ahead of me suggested that I try out for the freshman basketball team: I'd make the team because they were lousy, and I'd make friends. It was to be a social, not an athletic, endeavor.

So I went to tryouts. We each had little numbers clipped to our T-shirts as we waited in the Harvard gym.

"Number twenty-seven!" the coach called.

"Yes, sir," I answered.

"You're Schumer?"

"Yes, sir."

"You went to Madison?"

"Yes, sir."

"You play forward?"

"Yes, sir."

"How tall you are?

"Six-one, sir."

"Can you dribble?"

"Not very well, sir."

"Go home."

He moved on to the next kid without seeing me touch a single basketball.

I went back to my dorm room without having made a single friend. I sat down to write a letter to my parents. I told them I was already a flop here at Harvard; I should have gone to Brooklyn College.

That night someone from the Harvard Young Democrats knocked on my door. "How would you like to work on the presidential campaign of Senator Eugene McCarthy?"

I didn't have a political bone in my body. "Why not?" I sighed, throwing up my hands. "Who's Senator Eugene McCarthy?"

I spent much of the next several months in New Hampshire, knocking on doors for the McCarthy campaign. It was the most exhilarating feeling I had ever experienced: being part of this group, students and others who had never thought they had any power, all working together to stop a war that was unjust and defeat President Lyndon Baines Johnson, the most powerful man on earth.

Almost immediately, I caught the bug. To me, politics was the place where ideas and people met. I was elated to discover that it was possible to do good in the world—that a group of ragtag amateurs, fueled by students upset over the war, could truly change the course of history. The system that we had read about in textbooks really worked—you could actually make the world a better place!

By March, when McCarthy came close enough in New Hampshire to convince Johnson not to run for reelection, I had decided I wouldn't be an organic chemist, as I had planned, but would major in Social Studies and go to law school. I figured I had to be a lawyer to make a living, but politics, my true love, would be my avocation.

I was at Harvard for seven years, through undergrad and law school. I loved it. But I always identified more with Madison High School than with Harvard University. If anything, I felt closer to Brooklyn after I got to Cambridge. Up there, where there weren't that many people like me, I was the guy from Brooklyn. And that felt right. While I relished the intellectual challenges at school, I quickly realized that I was more at home, at home.

I had grown up in a middle-class household in a middle-class neighborhood. My father was an exterminator, my mother volunteered in the community. My block, East Twenty-Seventh Street, was a mixture of firefighters and cops, salesmen and teachers, small businessmen and homemakers. We were first-, second- and third-generation Irish, Italian and Jewish immigrants. My parents and my friends' parents worked hard. They cared for their families. They were honest, patriotic, decent and, all too often, under enormous strain. Life was good, but it was also tough.

As I was growing up, the government was distant from our daily lives, but we knew it was always there, behind the scenes. It was like a benevolent patriarch watching over us, protecting us from a distance; it was there when things went wrong. It provided security—for retirement, for safety, for health. And it represented a positive, moral force. When it became clear, in the aftermath of the Tet Offensive, that President Johnson had lied to the American people, I was depressed for two weeks. We were raised to have such trust in government leaders that learning they had lied for political gain was something new and absolutely devastating.

In Brooklyn, we could survive without the government, but we knew that at its best, it sure could help. Whether it was the safety offered to us kids by a caring police officer or the comfort our parents got in knowing that Social Security would be there when they retired—the government mattered and it was a good thing.

Now, after working for seven years at school and working in campaigns all over the Northeast, I wanted to be part of it. At home. Not as an avocation, as I had intially thought after that McCarthy campaign, but as my life's work—helping make things a little better for my parents, my friends' parents and all the families like them. I believed in them and wanted to serve them. To me, the life of a corporate lawyer seemed hardly different from running a mimeo; government was where I wanted to be.

Three aspects of public service swept me up in a tide that neither my parents nor I had a chance of fighting against: The excitement, which I had sought since my days in the mimeo room; the opportunity to do good, which I had experienced with the Young Democrats; and the chance to work for the people I most identified with, which is what I had craved doing while I was away at school.

My parents and I argued all the way to Brooklyn. When we got there, I stayed in the race.

My first election night, in September 1974, was probably the hardest of my career. When the polls closed, I had no idea what was going to happen—in part because my mother had told all her friends to vote against me!

Throughout my next thirty years in elective office, I was never again personally involved in a campaign in which I did not know the outcome by the time the polls closed.

Until 2006.

"How's it look?" I was on the phone with J.B. again.

"Missouri's good. Montana should be. Rhode Island's a win."

In Rhode Island, the Democratic candidate Sheldon Whitehouse was proving that even the most moderate Republican in the Senate, Lincoln Chafee, could not survive Bush's unpopularity. If Missouri, Montana and Rhode Island held, that would be three more pickups.

"Tennessee and Virginia?" We would still need one of them to take the majority.

"I don't think Ford can pull it off." Harold Ford, a moderate Democrat and a brilliant candidate, who would be the first African-

American senator elected in the South since Reconstruction. We had put everything we could into the contest, but he had been behind in polls for a couple of weeks.

"Virginia's not so good either," J.B. continued. Incumbent Republican George Allen, who only months before was considered a possible Republican presidential candidate, was holding on for dear life after a series of incidents that cast him as racially insensitive. The challenger, Jim Webb, was a former Republican and Reagan administration official who had spent his life working with the military. "It's close, but I don't think Webb can do it."

I hung up and sat down heavily on the couch. Wolf Blitzer on CNN slid Rhode Island into our column. The pundits weren't yet talking about it, but I knew that the whole night would come down to one state. "Virginia!" I called out, to no one in particular.

"Webb's down eleven thousand," someone answered. "Can we go over your speech?"

I leaned back and sighed. "Not now." We had won seats, but it looked like we were going to miss the majority by a couple of thousand votes. I was disconsolate. I don't play to lose.

A little while later, Harry Reid, the Senate Democrats' unflappable leader, and I were led by the Capitol Police through two hotel kitchens and down the room service elevator to a holding room. There, we met up with our House counterparts, Representatives Nancy Pelosi and Rahm Emanuel. They had won back the House and were exuberant. Harry and I put on our game faces. We congratulated them—they deserved it—and chatted with other members of Congress who had gathered. An aide and I huddled in the corner and looked at my speech for the first time, but my heart wasn't in it. I stuffed the papers in my jacket pocket—I could wing it. "Don't forget," he whispered as I walked away, "it's still a great night."

The other members of Congress and I were led to the edge of the stage. As we waited to be introduced, I looked out. The room was packed.

Suddenly, the crowd erupted. I figured they were cheering for Nancy, who was set to become the first female Speaker of the House.

I turned to Harry, but he was staring at the TV screen behind the stage. His eyes were wide and his mouth hung slightly open. I glanced at the screen. CNN was showing Virginia results. Guess they called it for Allen, I thought. Then I looked more closely.

Webb was up!

I did a double take. Webb was up! That's why they were cheering! With more than 90% of precincts reporting, Webb had gotten an edge—a couple of thousand votes—on Allen!

Harry and I slapped five and, with Rahm Emanuel by my side, I bounded onto the stage. For the first time all night, I really thought we might have a chance.

As Harry Reid and I stayed up in his hotel room watching returns into the early hours of the morning, it became clear that we would hold every Democratic Senate seat, including Washington and Maryland, where we felt challenged—both Maria Cantwell and Ben Cardin finished strong. In addition, J.B.'s positive predictions in Rhode Island and Missouri proved to be true. The one disappointment of the night was watching Harold Ford deliver a heartfelt concession speech in Tennessee.

By the time dawn broke, the balance of power in the Senate came down to nine thousand votes—seven thousand, out of more than two million cast, in Virginia and two thousand in Montana.

Four down. Two to go.

Two days later, on Thursday, November 9, George Allen and Conrad Burns, the Republican incumbents in Virginia and Montana, respectively, seeing the writing on the wall, conceded.

Six down. We had the majority! It seemed somehow appropriate that as a new majority dawned for Senate Democrats, two candidates who had been propelled by the growing "netroots" (Democratic-leaning bloggers), had made the difference in the end.

Of course, we did not just pick up the Senate and, thanks to Rahm's able stewardship, the House. We also picked up governorships and state legislatures across the country.

Just like 1974, election night 2006 was a great night for Democrats.

While trying to get some sleep a few days after the final results came in, I felt a familiar unease settling over me. As well as we had done, I was worried that the party I had grown up in, and in which I had a newly prominent role, would misinterpret the results. Just as Bush's reelection in 2004 was not the mandate that he claimed it was, Democrats' impressive victories in 2006 were not the sign of a lasting Democratic majority. If those eleven thousand voters (nine thousand in Virginia and two thousand in Montana), out of the millions who had cast their ballots, had made a different choice on election night, it would have been a good night—a four-seat pickup—but we would still have been the minority party.

As the celebration continued and newly emboldened Democrats strode across the country proudly proclaiming our party's rebirth, it seemed that in the euphoria we were forgetting a critical truth about the election: It *was* a great night for the Democrats, but mostly because it was such a tough year for the country—and because George W. Bush was stubborn and intransigent.

From the beginning, Harry Reid and I knew that 75% of the election would be about Bush and 25% would be about us. In the end, we played our 25% well and they played their 75% terribly. We recruited great candidates, spoke to the middle class and drew a sharp contrast with Bush's failures—from the continuing violence in Iraq, to the Republicans' culture of corruption, to Bush's assertions about the economy that were out of touch with the nagging financial concerns of most Americans. But nevertheless, the overwhelming reason for our victory was that Bush had screwed up.

In 2006, Republicans' mistakes and our campaigns made a lot of voters willing to consider Democrats, but in 2008 and beyond, we won't have George W. Bush or Tom DeLay to kick around anymore. It seemed obvious to me that the next couple of elections will be much more about what the Democratic Party offers; we will have to show voters why they should stick with us. Even if we are able to recruit the best candidates and raise more money again, it all too likely won't be enough. Unless we build on our values to generate better ideas, sharper policies and a clearer vision, we will be in trouble. Unless we are able to answer the question that Democrats are always asked—"What does the Democrat Party stand for?"—voters will go right back to voting for the Republican Party they have been supporting for the last twenty-five years.

Our victory was well deserved, but the Democratic Party still needs a new paradigm.

About a year before the election, during a particularly frustrating Democratic issues meeting—periodic gatherings of party leaders and strategists to help decide what the Democratic platform should be—a realization hit home. The meetings were always full of smart and dedicated people, each of whom I'm sure could have generated powerful and important ideas on his or her own. But the product of the meetings too often turned into pablum—big ideas were made small; tough choices were made weak; bold plans were made timid. A lot of our best stuff was drowned in a sea of consensus.

In this particular meeting, we were talking about energy independence. Of course, it was suggested that the Democratic platform should include higher CAFE standards. Short for *corporate average fuel economy* and pronounced *café*, these are the fuel-efficiency standards that are set for car companies. Raising CAFE standards should be a no-brainer for Democrats—it would save people money at the pump, reduce our dependence on foreign oil and help the environment.

"Let's do it!" I said. "It's a win, win, win."

"Hang on," someone stood up. "We can't do that. In Michigan, we depend on car companies and the United Auto Workers. They're against this. If CAFE standards are included, we'll walk out." So, CAFE standards were taken out. I left the meeting disturbed and pessimistic.

At these issues meetings, we were able to come up with some specific, trenchant proposals—raising the minimum wage, making college tuition tax deductible—that were meaningful and important and could win consensus in 2006. We rode them to victory against Bush, when voters just needed a feel for how we would govern. But they did not answer the essential question—what do Democrats stand for? Almost every Democrat, in every corner of the country, is still asked this question almost every day.

In 2008 and beyond, a greater percentage of the electorate will focus on our vision. We will need to be clearer, bolder, broader and more specific. In those meetings, I saw that it is just not possible by consensus.

The last time a political party created a new and successful model was in 1994. That year, Newt Gingrich did it with the Contract with America. After the meeting on CAFE standards, I kept asking myself, how did he do it? I wrestled with this conundrum for weeks. And then I had an epiphany. Newt Gingrich's Contract with America was not created as a consensus document of the Republican Party; it was the manifesto of a renegade who was trying to shake up his own party. It was aimed far more at Republicans than at Democrats—more at Bob Michel than at Bill Clinton. I became convinced that instead of calibrating our direction with careful tactical decisions made in private gatherings, the solution was to take a vision— a set of ideas uncompromised by countless chefs, each adding his or her favored spirit to the brew—present it to the public and see how it fared. If it caught on, the party would respond. If not, someone else would present a better one.

That's why I wrote this book.

For years, whenever friends or colleagues had suggested I write a book on the 1994 battle for gun control or my 1998 race against Senator Alfonse D'Amato for instance, I had demurred. But while sitting in that meeting watching the Democratic platform being whittled down, I decided to give it a shot. I had no ambition to create our entire vision on my own, nor any illusion that I alone could define a new paradigm. But I did have ideas and a perspective that I wanted to share. And I knew they would never make it out of those meetings intact.

I wrote this book, which is a reflection of my own particular perspective and vision, to try and help move the Democratic Party in the right direction. While I certainly do not have all the answers— I'm not even sure of all the questions—I feel that my background and my thirty years in politics give me a unique perspective that I yearn to share with my party and my fellow Americans.

Much of this book was written before election night 2006. But I am convinced that it is even more relevant now than it was when I started—after 2006, people are more open to our message. If Democrats hope to expand our razor-thin majority, if we want to win back the White House, if we dream of turning Democratic values into a paradigm and platform that will make our party the majority party for a generation, we have a long, long way to go. Bush's failures inspired Americans in blue, purple and red states to give us a chance. But now that we control Congress and because a presidential election with no incumbent is approaching, the onus is on us. Saying that we can do better is no longer enough—now we must prove it. In the wake of our victory, the Democratic Party needs additional ideas and policies even more than we did before we won.

In 2008 we must be able to respond to the question that we have not been able to answer sufficiently since Bill Clinton was on the top of our ticket in the mid-nineties: *What do Democrats really stand for?*

As I finally fell asleep that night, I was as convinced as ever that it was time to introduce my party and my country to some old friends—the same friends I came home to after graduating from law school.

So, without further ado, I'd like you to meet Joe and Eileen Bailey.

CHAPTER 2

IT'S THE MIDDLE CLASS, STUPID

EIGHT YEARS EARLIER, it was *my* Senate campaign that was being monitored from Washington, D.C. In 1998, my race was one of the most closely watched in the country. I was a locally known congressman from Brooklyn trying to unseat one of the most powerful men in New York State politics and a leader of the national Republican Party.

I had decided to run for the Senate for three reasons. For one thing, it was a good year to challenge Republican Alfonse D'Amato, the three-term incumbent. The Democratic nominee had lost six years earlier in a race that many had thought we could win. In 1998, the party was determined to finally unseat D'Amato. Second, I had amassed a significant war chest that would allow me to get my message out.

But the most important reason I decided to run for the Senate was the same one that caused me to turn my back on a law career in 1974. After almost twenty-five years in elective office, I loved legislating and still believed with every bone in my body that elected officials have a unique opportunity to make people's lives better. I loved the eighteen years I'd spent representing parts of Brooklyn and Queens in the House of Representatives—and my six years in the Assembly before that. If we had stayed in the majority, I might have spent my whole career in the House. But after '94 we were relegated to the minority. I didn't want to wake up every morning and go to the floor of the House just to beat up on Republicans; I wanted to get things done. In the House, as a member of the minority, that was rarely possible. In the Senate, where the rules ar emore flexible, whether we were in the majority or the minority, it would be different. I believed that I would have the chance to have a more positive influence in far more people's lives.

So, I chose to forgo almost guaranteed reelection to my Congressional seat and instead entered the Senate contest. At the outset, I was a decided underdog. In the Democratic primary, my potential opponents were national icon Geraldine Ferraro and well-known consumer advocate Mark Green.

Both Ferraro and Green had run statewide before, and both were well known and generally well liked. Ferraro, of course, gained national fame as Walter Mondale's vice presidential nominee. Green was the New York City Public Advocate; he had earned a lot of press over the years and was adored by the liberal base of the party.

Among people who followed politics closely, I was known in New York. The problem, I soon discovered, was that barely anyone followed politics closely.

In the House I had a record of achievement that put me in the news on a regular basis. I was a leader in writing and passing the Omnibus Crime Bill, which is the law that put 100,000 cops on the beat, the Brady Bill, the assault weapons ban and the Violence Against Women Act. I worked on the Freedom of Access to Clinic Entrances Act to ban violent protests at abortion clinics. I wrote and passed several consumer protection laws regarding credit and debit cards. I also held more press conferences than just about any other politician in the delegation.

So, when our first internal poll showed that I finished a distant third in a hypothetical matchup with Ferraro and Green, I was taken aback. Almost nobody outside of New York City knew who I was and less than half of likely Democratic voters in the five boroughs could identify me.

The secret was soon out. A local poll published in December 1997 had Ferraro at 48%, Green at 25% and Schumer at 12%—and Ferraro hadn't even announced she was running.

It wasn't all bad news, however. An internal poll that had me dead last also showed that once voters knew what I had accomplished in the House and hoped to accomplish in the Senate, my popularity soared. Still, with Ferraro waiting on the sidelines, the conventional wisdom was that she would enter the race and I would either quit or lose.

As Ferraro took her time deciding, I used her inactivity to get stronger. I had a reputation as a skilled fundraiser—it was the one edge that reporters and pundits were giving me—and by the end of 1997, I already had money in the bank. When I wasn't attending to Congressional business, I spent my time on the phone—calling donors to raise money and calling local politicians to gain endorsements. In my experience, there is no great magic to these calls. I enjoy people—on airplanes, I'll often ask the person next to me for his or her biography—and I'm goal oriented. My natural interest in people, along with discipline (working through the list), persistence (calling, calling and calling again) and directness (never hanging up without making a clear and concise request for support) made them easy.

"I hope you'll support me," I said to anyone who would take my call. "Green may be strong in the primary, but he's already lost once. I know how to beat D'Amato. And Ferraro probably isn't going to run."

I made the calls from a closet—literally, a closet—in the office of my consultant, Hank Morris. It had two phones, two metal folding chairs, a ledge for a desk and no windows. A tangle of wires from an old phone transfer box on the ceiling dangled just in front of my forehead, startling me every time I leaned forward. I'd sit in there for hours on end, going through endless computer printouts of names, phone numbers and bios of potential donors or supporters. I wouldn't stop until it got too late or I ran out of names.

I checked the news wires each afternoon for word whether Ferraro was getting in or staying out of the race. While our polls showed that I had a chance to beat her and I was telling donors that she probably wouldn't run, her possible entry into the race made me very nervous. I feared that she'd win the vast majority of the female vote with ease while Green and I slugged it out and split the male vote.

There's a test I use when I look at elections: If you do everything right and your opponent does everything right, who will win? If it's you, that means the race is in your hands. Against D'Amato, if I did everything right and he did everything right, I believed I would win. It was in my hands. The thing that gnawed at me about Gerry was that if I did everything right and she did everything right, she would win.

In January 1998, she got in. I had been happy to have three camera crews at my announcement; she must have had thirty at hers. It was an international news event. The next week, several polls showed Gerry with a huge lead, followed by Mark Green and then some guy named Schumer far, far back. A rumor started circulating—no doubt emanating from the Ferraro or Green camp—that I would quit and run for my old House seat.

I didn't quit, but soon after Ferraro announced, three of my senior Washington staffers did. Two had families and didn't want to risk having to look for a job if I lost. One simply thought I had no chance and didn't want to be around for the debacle.

As I was losing congressional staff, I was also having a hard time hiring campaign staff. I interviewed a dozen potential campaign managers, but no one was really enthused about working for me. They felt my race was a long shot and I had a reputation for being hard on staff. A few offered to work for me, but none for less than $20,000 a month. I couldn't stomach the notion of sitting in that air-locked prison in Hank's office, scouring call lists for money, pitching my heart out on the phone to potential donors, and seeing so much go to a single staffer. No, I said.

I couldn't find a campaign field director for many of the same reasons. I wasn't going to win; I wasn't the easiest boss to work with; I was tight when it came to salary.

Faced with a campaign without a team, I named Josh Isay, my chief of staff at the time, as campaign manager. Josh had one of the brightest minds of anyone I had ever met. He was fearless, strategic and tactical. He had a gift for press and was as quick with a quote as anyone you'll find in politics. But he was 28 years old, had never run a campaign in his life and was green as could be.

I settled on Mike Lynch as field director. Mike is a quiet, humble, calm Midwesterner—just the type of person I usually avoid hiring. I am drawn to people who sit on the edge of their seat and have a look of intensity in their eye. Mike had neither characteristic. But he was the only one who would take the job at the pay we were budgeting and had worked for Herb Kohl of Wisconsin, who has a knack for hiring good staff. I would later learn that he took the job expecting to be fired but wanted a chance to live in New York and see his beloved Yankees play in person. I would also learn that looks and manners can deceive. Lynch would one day become my most trusted staffer.

My policy director was Jim Kessler—a creative nonconformist who could write statements, speeches and talking points almost as quickly as he could talk. He worked for me for six years in the House and I could always rely on whatever he handed me. I would sometimes walk to the podium at a press conference in front of a bank of television cameras and reporters and read a statement he had written for the first time. But he had no campaign experience to speak of.

Over the next months I assembled a core of talented young people: press secretary Cathie Levine, upstate coordinator Jack O'Donnell, fundraisers Jeff Stewart and Jen Bayer and, as spokesman, a whip-smart young guy named Howard Wolfson, on leave from Congresswoman Nita Lowey's staff. Each was dogged, smart, cunning, aggressive—and very young. Not one of my senior staff had yet turned thirty-five, and most were in their twenties.

The only adults in my day-to-day operation were my pollster—first Tubby Harrison, then Geoff Garin—and my media and general campaign consultant, Hank Morris. Hank was a brilliant, argumentative political strategist who wore a sweater every day—no matter the weather. He wanted to win this race as badly as I did and had been waiting for this moment for a decade.

The race started out poorly. The dominant theme of the first month AGA (after Gerry announced) was whether I'd quit. This talk was having a stultifying effect on my efforts. I spent half of each fund-raising phone call convincing potential donors that I was in the race to stay. Then I would make a pitch for money that generally fell flat. Endorsements from labor leaders, county chairs, local party committees and prominent officials trickled to zero.

We decided to launch a series of campaign ads in February. The idea of the ads was to give the huge percentage of New Yorkers who didn't know me a sense of who I was. In every race I've ever run, I've believed that showing voters who I really am—where I come from, what I've accomplished and what drives me—is my best chance to win. You can only be successful in politics if you're comfortable with who you are. Voters can't stand politicians who aren't. Over the years, I've offered more than one Democratic presidential candidate this advice. "Be yourself!" I tell them, often to no avail. "I'm from Brooklyn—sometimes it helps me; sometimes it hurts me. But it's who I am. If I pretended to be anything different, I'd be a lot worse than whatever I am."

So, at the end of February we ran a week of biographical ads. New York's an expensive state for TV and it cost about a million dollars—nearly one-fifth of my entire war chest. If voters get to know me, I thought, I'll start to creep up.

The ads were a disaster. A new poll a week after they ran showed that I hadn't budged an inch. Now the question was whether my candidacy would be the most expensive bomb since *Ishtar*.

Reporters started to smell blood in the water; they began to circle and get ready to go in for the kill. I had been friendly with many of them during my eighteen-year career in the House. I asked after their spouses and their children. I chatted with them about their neighborhood in Kew Gardens, the Rockaways or Prospect Heights. But those pleasantries meant little at that moment. I was bleeding.

I entered the race as an underdog, but I was quickly becoming an also-ran. Reporters who had once written that I had potential were now musing that my career could be about to end. Our fundraising became lackluster and, to make matters worse, I had just poured one million dollars down the toilet on ads that had had little discernible effect.

I had to get out from under this cloud, and quickly. I had Josh Isay set up a meeting with Hank Morris and a couple of other trusted advisors. The mood was bleak.

I opened the meeting: "Houston, we have a problem." It was a wan attempt to lighten the mood.

Isay summed it up: "There's a negative buzz about our candidacy. It's not fatal, but it's a real problem. We are still early in the race, but this perception is giving people reasons to stay away rather than join up. We have to turn it around quickly, show positive momentum and quell any rumor that we're dropping out."

A poll we had just completed showed that my performance had improved among the few voters who remembered seeing the ad.

"We can show our numbers to reporters and let them know that our polls have us moving," said Hank. "It's not a great answer, but it's an answer. What we really need to do is move beyond polls and process and give them something to write that focuses on what you are about."

"Here's my gut," I said. "The truth is that Gerry, Mark and I would vote similarly on most bills in the Senate. We'd vote the same on guns and abortion; we'd all fight against poverty and for civil rights. The difference is that I'm a 'meat and potatoes' Democrat who cares about—"

"We polled 'meat and potatoes' Democrat and it just doesn't work," said Tubby.

"It's not polls! Look, there's a voter out there. He doesn't belong to the ACLU, he doesn't march for abortion rights, he isn't a member of the Sierra Club, but he votes. He's got a mortgage and property taxes. His wife works, in part because she wants to, but mostly because she has to. They have kids in the public schools and they lie awake at night wondering how they are going to afford college. These are the people I grew up with." I took a breath. "They're why I got into politics in the first place. I want to reach that family."

Hank smiled and looked at me. "It's the middle class, stupid."

After several hours of heated discussion, Isay brought the meeting to a close.

"We are going to quickly develop a two-week schedule of activities designed to change the focus of this race," he said. "It will be about who you are, what you stand for and what you will do as senator. It will be about the middle class and differentiate your candidacy from the others."

April and May were better months for the campaign. After the meeting, Isay designed a fourteen-day marathon sprint of activities that would let me and the campaign communicate our clear message. We held public events each day to highlight a new issue, announce an endorsement or deliver a speech. We quickly put together another upstate tour and hit all of the major cities.

I made sure that everyone on the team understood the middle-class couple I had conceptualized. It was easy for me to describe them. I had known them my whole life. They were the reason I had entered public service. Many of the bills I had passed and the speeches I had given were about them. As we went through the fourteen days, they started to become more concrete, more real and, at least to me, more alive.

Today, wherever I go, they are always at my side.

Joe and Eileen Bailey live in Massapequa, a medium-size suburb in Nassau County, Long Island. They are each 45 years old. Their home is about 30 minutes from the outskirts of New York City, but they don't go into town very often. They have a house, a mortgage, property taxes that never cease to go up, monthly payments for two cars, and three kids in the local public schools. They both work because they want to and because they need to. Joe works for an insurance company and Eileen is a part-time administrative assistant at a family physician's practice. They are middle class by New York standards, together earning about $75,000 per year, which translates to about $50,000 in a typical American community.

Both of Eileen's parents are in their seventies and healthy, although her father had a prostate cancer scare a few years ago. Joe's parents are in their early eighties. They still live in the same house they bought forty years ago, but they may need to move to assisted living soon.

The Baileys are generally optimists. They do not see impending clouds of doom on the horizon, though they sometimes worry that America's place in the world is under threat. Personally, they feel they are doing well. There are two cars in the garage, a family vacation each summer, a small positive balance in their bank account, and some retirement savings. Joe is able to get in a few rounds of golf during the summer. Eileen is able to splurge now and then at the mall.

But they are increasingly bothered by nagging worries. They're worried about terrorists who are hell-bent on killing Americans, though it doesn't feel like the kind of war that their parents lived through in the 1940s. They also worry about economic forces that are beyond their control. Health care is very expensive and not as personal as it was when they were younger. Property taxes go up every year. They don't see how they can possibly pay for college for their three children. They haven't lost jobs to outsourcing, but some neighbors have. If their parents get sick, Joe and Eileen will have to supplement their retirement income to pay for care.

They talk about these forces at night when they're in bed. They realize that a little belt tightening—Joe skipping the golf, Eileen forgoing a blouse—will not make a real difference in their economic situation.

Socially, the Baileys are not anti-authority; in fact, they respect authority. They attend church regularly, though not every week. They accept the structure brought to their lives by religion, work and governmental institutions. They want these structures to be successful and strong, and are leery of those who seem to always criticize them. Their children stand and put their hands over their hearts during the Pledge of Allegiance. Joe takes off his cap and sings along with the national anthem before the occasional Islanders game.

They are bothered by the corporate excesses they read about in the paper. But they are bothered even more when they read about someone burning the American flag. They feel there is a place in America for large, successful corporations and realize that they're needed—even if it's an unfortunate fact of life that some CEOs will always go too far. But they are infuriated by flag burners. That hits their emotional chord. The Baileys are angered by people who don't appreciate America and who exploit America's very freedoms to spit in its face—and in theirs. They are skeptical of anyone who defends such people.

They are concerned, and sometimes shocked, by the cultural influences that enter their home through television or the Internet. They are not prudish. They watch Sex and the City and Desperate Housewives (though Joe pretends not to like either show). But when Abby, their 11-year-old, made passing reference to something that they had not even heard of at her age, their fears about the effect of cultural influences beyond their control were affirmed. They do not always agree with all of the values expressed at church, but they are glad that someone is standing up to the moral excesses they see all around them.

They believe that everyone deserves a fair chance and are sympathetic to those who are less fortunate than they are. They gave money after the Asian tsunami and Hurricane Katrina. Eileen helps with the clothing drive at their church. But they are not driven by communal goals over self-interest. To them, there is nothing wrong with seeking what is good for yourself and your family. To them, it's part of the American credo. They believe in charity, but they also see nothing wrong with helping yourself do better. They instinctively believe in capitalism and democracy. To them, the capitalist precept that working in your self-interest and the democratic precept that voting in your self-interest lead to the greater good is fair, just and, just about, self-evident. Deep down, they believe that people who work hard and play by the rules will do fine in America.

They are proud of their country, their family and their faith. They are proud of their lives. They are nice people and good people. You'd be glad to call them your neighbors, coworkers or friends.

Politically, they are up for grabs. They don't follow politics particularly closely and are not ideological, but they always vote. They skim the newspapers and watch their local news. Their parents were New Deal Democrats. But the first presidential vote that Joe and Eileen ever cast was for Ronald Reagan, in 1980. They do not consider themselves Republicans or Democrats; they are part of the new wave of independents. After two votes for Reagan and one for George Bush, they twice voted for Clinton. In 2000, they voted for Bush over Gore, but it was the most difficult vote they ever cast. In 2004, they much more eagerly pulled the lever for Bush. In 2006, they crossed back to the Democratic side for the first time in years.

Over the years they have both benefited from government and been frustrated by it. They support government when they feel it supports them, which isn't often. They don't mind the government's help, but they hate it when politicians condescend to them. They're proud of what they've done and what they've accomplished, and they don't need government to treat them like basket cases. Most of the time, it seems to them that government's focused on someone else—the very poor or the very rich. So, most of the time, they tune government out.

They were my neighbors in Brooklyn and my classmates at Madison High School. They lived in the houses my father served as an exterminator. They chatted with my mom at the corner butcher shop. I played with them on the basketball courts and stood in line with them at the movie theaters.

By 1998 I felt that, too often, the Democratic Party ignored them. I made it my mission not to.

They became my constant companions and my heroes during the campaign.

I would see the Baileys in the row houses of Queens, the suburbs of Syracuse, the black churches of Brooklyn and the worn towns of western New York. They waited in line for beef on weck at Charlie the Butcher's in Buffalo, swam off the beaches in the Rockaways and took their family to see the Yankees a couple of times each summer. They sent their kids to SUNY Brockport for college.

 POLO PUBLIC LIBRARY DISTRICT
302 W. MASON ST.
POLO, IL 61064

I had called the couple Joe and Eileen since I started in the Assembly. That's the couple I knew best growing up. But in reality, they represented a much larger and more diverse middle class. Joe and Eileen are all the men and women whose lives are not a desperate struggle to survive, but a challenge to improve.

The Baileys of Massapequa could just as easily have been the Hancocks of Cazenovia, the Thompsons of Laurelton, the Ramirezes of Port Chester, the Pachinskis of Cheektowaga or the Shapiros of Riverdale. They were all the hardworking and often ignored families who were not tuned into special interest newsletters or the editorial page of the *New York Times*, but wanted a little something more from their government and their leaders.

In 1998, I thought about the Baileys all around New York State. Today, I think of many more. Across the country, the Baileys could be the Jensens of Roseville, Minnesota; the Kims of Elk Grove, California; the Coopers of Lebanon, Tennessee; the Salims of Dearborn, Michigan; the Montoyas of Lakewood, Colorado; the Giammarinos of Quincy, Massachusetts; and so many other families from so many other places. Though their locations and backgrounds are different, these families have mutual anxieties and aspirations and share a similar, and too often disappointing, relationship with the government.

We always had this family in the front of our minds. What would they think about what I was saying or proposing? Would it really make their lives better? How could I convince them that government could be their friend?

I would not act purely on the basis of what Joe and Eileen wanted, but I needed to listen to them and understand them so that when we had a difference of opinion, I could explain why I chose a different course in a way that they understood and respected.

No campaign can be successful unless it has a center, a core of beliefs that drives it forward. Staffers have joked to the press that I have imaginary friends, but Joe and Eileen Bailey centered my campaign.

Ferraro was likely to win many of the liberal New York City and suburban women who considered her a life-affirming role model. Mark Green had a strong base among environmentalists and other liberals. Liberals generally liked me and voted for me, but few would fall

POLO PUBLIC LIBRARY DISTRICT
302 W. MASON ST.
POLO, IL 61064

on their swords for me. I had taken positions that they had opposed—like supporting the death penalty and longer prison sentences.

I always had a middle-class focus in Congress; now I had actual, albeit imaginary, middle-class voters to talk to instead of an abstraction. It made a difference.

It also helped that Ferraro had started with a stumble. During her first Senate race, in 1992, Gerry was savagely, and in my opinion unfairly, attacked in the final days of the primary over her husband's alleged ties to organized crime. Those attacks cost her the race and caused her no small amount of personal heartache. She wanted her current opponents to swear off such tactics. So, she publicly asked Mark Green and me to sign a written pledge swearing off any negative campaign attacks during the primary.

It was a mistake. For starters, I had no intention of waging a personal assault on Ferraro's character. I believed that my only chance to win was not by going negative, but by letting voters know about my background, my accomplishments and my goals.

Furthermore, there is a "rule of three" in politics. It's a fact that negative attacks take a toll on the intended target, but they also have a rebound effect on the attacker. This is particularly so in primary races, where the ideological differences between candidates are generally small. In a three-way race, when one candidate goes negative on another, the candidate most likely to gain is the one who stays out of it. The candidate who attacked Ferraro most viciously in 1992, Liz Holtzman, ended up finishing third. In 2004, Dick Gephardt attacked Howard Dean in Iowa, and John Kerry ended up winning the caucus.

But the biggest problem with the pledge was not Gerry's opponents, it was that reporters thought her husband's alleged transgressions were fair game. They had proved that in the 1992 election, when they had covered those attacks with relish. If Green or I had brought them up in a press conference or an ad, it would have been huge news. When she brought the subject up herself, it was even bigger news. The press pounced on her as if she had something new to hide. She had to answer the kinds of questions no candidate wants to deal with. It was so bad that *New York Times* columnist Maureen Dowd wrote a scathing column called "Running like a Girl," in which she questioned whether Ferraro should be in the race.

By mid-spring, our campaign was cruising forward. We presented a series of middle-class initiatives focused on Joe and Eileen Bailey. We talked about real-life, kitchen-table economic concerns.

We released a report on skyrocketing college tuition and introduced a plan to make college costs tax deductible at press conferences around the state. We hammered banks for hiding outrageous ATM fees and introduced legislation requiring fee disclosure. We talked about property tax relief (traditionally a local issue), the ridiculously high cost of breakfast cereal (five bucks for a box of corn flakes!), usurious utility costs, and sky-high airfares from airports in midsize cities like Rochester, Buffalo, Albany and Syracuse.

Our events featured regular people—not local elected officials or interest groups. I stood with parents, not politicians; consumers, not consumer groups. I wanted to talk to people directly, not through intermediaries. When a burly Democratic Party official from Buffalo managed to get on stage with me at an event, Cathie Levine, my five-foot-one, 110-pound press secretary, nearly knocked him off the stage.

As spring turned to summer, my poll numbers started to creep up. We were still in third place, but we had gained about six points and Gerry had dropped about the same amount. I had gained full confidence in the campaign team that I had doubted only a few months earlier.

We were making news on our terms, about the subjects that defined what I was about—not about poll numbers, gaffes or attacks. Most important, we were a campaign that knew its center—Joe and Eileen Bailey.

As the race heated up, we attracted bigger crowds at our events. My basic stump speech was working—I could feel myself connecting with the audience.

I went to Irondequoit, in the suburbs of Rochester, where the Baileys are Bob and Susan Metcalf.

A flight from Rochester to Disney World should cost half as much, not twice as much, as a flight from Los Angeles to Tokyo . . .

I went to the Allen A.M.E. Church in Queens where the Baileys are Curtis and Angela Thompson.

My father was an exterminator and my mother worked in the home. They were able to send three children to college. That would be impossible today . . .

I went to a Union Hall in Tonawanda, where the Baileys are Al and Rose Bernardi.

This utility bill is from Buffalo and this one is from Pittsburgh. It's the same type of power, the same amount of power—why is it twice as much in Buffalo?

To be sure, I wasn't giving the Gettysburg Address. But I was talking about things that actually mattered to people in a way that proved I understood the world they lived in. As I gave variations of my basic stump speech, I noticed when the audience began nodding their heads "yes."

Why did I give up a safe seat in the House to run for the Senate? I love to legislate. It may not be what most people like to do, but it's what I like to do. I like taking an idea and then shaping and molding it into something that can become law and make a difference in people's lives. There's no better place to do that than in the Senate. I hope you give me the opportunity to do what I love and do what I do best.

That was how I ended most of my speeches. No pollster or political consultant would look at that finale and tell a politician to stick it into his speech. But it was honest. And as I stood on the podium, I could tell it was working with voters.

I didn't promise to end hunger. I promised I would love my job. I didn't promise to have all the answers. I promised that I would work to make a difference. And I didn't promise the moon and the stars. I promised to do what I believed in and what I had always done: Fight for Joe and Eileen Bailey.

Ferraro's problems mounted and Green couldn't gain a foothold. By July, I was in second place in the polls, a few points ahead of Green and about ten behind Ferraro. Her fundraising was lackluster, a factor of her late entrance in the race and my aggressive efforts at making phone calls. It was now certain that in the final stages of the race, I would have many times more money for ads than she would—all the hours in that little closet in Hank's office had paid off. And, because she had asked us to pledge not to attack her, she couldn't attack me. She had few options for regaining momentum.

We continued to talk to middle-class voters in all parts of the state. Every day began at seven in the morning and ended at ten in the evening. When I was on the road—as I often was—my staff and I stayed at Motel 6.

I didn't insist on Motel 6 for political reasons. I'm just cheap. When I was a teenager, whenever we'd go somewhere overnight, I'd argue with my mom about the hotel. I couldn't understand why we didn't stay at the least expensive place. They all had a bed, a pillow and a shower—what else did we need? Now that I was on my own, it was best value all the way. Anyway, Motel 6's firm mattresses, strong showerheads, and cable television were far superior to my digs in Washington. And, at $29 a night, you couldn't beat the price. Even though I was running for the Senate, I wasn't going to change.

It also had an ancillary effect. In the morning, I would greet dozens of voters as they checked out and loaded their cars. "I'm Chuck Schumer and I'm running for the Senate."

They were incredulous. "You're staying at a Motel 6?"

It revealed who I was: Someone you could call "Chuck" instead of (God willing) Senator Schumer. Someone who was frugal and, despite being a Democrat, wouldn't waste their money.

I traveled to Cheektowaga for the annual Polish festival and brought Brooklyn's own White Eagle sausage as an entry in the sausage-tasting competition. My staff told me not to go—they said "it wouldn't look senatorial."

I said, "So what?"

Cheektowaga is a middle-class suburb of Buffalo in Erie County. In Cheektowaga, Joe and Eileen Bailey are Stanley and Paula Pachinski. We went to the festival armed with the White Eagle sausage and entered the competition. Thankfully, Redlinski's Holiday Blend, produced by a local butcher, won the contest. It was a great day for the campaign—entering a sausage competition wouldn't win the

Pachinkis' votes, but it would get them to watch my ads instead of flicking the channel.

Everything was going well. My poll numbers continued to climb and by the beginning of August, I was even with Ferraro. By the middle of the month, I was ahead. I won the endorsements of the biggest newspapers in the state, from the *New York Times* to the *Buffalo News*. Hank Morris would take those endorsements and turn them into effective television ads. Success begat success as endorsements and fundraising dollars came my way. All of my ads were positive, and because of Ferraro's pledge, none of the ads by my opponents were negative. An internal poll by Geoff Garin just after Labor Day predicted a landslide victory.

Even though our polling from Labor Day through the election showed that we would win the primary, at noon on election day I did not have a victory speech. Many of my speeches, talking points and op-ed pieces during the campaign had been drafted by Jim Kessler, my longtime policy aide.

The reality of an intense campaign is that the candidate's time is filled with making fundraising calls to potential donors, answering questions from reporters, attending several events each night with large groups of voters, giving speeches, dashing off to meetings with political and community leaders, reviewing ad scripts, prepping for debates and hopping onto planes, trains and cars to get around the state. There is little time to personally draft speeches or newspaper op-eds. One of the big adjustments I had to make was to delegate the crafting of most of the written material and speeches—which I had usually drafted myself—to others.

For election night in the primary, we farmed out the speech to some consultants and professional speechwriters. This was to be a critical speech—a chance to introduce myself to the several million voters who do not tune in to campaigns until primary night and whose first glimmer of the campaign would be when they heard my speech that evening Although I trusted Kessler and felt he understood me and the Baileys as well as anyone, he was an amateur. We brought in the big guns.

On election day the speech was faxed to me at Hank's office. I read the first several paragraphs. I turned the page and read a few more paragraphs. I started frantically reading through the rest of it, tearing through the pages, then going back to earlier pages. I turned to Hank.

"Okay, I hate it. Do you understand? I hate it!" My face was purple.

"Okay, you hate it," Hank said. "We'll work on it; we'll fix it."

"This is . . . this is . . . It could be spoken by any Democrat. It's filled with the usual platitudes for every interest group under the sun. I'm not running for president of the teacher's union, NARAL or the League of Conservation Voters. I'm running for Senate. The Baileys brought us this far; we can't abandon them now. Joe's going to hear this and switch to *SportsCenter.*"

Hank called up Kessler. "Congratulations, you're writing tonight's speech."

Election day, as it always is in important races, was torture. Some candidates take the afternoon off and see a movie; I spent most of the day in Hank's office, leaving only to drop by the campaign office to thank the team.

Josh Isay spent the day pacing nervously and incessantly. He had nothing to do, and that brought out the worst in him. He chewed on the back of a pen—his office was filled with chewed pens—and called Kessler for the fifth time that day.

"How's the speech? When can Chuck see it? Do you think it's good? How many more hours will it be? Can I do anything to help?"

At 1:00 p.m., Kessler had not written a single word. Sitting in Hank's office, I started to draft something in my head. "If worse comes to worst," I thought, "I can always wing it."

At 8:00 p.m., I moved to a hotel suite above the ballroom where I would soon give my speech. I had still not seen a word of it. The polls would close in an hour.

Kessler came in.

"I couldn't get anything done. The office was a zoo. I was drawing a blank. At four o'clock, I took a pad of paper to the only quiet place I could find—the bathroom. I spent three hours sitting on the toilet writing it longhand. I barely had a chance to type it up. The irony is I have to, you know . . . go."

I spent the next hour rewriting the speech, changing lines, moving paragraphs around with a felt-tip pen and inserting notes. We did not have the time or the technical ability to make edits on a computer at the hotel. I made all the changes by hand.

The networks called the race for me at 9:01—a minute after the polls closed. Mark Green and Geraldine Ferraro called right away to concede defeat. On the day of an election, the campaign managers generally call each other to get all of the relevant phone numbers for just this occasion.

My conversation with Green was rather short. He congratulated me and pledged his support. Green and I have never been particularly close. There was no love lost between the two of us. But, to Mark's credit, he was friendly and generous.

Geraldine was disappointed but displayed the grace that marked her career. We ran a civil race based on the issues and I think she appreciated that I never said anything bad about her—publicly or privately. Both she and Mark agreed to attend a unity breakfast the next morning and they both pledged their support in the race against D'Amato.

It was time to take the stage in the ballroom. It was packed. The place was electric. As I walked toward the podium, Bachman Turner Overdrive's "You Ain't Seen Nothin' Yet" blared from the sound system. The crowd was delirious.

My wife, Iris, and my daughters, Jessica and Alison, formed a ring behind me. Behind them were about three dozen Democratic politicians, including many of the people with whom I served in the House. I exchanged a few words with Jerry Nadler, a congressman from the west side of Manhattan who represented one of the most liberal districts in America. He supported me over the more liberal Green and I wanted him to know I'd never forget it.

The crowd continued to thunder. It was a moment unlike any I had ever experienced in politics.

After several false starts the crowd finally quieted down. I no longer have my heavily marked-up copy, but I remember the speech went something like this:

This election—the next seven weeks—comes down to one word: trust. Who do you trust to fight for New York families? Who do you trust to stand up for what is right?

Who do you trust to make college more affordable? Who do you trust to put 100,000 cops on the street so you can live, work, play and go to school with peace of mind? Who do you trust to protect Medicare for your parents? Who do you trust to fight every waking hour of the day to attract jobs and businesses to the ravaged upstate economy? Who do you trust to reform education so that your children can go to a public school that is worthy of the property taxes you pay?

There were references to issues like a woman's right to choose, gun control and affirmative action—they were in my speech and they were not buried. But I wanted Joe and Eileen to know I was focused on them. To know that I believed in their America. To know that I honored the world they had created for their children, that I was humbled by the contributions they made to their community, and that I would fight for them like no one else would.

The use of the word *trust* was a warning to all, including D'Amato, that we might someday use the ethics issues that had plagued him his whole career. But on this day, the word *trust* was an indictment of D'Amato's failures to address the real problems New Yorkers faced.

That afternoon, while Kessler had been in the bathroom writing the speech, I had left Hank's office to pay a visit to the sweltering headquarters. I gathered the entire campaign team—from campaign manager Josh Isay, who had methodically and brilliantly commandeered the effort, to the developmentally disabled man who volunteered in the office every day.

"I think we're going to win tonight. Our tracking polls look really good. But whether we win or not, I want you to know that this is the greatest group of people I've ever been associated with. It's the greatest group of people anyone has even been associated with," I actually started to cry. "We'll have a lot of work to do over the next seven weeks, but this group of people can do anything."

My ragtag staff of castoffs looked every bit as exhausted as I did. They hadn't yet realized what they had accomplished and had no idea what would come next. As the group broke up and walked backed to their desks, Mike Lynch, the field director whom I hadn't wanted to hire put his hand on my shoulder and pulled my head down toward his.

"Don't ever tell the staff that we've won. Now they won't bust their ass for the rest of the day."

Maybe they were more ready than I thought.

CHAPTER 3

THE FONZ

IN DECEMBER 1997, I had trailed Geraldine Ferraro by thirty-six points in the first public opinion poll of the race. In March, my campaign had been sputtering and left for dead. On election night, I won by twenty-five points.

There is no single reason I won. My background, my record and my fundraising advantage were all significant. But there is no question that, at least in part, I owed my win to the Baileys—the Baileys in the row houses of the East Bronx and the suburbs of Binghamton, the black churches of Mount Vernon and the worn towns of the Mohawk Valley. Those who were doing fine but needed a little more. Those who were confident that their children would go to college but were petrified about the prospect of paying for it. Those who owned a home—a piece of the American Dream—but were saddled with property taxes and bills that kept them on an economic treadmill.

I had spoken to the voter who works fifty weeks a year, speeds through breakfast and rushes her kids to the bus stop every morning, stays married through the pressures of raising a family and saving for the future, puts a few dollars aside each month for a college fund, looks in on and supports her elderly parents—and gets little or no appreciation from government. This is the voter who is too "rich" to benefit from most government programs but too "poor" to benefit from rifle shot tax breaks like estate tax relief. On September 15, 1998, these voters—at least those registered as Democrats—voted for me.

The reward for winning the Democratic primary was taking on Senator Alfonse D'Amato in a seven-week brawl until election day. Most states leave ample room between the primary and general elections. Not New York. After expending every ounce of energy I could summon to defeat Ferraro and Green, I would have about five hours of sleep to rest up for D'Amato.

I had told thousands of potential donors, elected officials, union leaders, newspaper editorial boards and voters that I knew how to beat D'Amato. Now I had my chance.

Alfonse was a legend in New York. He was a former town supervisor from Nassau County who stunned the nation in 1980 by defeating fellow Republican Jacob Javits in a primary and then winning a three-way race in the general. He was a pure power politician who controlled all levers of the New York State Republican Party.

Years earlier, he had handpicked a political unknown, George Pataki, to take on and defeat Mario Cuomo for governor. To his detractors, including many in the media, D'Amato had a reputation for tolerating corruption. One of his nicknames was Senator Pothole, to some a disparaging sobriquet for a senator who was no match in academic erudition to his senior colleague Pat Moynihan, but a nickname that D'Amato wore proudly.

D'Amato was truly a Joe and Eileen Bailey politician. He was called Senator Pothole because he had honed a reputation for solving people's everyday problems. He fought for federal money for bridges, ports, roads, hospitals and political cronies. Everyone knew to leave the truly brilliant speeches to Moynihan, but if your Social Security check was late, you'd call D'Amato's office. Though he was a rogue and could be a bully, he was colorful and confident and he had character.

His other nickname was "the Fonz"—a nod to the famous *Happy Days* character. It was short for Alfonse and a tribute to his ability to intimidate and still win admirers.

D'Amato was a master politician and one of the toughest players in the game. His strategist, Arthur Finkelstein, created the spots for people like North Carolina segregationist Jesse Helms. Finkelstein had no compunction about playing the race card if it helped his candidates win an election. His forte was creating hard-hitting negative spots that would simply rip the bark off his foe. More than any other media consultant, Finkelstein is responsible for tarring the word "liberal." Democrats were embarrassingly liberal, pathetically liberal, shamefully liberal and too liberal for too long.

Unlike the primary, there would be no politeness in this race—false or otherwise. This would be a bare-knuckle chess match. Hard hits and smart tactics.

My plan to defeat D'Amato was unorthodox. Everyone expected me to go after his ethics. That, according to conventional wisdom, was D'Amato's Achilles heel.

But our campaign was in a different mindset than the experts. We didn't think the Baileys particularly cared about D'Amato's ethics. That's not to say Joe and Eileen Bailey are not honest people—they are very honest. Eileen was appalled when their oldest daughter, Megan, told her a friend had been caught cheating on a quiz. Eileen, Joe and the children believe in the values they learned from their parents and from their church. Lying is not tolerated in the house—ever.

Still, the Baileys think most politicians are probably dishonest, just as they think most baseball players probably take steroids. They are skeptical of politicians who act holier than thou—because they think it is an act. They don't believe that every politician takes a brown bag full of money, but they do think most are overly influenced by big donors and other powerful people who don't have the interests of the middle class at heart. Despite their negative view of politicians in the abstract, they always vote—more often than not for the incumbent—and continue to feel some respect for governmental authority.

Besides, calling out D'Amato on ethics, whether it was fair or not, was like calling Bush a good ole boy—Joe, Eileen and everyone else across the state had already made up their minds on the subject. They either accepted or rejected it. It already factored or would never factor into their decision about how to vote. During my year traveling around the state, it became obvious that the only people whose votes were swung by attacks on D'Amato's ethics were those who always supported the Democrat anyway.

No, the plan to defeat D'Amato was to convince Joe and Eileen Bailey that the Fonz was out of touch with their views on the major issues of the day and was unconcerned about their daily life challenges.

Even before the primary was over, we had started communicating this message. Hank put together an ad called "Senator Pothole." He found an actor who had an uncanny resemblance to D'Amato, put him in a suit, and showed him directing a road crew fixing up potholes. The idea was to show middle-class voters that D'Amato's greatest asset, his much-vaunted constituent services operation, was an obfuscation to distract them from the real effect of his positions in the Senate—he would replace a lost Medicare check and at the same time vote to cut Medicare. In the ad, I spoke to Joe and Eileen. "He calls himself the pothole senator," I said. "But D'Amato's votes in Washington create thousands of potholes here in New York. Then he fills a few near election time, and he wants our vote?!"

That was our opening salvo and it had nothing to do with corruption. Instead, it had everything to do with what government could do for Joe and Eileen Bailey.

At nine on the morning after the primary, Ferraro, Green and I sat down for a public unity breakfast. In front of the media, both of the defeated candidates pledged their enthusiastic support for my race against D'Amato. This could not have been easy for them and was hugely significant for my campaign. In 1992, the Democratic primary had been so venomous that it took nearly a month to bring the candidates together for a grudging handshake. In 1998, the cameras clicked as Gerry, Mark and I chatted amiably over breakfast.

Also by nine o'clock, D'Amato's ads were airing throughout the state. We had already decided that when D'Amato hit us, we could not wait, analyze or hesitate—we had to hit back, immediately and with all our strength. His first shot predictably depicted me as being liberal on taxes, welfare and crime. We were prepared. We already had two ads in the can—one on taxes, one on crime. They were on the air within a day:

> Al D'Amato's lying about Chuck Schumer on crime.
> The truth? Chuck Schumer's the tough-on-crime Democrat who wrote the law that put thousands of new police on the street and banned assault weapons. D'Amato voted no.
> Al D'Amato—too many lies for too long.

The *too many lies for too long* line was a gamble. We had said this campaign was not going to be about ethics, and this skirted dangerously close to the line. It was also a very negative attack that had the potential to turn voters off to the attacker.

Kessler thought the line was too harsh. "Shouldn't we tone it down a bit? Maybe we should say something like 'There goes Al, playing loose with facts.'"

Hank would have none of that. "Where does that lead us? Reporters will ask Chuck, 'Are you calling D'Amato a liar?' And Chuck will say, 'No, I'm just saying he's loose with the facts.' Reporters will continue to hound Chuck until he says either 'Yes, D'Amato is a liar' or 'No, he is not.' Adam Nagourney will have a field day with that," Hank said, referring to a *New York Times* reporter who was covering the race.

"We will look weak and unsteady," Hank continued. "And the fact is, D'Amato is lying about your record. He's lying about your record on taxes. He's lying about your record on crime. Let's just say it and be done with it. No one will ask Chuck what he means. It will be obvious and he will look strong instead of weak."

I turned to Carol Kellermann. I had met Carol in college when I was organizing for the Harvard Young Democrats. I had suggested to a friend that we go up to Radcliffe to recruit new members and, as long as we were there, maybe check out the freshman class of women.

The two of us—my friend E. J. Dionne (the future columnist) and I—happened to knock on Carol's dorm room door. While the trip wasn't romantically successful, Carol and I have been best friends ever since. She ran my first campaign for Congress and is one of my closest confidants. She is a contrarian and one of the only people who will hit me with a verbal two-by-four. I especially turn to her whenever I'm afraid I might be going too far. By nature, I'm a *yes* person. If I have to choose between holding still and driving forward, my instinct is always the latter. Carol's the opposite. She's cautious by nature. If there's unnecessary risk or a less than compelling reason for something, she'll say no; she'll hold her fire. When Carol says I should go ahead and do something, I know it's okay. She's kept me out of more trouble than I care to imagine. For this reason and many more, I trust her and depend on her.

"Carol, what do you think of 'too many lies for too long'?"

"I like it." She parcels out compliments as if they are precious stones, so this was high praise.

"Does it go too far?"

"Let's do it," she said.

They were right. I wasn't challenged by a reporter even once about the ads. No one asked me to clarify my position about whether I thought D'Amato was a liar or not. It showed that I was ready to brawl with the toughest politician in the state. And I had a hunch that in the eyes of Joe and Eileen Bailey I had grown a little bit taller.

But we made sure that the *too many lies for too long* line was used only in reference to D'Amato's failure to deliver on his promises for New York or to rebut his attacks on me—not to bring up charges of steering federal contracts to favored friends or alleged wrongdoing. We were not about to touch the thorny ethics issues that dogged D'Amato's career. We were going to keep our eye on the ball—focus on the Baileys, make the campaign about meat and potatoes issues and show that the Fonz couldn't intimidate me.

After the unity breakfast, I rushed to the airport and got on the little one-engine prop plane that the campaign had hired to fly me around the state. The plan was to hit all the big upstate cities—Buffalo, Rochester, Syracuse and Albany—in the first few days after the primary.

When we took off, I asked pilot Mike Ezzo to fly low so my cell phone would work. Throughout the flight, I hurriedly raised money. I called the top donors for Green and Ferraro, dispensed with the chitchat and made my pitch.

"I know you gave to Gerry in the primary; if you still want to beat D'Amato, why don't you help me out? Costa will tell you where to send the check." I would trade phones with my aide, Costa Dimas, and begin another call.

I arrived at our first event in Buffalo with the phone still to my ear. I passed it to Costa and strode to the podium. Several hundred potential supporters and the news media had come out to see the new Democratic nominee.

I am a tough-on-crime, law-and-order Democrat. I have been all along. I believe in people's rights. But I also believe that criminals, particularly violent criminals, should be treated with the punishment that their crimes deserve. And despite his bluster, Al D'Amato is not close to being as tough on crime as Chuck Schumer.

He's been in the Senate too long. He's out of touch with ordinary voters. It's time for him to go.

Over the next few days, I touched on all the Bailey issues.

College is a necessity that is priced like a luxury. If you elect me, we'll fight together to make college tuition tax deductible, just like your home mortgage. Lord knows you've earned the right to a middle-class tax break . . .

Our electricity costs are the highest in the nation. It's bad enough that it eats away at your bank account, but it's also chasing jobs to other states . . .

A plane ticket from Albany to Disney World costs as much as a trip from Chicago to Paris. I will leave no stone unturned to find a Southwest Airlines for the Northeast so that your vacation doesn't break your bank account . . .

I would sometimes bring up the standard Democratic issues, but I could sense the audience starting to drift. They had heard the same platform from Democrats for years and they were tired of it. Maybe they thought our traditional solutions weren't believable. Maybe they thought the problems were unsolvable. All I can tell you is that by 1998, I had been speaking in front of audiences for twenty-five years and I knew when a segment of a speech fell flat. The traditional Democratic themes had lost their potency.

I had my own theory about why average people tuned out when Democrats talked about so many issues. When Joe and Eileen heard Democrats talk about the schools or health care or jobs, they felt we were talking about someone else's health care and another neighborhood's schools.

How many times have you heard Democrats, particularly in the '90s, talk about "the crumbling public schools"? The school in Massapequa that the Bailey children attend is not crumbling. The building is rather nice. The lawn is mowed. There is no graffiti on the walls. The ball field is in good condition. The school is not crumbling; it's just becoming crushingly okay. And the Baileys know that in this new, global, competitive economy, *okay* just won't do. When we, as Democrats, talk about crumbling schools, the story we tell is of a building that is far, far away from the brick and glass structure the Baileys' children are educated in.

This does not mean that Democrats should ignore crumbling schools or any other hardship suffered by the poorest Americans—we must never forget those who are most in need. Beginning to address the middle class does not—must not—mean ceasing to address those below them on the economic ladder. As much as I reached out to the Baileys, I was equally sure never to turn my back on the poor. Instead of pretending that the interests of one were always the interests of the other, I tried to address the issues that concerned the poor and the issues that concerned the middle class—both crumbling schools and crushingly okay ones.

After the event in Buffalo, it was back to the phone. I called Bob Kerrey, a senator from Nebraska and chairman of the DSCC. Now that I had won the primary, I was eligible to receive money from the DSCC. Based on the size of my state, the likelihood of my winning and the wishes of major donors to the DSCC, my share was a little less than $3 million.

"Bob, I need it today," I said.

"Chuck, you don't want to spend this too early. You'll need it in the last weeks in the race. You cannot afford to be outspent in the final days," said Kerrey.

"Bob, I can't afford to go dark now." *Going dark* means not having any ads on the air. "D'Amato will air a blizzard of negative ads to define me. He thinks I've spent everything to win the primary. Well, I saved a couple million to go spot for spot in the first two weeks. I've got D'Amato by the throat and he doesn't know it yet. I'll raise the money for the final weeks. I just need something for weeks three and four."

"I'll see what I can do."

Thankfully, the check arrived a few days later. We needed every penny of it. D'Amato ran an ad in upstate New York that accused me of taking upstate taxpayer dollars and funneling them down to New

York City. It was a clever ad that used computer graphics to depict a school of dollar signs flowing down the Hudson River to New York City. Hank quickly acquired a copy of the ad and ran it—much to D'Amato's chagrin—in New York City.

The first polls showed us statistically neck and neck, with each garnering slightly more than 40%. Our own internal polls showed me down by four points—not a bad place to be seven weeks out. Even more encouraging, my *positives to negatives*—the percentage of voters who had a positive view of me versus the percentage who had a negative view—were pretty good. Meanwhile, D'Amato's negatives were much higher than his positives. Pollsters will tell you that these positive and negative perceptions of each candidate, numbers they call *internals*, are much more important for predicting a winner than the *horse race* ("D'Amato or Schumer?") is.

I asked my pollster, Geoff Garin, a question I would repeat almost every day in the campaign.

"Who would you rather be, me or him?"

"You," Garin said.

A general rule for campaigns is that if you are able to talk about the things you want to talk about and if the news coverage reflects those things, you'll win. If the coverage is about other things—maybe an opponent's attack, maybe a self-inflicted gaffe or maybe an unexpected event—you'll probably lose.

The unexpected event was the impeachment of President Clinton and the Monica Lewinsky scandal. Because I sat on the Judiciary Committee, I had to return to Washington regularly to attend impeachment hearings. While the campaign dictated that I should be in New York campaigning every waking moment, the matter was of such national consequence that there was no question I needed to be in Washington. And I had to prepare by spending precious hours reading and rereading Clinton depositions, grand jury testimony, the Federalist Papers and judicial precedent.

Liberal Democrats in New York were outraged about the attacks on the president. They looked at the impeachment hearings as a right-wing coup. My liberal base was encouraging me, even counting on me, to stand with Clinton and use my senior position on Judiciary to stick it to the Republicans.

Joe Bailey wasn't overly bothered by the scandal. He thought it was sleazy but didn't think it made Clinton a worse president. What bothered him more were the holier-than-thou politicians on both sides. To him, they were hypocrites who should get off their high horses.

Eileen was more bothered. She thought the scandal represented a culture of dishonesty and corruption. She worried about the message the president's actions would send to her children and believed he should be impeached. At an event in Buffalo, a middle-aged woman offered me a vivid articulation of Eileen's view. "'Too many lies for too long,'" she said. "Are you talking about the president?"

I spent much of the next two weeks in Washington. After several days of hearings, including the questioning of witnesses like Kenneth Starr, and many hours locked in a room reading grand jury testimony, I gave a short speech in the Judiciary Committee and, for the first time, laid out my position:

> To me, it is clear that the president lied when he testified before the grand jury—not to cover a crime, but to cover embarrassing personal behavior. And yes, an ordinary person in most instances would not be punished for lying about an extramarital affair. But the president has to be held to a higher standard and the president must be held accountable. That said, the punishment for lying about an improper sexual relationship should fit the crime. . . .
>
> Article II Section 4 of the Constitution states that the president may be removed from office on impeachment for and conviction of treason, bribery or other high crimes and misdemeanors. The framers intended impeachment to apply to public actions related to or affecting the operations of the government and not to personal or private conduct even if that conduct is wrong or may be considered criminal. . . .
>
> I would support a motion to censure, or a motion to rebuke as President Ford suggested yesterday—not because it is the politically expedient to do—but because the president's actions cry out for punishment. And because censure or rebuke, not impeachment, is the right punishment. . . .

It is time to move forward and not have the Congress and the American people endure the specter of what could be a yearlong focus on a tawdry but not impeachable affair. . . . The American people cry out for us to solve the problems facing America—like health care, education and ensuring that seniors have a decent retirement.

In politics, as in life, you have to see the world for what it is and not for what you want it to be. On difficult questions, you have to follow your internal gyroscope. Bill Clinton went before a grand jury and lied. It's true that he never should have been put there in the first place. It's true that Ken Starr's investigation was a witch hunt. It's true that the Lewinsky question had nothing to do with Whitewater or any other matter under investigation. But he still lied before a grand jury and that was wrong.

I went back up to New York to campaign. In speeches, on television and in the newspaper, I was constantly asked about the Clinton impeachment. My answer was always some variation of the statement above: He lied. He may have committed a crime. It does not justify overturning the vote of the American people. Let's not fall into the trap where Congress tries to find a character flaw in every president for the purpose of impeaching him or her. I thought he should be censured, not impeached.

It passed the Bailey test. Even though Joe did not fully agree with me and Eileen disagreed with me, they felt I was being reasonable. They could see that my reaction was thoughtful and, more important, honest. Like Joe, I did not feign moral shock; unlike him, I thought that there was a legitimate reason to talk about the issue. Like Eileen, I believed that the president's behavior was entirely inappropriate, perhaps even criminal. I did not turn it into a partisan counterattack and I did not throw myself on the train tracks for him. But unlike her, I didn't think his actions reached the constitutional standard for impeachment.

You don't always have to agree with the Baileys, but you always have to listen to them.

Though the White House was upset with me, it didn't stop Hillary Clinton from coming up to New York to campaign for me. I could not begin to imagine the stress that was going on in her life. But she came up four times. She couldn't have been received more warmly or enthusiastically if she were Eleanor Roosevelt or the Beatles. Her presence simply shook the venues and the press couldn't resist her. Her strength and indomitable spirit knocked my socks off.

She lit into D'Amato, who had been the ringleader of the original Whitewater hearings. She highlighted the Brady Bill and 100,000 Cops on the Beat. She brought the house down and dominated the news. Reporters asked me questions about impeachment and whether it was a conflict of interest to have her campaigning for me.

Standing beside Hillary, I gave the same answer I'd given before, adding that the White House was not happy with me and noting that the First Lady was not on trial.

And whenever I was asked about it, whether Hillary was campaigning with me or not, I would turn as quickly as I could to issues that the Baileys really cared about. "That's what I think on impeachment, but let's talk about bringing low-cost airfares to upstate."

We took another poll. I had a lead of three points—my first lead in our internal polls. A majority of voters were able to identify my major accomplishments and what I hoped to do in the Senate—which was progress.

"Who would you rather be, him or me?"

"You," Garin said.

As the ad wars and press conference wars continued, I prepared for two back-to-back debates scheduled with D'Amato.

One of my former staffers, Tom Freedman, flew up from Washington to play the role of D'Amato in our prep sessions. After Tom left my office, he worked on the Clinton campaign as a policy advisor and rose to a prominent position in the White House domestic policy shop.

Isay played the role of moderator. Hank, Kessler and my other advisors sat on couches jotting down notes. Carol Kellermann sat on the edge of a table.

Freedman's portrayal of D'Amato was dead-on. He had the voice, the hand motions, the impatient sighs, and the brusqueness of the Fonz. For the first thirty minutes, his portrayal was amusing. It became exasperating once he started beating the pants off me.

"You know, Chuck," said Freedman as D'Amato, "you should be ashamed of those ads you're running. You have voted for over a trillion dollars in tax hikes and I've voted for over a trillion dollars in tax cuts and you call me a liar for pointing out the hard facts. You know, Chuck, facts are a stubborn thing. Now, you just misled the voters of New York by about two trillion dollars. Who's telling 'too many lies for too long' now, Chuck?"

I don't remember how I answered. I just know it wasn't a strong answer. I was flat. I was off.

"You're terrible," said Carol. "You are absolutely terrible. If you perform like that next week, the race is over. Who are you talking to—the moderator? Who are you trying to convince—D'Amato? Who is your target audience—the press?"

"Okay, let me try it again."

Freedman repeated his attack, now calling it the biggest lie in terms of dollars in the history of American politics. This time I did not respond to Freedman, D'Amato or the *New York Times*. Instead, I resumed my conversation with Joe and Eileen Bailey.

"Senator, it is true that you have voted to cut the taxes of people so wealthy that they, their children and their grandchildren will never need to work. And I have opposed them. Just as I have voted for middle-class tax cuts and you have opposed them. Instead of arguing about who's right and who's wrong, why don't you endorse my plan to make college tuition tax deductible? That would be the most important middle-class tax break since the home mortgage deduction. Are you for or against making college tuition deductible, Senator?"

Freedman responded by accusing me of changing the subject and repeated the same charge.

"Senator, the subject is taxes. I think it is clear to the viewers sitting at home that Al D'Amato will not commit to making college tuition tax deductible."

The first debate was Saturday night in Schenectady, just up the New York State Thruway from Albany. The second, the following day, was in New York City, moderated by veteran political reporter Gabe Pressman. They were the first face-to-face meetings between

D'Amato and me in the race, primary included. I felt prepared and confident. I had learned my lesson during the prep session. My goal wasn't to score debate-club points, impress reporters with clever repartee or have the best zinger. It was to convince Joe and Eileen Bailey that I understood their problems, knew how to make their lives better and would fight harder for them than Senator Pothole.

I don't remember much of the debates, except this: I knew I was talking to the Baileys. I wasn't overly argumentative—a trap I can fall into. D'Amato was a bit off, even more so on Sunday afternoon than Saturday night. He was not as tough a debater as Tom Freedman. For some reason, he was not on top of his game. I left the TV studio Sunday afternoon feeling that, as much as there are winners and losers in debates, I was the winner of these two. I talked to the Baileys (if they were watching) and, according to the coverage, I impressed the reporters (though I had pledged not to make them my intended audience). A few months later, *New York Times* reporter Adam Nagourney told me that my performance in the debates convinced him I had a chance to win.

The voters had seen that I was able to stand up to D'Amato and that I was focused on the issues they cared about. But they didn't know me very well. They had known the Fonz for eighteen years; most had only known me for a few weeks, during a brutal campaign. So, as I traveled the state talking to the Baileys, D'Amato had only one play left: the character card.

It's often the case in campaigns that the attack that ends up being the most effective is the one you least expect. We were taken by surprise when D'Amato started hammering me on having missed more than eight hundred votes in my career (a tiny percentage of the many thousands I had cast). The charge focused on a simple, if misleading, fact: In 1998, I had missed scores of committee and procedural votes because I had been in New York for the campaign; D'Amato had missed very few.

We couldn't believe the attack would resonate. It seemed to suggest that I was lazy and didn't do my job. And, while there are a lot of bad things you can say about me, lazy isn't one of them. Throughout my career I have regarded voting as almost a religious obligation; I flew down to Washington if there was even a chance a vote would be called. It troubled me that when the campaign got intense I would have to miss votes. Even so I made sure that I never missed one that was important or those I could make the difference in. Many of the votes I had missed were unanimous or were on the most trivial procedural issues.

Hurriedly, we put together a response attesting to my effectiveness in Congress. It pointed out my legislative accomplishments and noted that I had garnered support from objective observers. It was a pretty good response. And, as Henry Kissinger has said, it had the added benefit of being true.

But we had missed the point of the ads. They were about my character, not my work ethic. I was a craven, ambitious politician who put my own personal quest ahead of the needs of the Baileys. If D'Amato could make this stick, it didn't matter what issues I was talking about. To the Baileys, it wouldn't matter—when I got to Washington, I would forget about them and only be out for myself.

D'Amato flooded the airwaves in English and Spanish. His ads claimed that I wasn't there to support Social Security, breast cancer victims or veterans. The ads were everywhere—in every part of the state, on all the popular channels, at every hour of the day. Our response ads, showing what I had accomplished, highlighting the accolades that others had bestowed on me and illustrating how out of step D'Amato was with New York voters, did not attest to my character.

D'Amato even held an event with Holocaust survivors in front of the Holocaust Memorial Wall in New York.

"He missed the vote to make the Capitol Rotunda available for a magnificent Holocaust commemoration ceremony," the Fonz said. "I understand that you've got to be there—even if it means that there are political events that you'd like to make but you can't—if it comes to missing your duty and your obligation."

I had relatives who suffered and perished in the camps.

And that bill he mentioned? It passed 406 to zero.

But it didn't matter. In D'Amato's telling, I cared more about campaigning than about the victims of the Holocaust.

At first, the polls showed no movement at all. We were still neck and neck. But I could feel a change. I was getting large crowds and warm receptions, but I was also hearing voters call out or mutter under their breath "missed votes" at nearly every stop. Even supporters were bringing it up.

"What's the deal with the missed votes? You're gonna hit D'Amato for missed votes too, right?"

We quickly put another poll in the field. There was a tiny bit of movement toward D'Amato—all within the standard margin of error. We were now dead even, a loss of about three points. That could be real movement or simply the standard statistical anomalies that come with polling. My negative rating was up a little bit, but not too much. My positive rating was down a tick—again, it could be real movement or simply the margin of error.

"Who would you rather be, me or him?" I asked Garin.

"Uh, you. You. I think, you."

Oh, God.

For weeks, I had pummeled D'Amato with Bailey issues—college tuition, upstate airfares, electric rates, cops on the beat, jobs and pensions. I had higher positive ratings and lower negatives.

Now D'Amato had a Bailey issue that trumped mine. Mine were about policy positions; his were about character. For the first time since those bleak February days, I thought I might lose this race.

Some of my closest friends began to wonder why I had gotten into the race in the first place. But even in the darkest moments, I never questioned my decision. For me, it would either be up or out; I did not want to return to the partisanship-poisoned House. If the campaign didn't work out, I would take up teaching. Too often, candidates in tough races fear losing so much that they make serious missteps. I didn't realize it at the time, but my comfort with my decision to run—win or lose—was a critical asset against D'Amato.

A new internal poll showed further erosion of my support. I didn't bother to ask Garin who he'd rather be. I knew the answer.

I hate to admit it, but as hard as you work and as right as you think you are, you still always need a little luck.

Two weeks before election day, as the pressure weighed on both of us, D'Amato made a mistake. In a private meeting with Jewish supporters, including former New York City Mayor Ed Koch, he referred to me as a "putzhead." The comment made its way to the news media. D'Amato was asked about it.

"I have no knowledge of ever doing it. I just don't," he stammered. "I have not engaged in that. I wouldn't engage in it. It's wrong. I haven't done it."

But to Ed Koch's everlasting credit, even though he was a D'Amato supporter, he admitted the Fonz had made the comment.

The press went into a feeding frenzy. The story dominated the nightly broadcasts and was in all the downstate papers. The *New York Times*, in its own inimitable way, called D'Amato's comment a "Yiddish vulgarism."

I didn't ask for an apology. Instead, I focused on the fact that he had lied. The Baileys didn't care if my feelings were hurt (they weren't)—they wanted to see if I would stand up to the bully.

But for the Baileys, my reaction was less important than the fact that D'Amato had lied to their faces. They already understood that he sometimes cut corners in political affairs—to them, that was politics. But no one, politician or anyone else, can maintain their trust if he lies to them. When the Fonz lied, it created a character issue that trumped the missed votes he had wielded against me.

We got a final bit of luck a few days later.

A reporter from the *Village Voice,* Wayne Barrett, uncovered D'Amato's pre-Senate voting records, from his time on the Nassau County Board of Supervisors. My team had tried but been unable to find them. Barrett discovered that during D'Amato's 1980 campaign for Senate, he had missed more than 900 board votes. An enterprising reporter helped save us.

When the story broke, Howard Wolfson's quote was perfect: "This demonstrates Al D'Amato's whole campaign has been a fraud. He's clearly been living in a glasshouse and throwing stones. And today, the glasshouse shattered."

Or, as our ads had put it, *too many lies for too long.*

I welcomed Joe and Eileen Bailey back to my side of the ledger.

Journalists were going in for the kill. They wrote about how stupid D'Amato was to attack me on missed votes when his record was sure to come out. I don't think D'Amato acted stupidly at all. We had blunted all of his conventional attacks. We had won the loyalty of a large share of the Baileys, voters whom he had counted among his supporters. He was playing a losing hand and he had to take a risk, even if it might blow up in his face. In politics, sometimes you have to gamble. I did it on several occasions and was fortunate that I had the odds on my side. In this race, D'Amato was playing against the odds. He had to roll the dice, and eventually he rolled snake eyes.

And, while it was lucky that Wayne Barrett had found those records and that Ed Koch had had the courage to tell the truth when D'Amato lied, it wasn't luck alone that brought Joe and Eileen back. Although they get by without it, the Baileys have a persistent hope for a new type of politics, one that speaks to them. Of course, they have frequently been disappointed by politicians, so they are wary of any who claim to carry the torch. But since I had spent my life—and my campaign—working on their behalf, they were more willing to cut me some slack once there were two sides to the story. I know that Wayne Barrett and Ed Koch opened the door, but I like to believe that a flicker of hope sparked by my campaign is what brought the Baileys back.

On the Sunday before election night, Garin called me with the last of our nightly tracking polls. I was up by a half-dozen points and the lead seemed to be widening.

For the last time, I asked him: "Who would you rather be, me or him?"

"You, Chuck."

My apartment was quiet. Iris and the kids were sleeping down the hall. I walked to the window and stood staring out over the scattered lights of Brooklyn—Bay Ridge to the south, Williamsburg to the north—and the Manhattan skyline beyond. For the first time in eight months, I was still.

In 1974, fresh out of law school, I ran for the New York State Assembly. Every day I went door-to-door looking for support among my neighbors, the original Baileys. My mother thought it was such a foolhardy career move that she told her friends to vote against me. When I asked my local barber to put a Schumer sign in the window, I was rebuffed. "Chuck, I'm not only a barber, I'm also a bookie. We're giving you fifty-to-one odds."

This race and my first race were similar in one way—they both proved that campaigns are unpredictable beasts.

At the beginning of 1998, I was struggling. We took the measure of who I was—why I was in the race—and we committed to run a campaign dedicated to those for whom I had entered politics in the first place. Twenty-five years after my first election, and with a state-wide electorate so seemingly dissimilar but in reality so much like the constituents in my first Assembly District, it had started to work. Then, unpredictable events had threatened to knock me off track. Impeachment was a minefield—but I followed my conscience and explained myself to the Baileys. For a time, missed votes looked to be my downfall—but a stupid comment and exhumed voting records saved me.

Now I was poised to become the first U.S. senator from Brooklyn in 140 years. For all the hard work, life lessons and legislative accomplishments that had filled a quarter century, I was right back where I started in 1974—with the Baileys.

After a moment, I turned from the window and headed for bed. There was a lot of work to do.

On the final two days, I didn't leave anything to chance. I campaigned like I was six points behind, not six points ahead. We hit every part of the state. On election day eve, Hillary Clinton flew up to Manhattan for a three o'clock rally. It was her fourth visit of the campaign, and the crowd simply erupted at her presence.

It was obvious from the reception how many New Yorkers already loved her. When Senator Moynihan announced his retirement and Representative Charlie Rangel and others begged her to run, I like to think she remembered the tremendous reception she'd received that fall. She helped me win then, and I hope her visits were a factor in her decision to run in 2000. One of the open secrets in Washington is that senators of the same party and same state rarely get along. Hillary and I are both ambitious, hardworking politicians who occasionally step on each other's toes. We have had our high points and our low points. But we have the bonds of my campaign in 1998 and hers in 2000 that are unique to our relationship. She's a great senator and I'm glad we are partners in the Senate.

After Hillary left, I decided to fly back up to Buffalo for a final campaign rally in West Seneca, a middle-class suburb. As I took to the podium, my staffer Jack O'Donnell handed me a box of Flutie Flakes.

I held up the cereal box with local football legend Doug Flutie on the front. "They said Flutie was too short, too light and too fragile to win. And they said I was too downstate, too unknown and too much of an underdog," I remember saying. "I'm no Doug Flutie, but tomorrow we'll see who deserves the breakfast of champions."

On election day, the polls closed at 9:00 p.m. Within half an hour the race was over. I beat D'Amato in New York City and the counties of Erie, Monroe and Albany—homes of three of the biggest upstate cities. I lost the county where Joe and Eileen Bailey live— Nassau—by only six points. That was D'Amato's home base and his margin was far, far smaller than necessary. D'Amato also took many of the more rural and suburban upstate counties, but there his margins were too thin, as well.

My connection to the Baileys and all the families like them, from southeastern Queens to the northern and western reaches of the state—the Wilsons, Pachinskis, Ramirezes, Bernardis and so many others—was critical. In the end, with their help, I beat Alfonse "the Fonz" D'Amato by nine points.

A few months later, D'Amato and I had our first real conversation since the election. In talking about why I had won, he offered what he said was an enormous compliment. "I couldn't scare you, Chuck," he said. "You've got the two biggest ones in the state."

Then, he told me about the new lobbying firm he was putting together and proceeded to lobby me on behalf of a New York client.

He had quite a pair himself.

CHAPTER 4

OHIO 4 BUSH

ON ELECTION NIGHT 2004, I was on the ballot again—for my first reelection to the Senate. This time, the national focus was not on New York, where my race and the presidential vote were both foregone conclusions. Instead, everyone, including my team, was focused on a number of presidential swing states and close Senate elections throughout the country.

My aides and I spent the night monitoring BlackBerries for updates on national results.

> *Message: Carson, no. Bowles, no. Castor, 2 close. Daschle, no.*
> *Reply: Daschle no?*
> *Message: Daschle no. Florida 4 Bush. Ohio 2 close.*

I handed the BlackBerry back to a staffer as an aide poked her head inside the hotel room door to tell me I had fifteen minutes to get downstairs, be introduced and start speaking in time to be covered on the local news.

"How's the crowd?"

"They're beginning to realize it's going to be a bad night."

I grabbed a marked-up copy of my victory speech and, with my family behind me, walked past the police officer guarding my hotel room. We took a service elevator to the ground floor, where we were led by a handful of staff members to a roped-off area behind the podium.

After telling me that my forehead looked shiny, a staffer dabbed a little pancake makeup on my brow. Hillary Clinton, now my colleague in the Senate, walked over, trailed by a clutch of staffers.

"Daschle lost," she said.

"I know."

I was planning to give a serious speech. So much of campaigns devolve into thirty-second ads and daily attacks that I like to conclude each of my reelections with something forward looking. It's a great opportunity to speak to people and I like them to hear something of substance.

I took the stage in front of a crowd of more than a thousand supporters, thanked the voters, my staff and my family, and began to talk about election reform. It was an issue on which I had taken a leadership role since the Florida fiasco in the 2000 election. As was predictable, there were indications of shenanigans in Florida and Ohio on this night as well. But the crowd was clearly antsy. They had come not to celebrate my victory or to hear an allocution on ballot boxes, but to revel in the defeat of George Bush. The early optimism in the ballroom had bordered on euphoric. Now the worm was turning.

The television election coverage—projected on two large screens astride the stage—was decidedly cautious. But the body language in the respective presidential campaign parties told a different story. At the Kerry party, the boisterous crowds of an hour earlier had been reduced to grim stares and stage murmurs. The worried looks at the Bush gala had turned into confident grins.

On television, Florida was still among a handful of key presidential states that were too close to call. The critical Senate races in South Dakota, Florida, North Carolina, Kentucky and elsewhere were still being listed as toss-ups.

But those of us on the inside—those with campaign aides holding BlackBerries containing urgent messages from campaign consultants and pollsters—knew better. The networks were merely trying to save themselves from the embarrassment of 2000, when they mistakenly projected Florida for Gore.

I cut my speech down to about half the size and spent thirty minutes in the crowd—sneaking glances down at the borrowed Black-Berry—assuring supporters that many of the key races were still too close to call.

Castor, no. Mongiardo, no.

By the time we made it back to the hotel room, the television coverage and the BlackBerry messages were in sync. Florida was colored red on the map. Daschle went from "could lose" to "will lose." Ohio stayed in the toss-up column, but Bush's lead was not contracting at anywhere near the rate necessary to turn the tide toward Kerry.

A bit of gallows humor lightened the moment. "Well, you'll move up in seniority," said Iris.

"There's an opening on Finance," said Mike Lynch, now my chief of staff.

"If you run for governor, you'd win," said Hank Morris, still my top campaign advisor. He wasn't being light.

On the ride home, while noshing on a few cold chicken wings, I weighed two contradictory thoughts. The first was that in purely numerical voting terms, we didn't fare so badly. This is a truly divided nation, I thought. The left and right are evenly matched—a couple of breaks here, a few bobbles there, and it's Republicans who are eating cold chicken wings and Democrats who are measuring the drapes in the Oval Office.

The second thought was, Who am I kidding? As close as the election seemed, there were far greater fundamental problems afflicting the Democratic Party (problems that still must be solved today, despite our victory in 2006).

In Alaska, we ran a popular former governor against a political newcomer who was appointed to the U.S. Senate by her dad—the current governor. We lost.

In Oklahoma, we fielded a brilliant and moderate Democratic House member against one of the most conservative congressmen of the last ten years. We lost.

In North Carolina, we nominated a former White House chief of staff against an ardently pro-business congressman. We lost. In South Dakota, we had the most powerful Democrat in the Senate running against a Republican who had lost a run for the same office only two years earlier. We lost.

We lost in Florida despite a divisive, mudslinging GOP primary. We lost in South Carolina against a candidate who called for a 22% sales tax. We lost in Kentucky against an incumbent who had seemed suddenly vulnerable.

All of my lessons from thirty years in politics told me this: Democrats weren't simply victims of bad luck—there was something more seriously wrong.

The sobering truth is that we had no excuses. We lost every contested race except for one lone victory, by the capable and honorable Colorado attorney general, Ken Salazar. The only other bright spot was the landslide win by a promising young politician who had taken that summer's Democratic Convention by storm, Barack Obama of Illinois.

We pulled up in front of our apartment building in Brooklyn. I said goodnight to the New York City police detective who had been assigned to me since my election to the Senate. Iris, Jessica and Alison groggily trudged to our front door. The borrowed BlackBerry buzzed one last time.

Ohio 4 Bush.

Now the night was officially a total loss.

I did not think we would lose as badly as we had. Democrats now controlled only forty-four seats (forty-five, if you counted Vermont Independent Jim Jeffords). I was left with the queasy feeling that the party I had grown up with as a child and belonged to as an elected officeholder for thirty years was no longer competitive with too many voters in too many parts of the country.

I knew that the next morning the recriminations would begin. The liberals would blame the moderates for the Democrats' dismal showing. The moderates would blame the liberals. Everyone would blame John Kerry. A few would blame the Democratic pollsters and media consultants.

I couldn't help but feel that they were all wrong—that they were all missing an essential element of what had brought us to this disastrous night. I drifted off to sleep bothered by a nagging thought, a sense of unsettling déjà vu.

Nationally, the Democratic Party had forgotten Joe and Eileen Bailey.

Over the previous six years, during my first term in the Senate, I thought of the Baileys just about every day. They had not always agreed with me. But I had made sure they always understood where I was coming from.

At the end of 1998, after the excitement of the election had died down and shortly before I was sworn in as senator, we began to plan for the future. Josh Isay and Mike Lynch—who were soon to be in charge of my D.C. and New York operations—gathered my close circle of advisors. It was the first time we had all been together since election night. The idea was to lay out goals for year one and my whole term.

That meeting was the first of what would become an annual tradition. Josh and Mike called it Festivus—a reference to the holiday invented by the Jerry Stiller character on *Seinfeld*. (And an appropriate allusion to the spirited debate that was a hallmark of our annual gatherings.)

Josh called the meeting to order. "Welcome to Festivus," he announced. "Let's start with campaign promises."

Campaign promises can be tricky things. In every campaign, many are made; generally, right after the election, too many are forgotten—until the next campaign rolls around and a challenger inevitably hits the incumbent with promises made and promises broken.

I didn't want to make that mistake.

"First promise—" Josh continued, "to counter D'Amato's claim that you'd never be seen west of the Hudson, you said you'd go to every county in your first term."

During the campaign, I had promised to visit all sixty-two counties during one six-year term. As a Brooklyn-born and -bred politician, I issued this pledge to the neglected upstate New York voters. They felt ignored by national politicians in general and by Democrats in particular. Even Mario Cuomo barely got above 30% among the rural counties.

"That's easy," said Carol. "It's only ten a year."

"Less if you count the fifteen high-population ones," Hank said. "What's next?"

Lynch put up his hand. "One second," he said. "Sixty-two counties in a term *is* too easy. What is that—you visit once every six years? If you really care about upstate then really spend time upstate. You should visit all sixty-two counties *every year*."

"What about Hamilton?" someone screamed. "It has five thousand people!"

Lynch smiled. "So what?"

Hank smiled too. "Woody Allen says 80% of life is just showing up."

I love traveling, going to events and meeting people. As a congressman, I traveled around my district as much as I could, even though my seat was safe. Visiting people where they live is one of my favorite parts of the job. "Let's do it," I said. "Sounds like fun."

It's one of the best decisions I've ever made. Visiting sixty-two counties every year isn't always easy. Some years, it can be grueling. But it's always valuable. There is nothing like getting out of the big cities and spending time in towns, villages and everything in between. You get to walk Main Streets. Shake hands on front porches. Smell freshly tilled fields. See challenges and achievements up close.

While visiting Seneca County during my first summer in the Senate, I realized what the sixty-two-county tour was really all about. A drought was ravaging the Finger Lakes that year. I'll never forget standing in a field of dying corn, a few hundred yards from the shores of Lake Seneca. The farmer who owned the field stood next to me, stoic amid his shriveling stalks. All that fresh water was so close, but he couldn't make use of it. There was nothing he could do to save his crop. He accepted the power of nature and God in his life and, though he couldn't do anything, he persevered. It was the first of many lessons about farmers, their relationship with nature and their outlook that I never could have learned on the tried-and-true political circuit. It's also why I was so touched when the New York Farm Bureau, a largely Republican group, made me Man of the Year—they dubbed me the "Brooklyn Farmer."

Traveling the state has not only changed my perspective, it has also sparked some of my most important initiatives. The city of Cortland, in Cortland County, is an industrial town that has suffered a huge number of layoffs over the years. Today, its last best hope is a company called Marietta. Few have heard of it, but we've all used its products: those little shampoo bottles you get at hotels. Marietta's CEO told me that the company is able to get those little bottles into every hotel room, in every hotel in the world. The only place they can't go, he said, is China. Protectionist Chinese trade policies keep them out. Worse still, with no competition and huge profits in a protected domestic market, their Chinese counterpart is now taking advantage of open trade policies in other countries to compete with Marietta all over the world. My visit to Cortland County is what pushed me to start fighting in the Senate against China's unfair trade policies.

My annual sixty-two-county tour is a lot better than just showing up; it's more than demonstrating to families all over the state that I still have time for local issues. It's allowed me to learn about my constituents—and the world—in a way that would not have been possible if I'd stayed on the beaten path.

It's not always easy, but it's always a joy. I enjoy it so much that I'm still doing it in my second term, even though my pledge has expired.

The next decision at that first Festivus was not as easily accepted. As a congressman, I had become famous among reporters for my Sunday press conferences. Sunday is a slow news day, so I had made a regular habit of calling press conferences to talk about important issues that might not otherwise get covered. I would highlight consumer fraud, release a health study or publicize a federal program that would benefit the Baileys. Sunday press conferences were my chance to talk to the Baileys about the things they cared about most.

Though I was now going to be a senator, I wanted to continue holding Sunday press conferences. At Festivus, people were worried. They made three arguments. First, Sunday press conferences are not senatorial. Second, pundits mock them. Third, if I held too many, the *New York Times* editorial page would find it harder to take me seriously.

Each of the arguments had validity. The thing was, though, that none of the arguments had anything to do with the Baileys. I didn't believe that the Baileys focused on my senatorial image, the pundits' opinions or the *Times* editorial page. They cared that I was out there fighting for and delivering on issues that mattered to them. That was my job, after all.

I could see that it was sometimes important to be senatorial, I grudgingly admitted that pundits occasionally mattered, and I agreed that being taken seriously by the *Times* and other editorial pages was important. I wanted to win each of those battles. I just wasn't willing to ignore the Baileys for any of them.

So, throughout my term I held regular Sunday press conferences. Each spoke to the Joe and Eileen of the local region—not to the pundits or the editorialists. I would talk about something that they cared about. Something that affected their lives directly. All too often, the things I talked about had nothing to do with the issue du jour in Washington.

I liked demonstrating to the Baileys that government can be a force for good in their lives, that politicians are able to get beyond partisan squabbling. Government and politics so frequently seem irrelevant; when the Baileys watch the local news on Sunday nights, I hope they see that government can indeed make a difference for them. Sometimes a Sunday press conference and a little follow-up pressure were all it took to solve a problem; shining sunlight on it was enough. I convinced Presidents Clinton and Bush to dip into the Strategic Petroleum Reserve to reduce gasoline price spikes, successfully pressured the FDA to warn patients about the suicide risk of antidepressants and forced companies to make holiday gift cards more honest and fair.

The Sunday press conferences regularly earned snickers among the pundits. But any doubt I had about them vanished a couple of years into my term. My daughter Alison, a natural athlete, got a concussion while playing basketball at school. They rushed her to the hospital. Iris met her there. When the intake nurse, an immigrant, heard Alison's last name, she peered at my daughter.

"Schumer?" She asked. "Any relation to the senator?"

Iris said that yes, I was the patient's father.

"Tell that man I love what he does. Usually the politicians talk blather," she said with a touch of anger, emphatically poking the air. "But Schumer, he's on the TV every Sunday night talking about something that matters to *me*."

The final thing we did at the first Festivus was to make a legislative priority list. In some ways, this was the easiest thing we did all day. I knew I would keep my campaign promises. I knew I would never forget the middle class.

So, as soon as we started, the list flowed. It was the work I had been doing throughout my adult life and the message we had been talking about for a year. Cheap airfare, generic drugs and college tuition deductibility immediately went to the top of the priority list.

We didn't forget the grander, more sweeping issues, nor did we forsake traditional Democratic concerns. I had a lot of energy and was planning to work both in the trenches and on the mountaintops. My two predecessors in the senate, D'Amato and Moynihan, were each known for one or the other. But I aspired to model my Senate career on that of Jacob Javits, whom I had known only in the twilight of his. If you had put Javits in a centrifuge, you would have gotten Moynihan *and* D'Amato. He had been able to amass impressive legislative accomplishments and deliver on the local needs of regular people.

Isay summarized the meeting. In addition to staffing decisions, three things stood out: the Sixty-Two-County Pledge, Sunday press conferences, and a legislative priority list heavily studded with middle-class issues.

It was a great six years. I was with the Baileys and they were on my side. I visited all sixty-two counties every year. I held regular Sunday press conferences. And, I was able to compile a legislative record that encompassed the larger issues—such as the fight to keep extreme judges off the bench—and issues that worked more directly for the Baileys—such as making college tuition tax deductible.

As my reelection approached, I thought it was possible that I might win every county and win by the largest margin in the history of New York State. (An achievement made possible by a weak opponent and a Republican Party machine in New York that, post–Al D'Amato, is, frankly, moribund.) Mike Lynch was obsessed with both goals—especially after his beloved Yankees were beaten in Boston's march to the World Series title.

Lynch figured that to achieve the goals we would need a slight margin in rural upstate counties and a big margin in the expanding exurbs. The rural counties vote very much like central Pennsylvania or rural Ohio. At first glance, these voters—Tom and Ann Hancock—seem much more conservative than the Baileys. But they're not. They're middle-class and traditional and carry a touch of populism. It became clear that I'd do well with the Hancocks when the rural papers, one by one, put aside some of their disagreements with me on national issues to endorse me.

On election day, we did set the record for the all-time largest margin, winning with 71% of the vote. About four out of every ten people who voted for Bush made the active choice of crossing over from the Republican line to the Democratic line and voting for me.

And, we came close to Lynch's goal of winning every county. We won sixty-one of sixty-two—the blue ones, the purple ones and all the red ones except one. Hamilton, population five thousand and the only county without a local daily newspaper, went for my opponent. Thanks to my every-county-every-year promise, I had visited Hamilton more times in my one term than any previous senator had in his entire career. One staffer joked that the problem in Hamilton was that I had met each of the voters personally.

Despite Hamilton, I felt vindicated.

In 1998, as a little-known congressman from a corner of Brooklyn, I had asked the Baileys to give me the benefit of the doubt; in 2004, the election results showed that after six years of working hard to make government work for them, their doubts were gone.

The morning after election day 2004, I was eating a bowl of corn flakes in my Park Slope apartment when my youngest daughter, Alison, came in and announced that Harry Reid was on the phone.

With Tom Daschle defeated, there were vacancies throughout the Democratic Senate leadership. Harry Reid, a soft-spoken Nevadan, was the odds-on choice to replace Tom as minority leader.

I had spoken to Daschle right after his defeat. I was never personally close to him, but I felt that he embodied much of what is good about politics. He was in the business for the right reasons—to make a difference in people's lives. As Democratic leader in the Senate, he was constantly required to put his own career at cross-purposes with the wishes of his constituents in South Dakota.

The way he had lost also really bothered me. Millions of dollars had been raised and spent by outside groups to demonize one of the most honest and gentlemanly people I had ever known in politics. Daschle's defeat had been largely due to a series of nasty, personal attack ads meant to convince South Dakotans that the Democratic leader had "gone Washington."

When I called Daschle, I told him that he was going to be happy in his new life because he had a wife and children who loved him and he, unlike many in politics, was a balanced person. My sense from him was that he was still in shock about his defeat, but relieved that he could finally lead a normal life without worrying about eking out a slim victory in a deeply red state every six years against a well-financed opponent and brutal attack machine.

Now, the day after the election night debacle, I was shoveling spoonfuls of corn flakes into my mouth and on the line with Harry Reid. We did not talk about Daschle. In politics, when you lose, everyone else just moves on.

Actually, it's even worse. After a defeat, other elected politicians look upon the vanquished sympathetically but as if they were inflicted with a communicable disease—the loser's disease. Politicians like to choose their own exit from the arena, but it rarely occurs as planned. In Tom Daschle's defeat, every Democratic senator saw his or her own political mortality. Rather than dwell on the uncomfortable, we chit-chatted for a little bit before Harry got to the point.

"Chuck, I'm running for leader and I'd like your vote."

Reid is a political junkie, a consummate insider and a masterful Senate tactician. He is soft-spoken and polite and is a deeply religious Mormon. He will also kneecap you if you cross him.

When I was first elected to the Senate, I was advised to get to know and make friends with him. As an eighteen-year veteran of the House, I was told repeatedly that the Senate worked much differently than the chaotic, turf-conscious House. In the House, bipartisanship is rare and there were members with whom I served but could not even name.

The Senate is a club steeped in tradition and civility. Personal relationships matter a great deal. Debate is deliberate and, at times, even scholarly. In the House, the maximum any one representative usually may speak on a bill is five minutes, and that's only for the most senior House members. The first time I came to speak in the Senate, the clerk asked me how much time I would need. I figured

I'd go for the maximum. "Do you think I could have five minutes?" I asked.

"Only five?" she replied. "Guess you don't have much to say." In my eighteen-year career in the House, I was probably afforded the right to speak for five minutes fewer than thirty times. In the Senate, you can go on forever—a great luxury for senators and a bad habit for politicians.

Even though the Senate is a civil place, civility and politeness should not be confused with weakness or timidity. The civility hides the ferocity of the debate and the many layers of calculations that go into certain bills or nominations. The rules of the Senate give incredible parliamentary powers to each of us. One senator can block a bill or hold up a presidential appointment. Any senator can gum up the works for days at a time. There is no one in the Senate who doesn't matter. But, as minority whip and the senator who knew floor procedures better than anyone but West Virginia's Senator Robert Byrd, Harry Reid mattered more than most. He could help you bring a bill to the floor or get a plum committee assignment.

When I arrived in the Senate, I struck up several conversations with Reid. He knew everything that was going on in the Senate; I could learn something by talking to him. And as the whip, he alone could tell me when votes would end—information I pumped him for on the frequent days when I had a drum-tight schedule back in New York. But most important, I liked him. Two men in the same career couldn't be more different, yet we quickly became buddies. Today, we are the best of friends.

"I'm with you," I told him. "Who can I call?"

Reid gave me a list of senators; I made the calls.

Within two days, it was clear that Reid would be the leader; the race would be uncontested.

The moment it was sewn up, Reid called to thank me. Seamlessly, he turned the conversation to my future.

During my campaign, I was constantly asked if I had future plans to run for governor. The morning Reid called to thank me, the *New York Times* had run a story speculating that three Democratic Northeastern politicians could be trading in their Senate seats for homes in their respective governor's mansions.

"Our backs are against the wall," Reid said. "Corzine is thinking of running for governor. Dodd is thinking of running for governor. And it looks like you're thinking of running for governor. We've got a hell of a fight on our hands, and we really need you." He didn't pressure me. He didn't ask me what I was thinking. All he said was that they would need me.

If Reid had asked what I was thinking, I knew exactly what I would have said. It made me laugh to think about it. Over the previous three months, I had probably been asked about running for governor a thousand times. Each time, I gave the same answer: "The only thing on my radar screen is being a good senator and helping New York. That's my only focus."

I said it so much, it became a joke. Some reporters started finishing the thought for me. But they kept asking. In an election that didn't offer much in terms of competition or scandal, they were hoping for a scoop. There wasn't one to give, so my answer left just enough daylight to allow them to keep filing stories.

The thing is, I wasn't being coy. No reporter believed it, but I was being cautious. The question of whether I would, or even could, run for governor would only be relevant if I was reelected—I refused to address the question before this election was in the bag.

One of my favorite political lessons has nothing to do with politics—it's the story of Mike Tyson and Buster Douglas. When he was champion of the world, Tyson agreed to face an unranked fighter named Buster Douglas in a match in Tokyo. The fight was the most punishing of Tyson's career to that point. Incredibly, Douglas won. The next day, the bloody and bowed champ was asked how he could have lost to an unranked fighter, a nobody.

The answer was obvious: Tyson had been looking past the easy opponent to the next fight. He lost because he wasn't prepared for the task at hand. Douglas, like most challengers, was hungry. His sole focus was on competing against the champ. He ended up giving enough to take him out.

In every election season there is one Mike Tyson—a sure-bet candidate who goes down or almost goes down. In 2004, it was Senator Jim Bunning of Kentucky, who came within a hair of losing his seat. Bunning didn't think he had a race. For much of the night it looked like he shortly would not have a job.

The truth was that I wasn't just refusing to talk about running for governor. I was refusing to think about it, too.

Now, for the first time, I started to think about it.

There's no question that a governor has much more immediate impact than a senator does. You are in charge of an enormous and powerful bureaucracy. There are a thousand decisions you can make on your own—both big and small. You decide if we need new roads. If we do, you decide if they should run through Chemung County or Steuben County. (And then you have to make it up to the county that lost.)

Still, over the last fifty years, only one New York governor has left a lasting legacy—Nelson Rockefeller. Meanwhile, both Pat Moynihan and Jacob Javits left a legacy with their work in the Senate. This is not any governor's fault—it's the nature of the job. Inevitably, a huge amount of energy is spent on issues that are not of your choosing.

I knew that my decision would come down to one question. With my thirty years of experience as a legislator and my ability to get things done for the Baileys, did it make any sense to drastically change course now? With my particular set of strengths and weaknesses, where could I do the most for the state and country I loved?

The week after the election, I flew down to Washington for organizational meetings among the remaining Senate Democrats. There were also a few votes that needed to be taken before Congress officially adjourned for the year.

The mood was bleak. Tom Daschle dropped by the Tuesday Democratic Caucus lunch and received a loud, sustained standing ovation. There were tears in the room upon seeing him and he was clearly moved, as was I.

Then Harry Reid sauntered over to me, put his hand on my shoulder, bent his head toward mine and said in a voice barely above a whisper, "You're on the Finance Committee. It doesn't matter what you decide. You're on Finance." Then he walked away. This was the committee assignment I'd wanted for twenty-four years—eighteen in the House and six in the Senate.

When I was first elected to the Senate in 1998, former New Jersey Senator Bill Bradley called me up and said, "I have three words of advice for you: Finance, Finance, Finance." One week after taking my Senate seat, I went to pay homage to New York's senior senator Pat Moynihan. I had a special fondness for Moynihan dating back to my college days, when I had had him for a professor. Although he generally ignored the House and paid almost no attention to New York's congressional delegation—I doubt he could name half of us—because of our early acquaintance, we became friends.

Moynihan was getting frail at this point—the pain from the back injury he had suffered in World War II never left him. But he was still exceptionally quick-witted and brilliant. "I'm going to retire," he told me confidentially. "But, Chuck, you must get on the Finance Committee. It controls 80% of tax policy and 50% of spending policy." He was the only New York senator ever to hold a seat on the coveted committee.

Freshman year of college, I took Economics 1 with Otto Eckstein. I was struck by the power of economic levers on meat-and-potatoes issues. Ever since, economic issues have fascinated me. To me, there is no better place than Finance. You control large economic levers—such as tax policy—and smaller ones—a large share of discretionary spending. No other committee has as potent a combination of issues. I don't believe that any other offers the same opportunity to benefit New York and America or to help bring the Democratic Party back to Joe and Eileen Bailey.

Now a seat on the Finance Committee was mine for as long as I stayed.

Later in the week, Reid asked me to take the helm of the Democratic Senatorial Campaign Committee—the campaign arm for Senate Democrats. I had been asked to chair the DSCC before, but felt that the timing wasn't right for me. It's a very political job that includes an intense fundraising component. I didn't want to take the position until I had been reelected first.

The DSCC job is not necessarily a plum assignment. It's like being elected president of your condo association—someone's got to do it. It requires a lot of travel and a lot of time dialing for dollars.

Reid is a clever guy and a great psychologist. He spent one year courting disgruntled Vermont Republican Jim Jeffords before finally sitting down and opening a dialogue to get the New England icono-clast to switch parties. Here, he was playing it smart with me. He gave me the Finance Committee first so that if I decided I didn't want the DSCC job, I'd still get the committee post I desired. There was no quid pro quo. He was telling me that my staying was so important to him that he wasn't going to play the usual games and cut the usual deals.

I hadn't told anyone yet, but Reid didn't need to be so careful. For me, there was no question. I was staying in the Senate.

I felt that in the Senate I would have more freedom to focus on the large and small issues that I believe are most important. I wouldn't have to keep the bureaucracy humming; I could devote a greater percentage of my time to things I truly cared about. And, in Attor-ney General Eliot Spitzer, New York already had an accomplished and popular candidate for governor. Whether I ran or not, a Demo-crat would finally win back the governor's mansion and begin to fix our often dysfunctional state government.

The truth was, I was eager to do the DSCC job. While it wouldn't be easy, it was the right job for me. I love campaigns and I don't mind calling donors for money. I hoped that my ability to craft a message, frame issues and fight with passion would serve me well in the post.

The number-one reason that I decided to take the job was because I worried that if we had another bad election, if we lost another two or three seats, it would be over. Conservative Republi-cans, with their harsh social and economic agendas, would run roughshod over the entire country. The Supreme Court would take this nation backward 130 years. I took the job because I felt I had an obligation to do everything I possibly could to stop that from hap-pening.

I had a philosophy about what the Democrats were doing wrong and how to correct it. In my view, we had forgotten the middle class. We talked about them, but we didn't listen to them. Even worse, we were under the illusion that they liked what we had to say. In the 2004 election, the middle class was the runaway bride and Democrats were left standing at the altar. I had built my career by working for and communicating with the middle class. I wanted the chance to help the Democratic Party patch up the relationship.

A few days later I went in to see Harry Reid. "I'm going to stay in the Senate," I said. Reid was visibly relieved. "And I'm going to take the DSCC job, on two conditions."

Reid nodded for me to continue.

"First, I want to run the DSCC like a business. If I take over, I want us to win."

"Me, too," Reid said with his quiet determination. In the last six years, I had learned that Reid says what he means, knows the buck stops with him and has a backbone that's tougher than iron. He had come to remind me of President Truman—another great Democratic Harry. "They are five changes we should make," I continued. "First, as you've said, we shouldn't ask donors to retire our debt—they don't want to pay for past mistakes, they want to pay for future victories."

"I'm already there."

"Second, we can't let red-state Democrats retire—in '04 we lost every race where they did. Third, I don't want to give money to incumbents in safe seats just because they have seniority in the caucus—we have to spend money where it counts. Fourth, we have to recruit candidates and mix in in the primaries—no more throwing up the cards and seeing where they land; we have to get candidates who understand average voters. And finally, if we're funding the campaigns, we get a say in how they're run—senior staffs have to be okayed by us. I'm not paying for hacks to run our candidates into the ground."

Reid nodded. "Chuck, I wouldn't want it any other way."

Both of us kept our word—each of the five points became a reality.

On the strength of Harry Reid's brilliance with people, the first was surprisingly quick. Within the first three months, incumbent Democratic senators had generously paid down our debt to zero. Not a dime of debt was paid for by contributors.

To keep red-state Democrats from retiring, Harry and I hounded Kent Conrad of North Dakota, Ben Nelson of Nebraska and Bill Nelson of Florida for most of the first session. We negotiated, we begged, we appealed to their higher aspirations for the country. In the end, none retired. And every one of them coasted to easy reelection.

Before announcing the third point—that we were no longer going to give money to those running for safe Senate seats—I approached Ted Kennedy and Hillary Clinton. They are two of the biggest names in the caucus and both were up for reelection in 2006. I told each of them that I wanted to spend money on seats we *could* win, not seats we *would* win, like theirs. They both agreed immediately. And they promised to have a talk with any colleague who didn't.

On the fourth point, in each contested state, we did our research and picked the best candidate. In some cases, I took flak for it. The first candidate we sought was in Pennsylvania—we felt we had to beat Rick Santorum. I called Governor Ed Rendell and asked who in his state could beat Santorum.

"There's only one guy who can win," Rendell told me. "Except he doesn't want to run and you wouldn't want him if he did."

"If he'd win, why wouldn't we want him?"

"Because he's Bob Casey and he's anti-abortion."

I took a deep breath. "Ed, the days when Democratic candidates had to check off twenty boxes before getting our support are over. Maybe if we had sixty seats, we could do that. But not this year. Not with our backs against the wall."

Casey was the guy who best represented the Joe and Eileen Baileys of Pennsylvania. In fact, in some ways, he is the living embodiment of Joe. A lot of time was spent convincing him to run. But it took no time to call the election in his favor when the polls closed. His dominance from the first day of the campaign to the last hour of the election allowed us to focus resources on other states. Now, even my most liberal friends, who had been angry at me for choosing him, admit it was the right thing to do.

In going out of our way to choose candidates, we looked for people who understood and could talk to the Baileys of their home state. Bob Casey wasn't the only candidate who reminded me of a state's Joe or Eileen Bailey. Jon Tester wouldn't have played in Rhode Island, but he is the embodiment of the Montana farmer; Sheldon Whitehouse could never have competed in Billings, but he was the perfect candidate to talk to the average Rhode Islander.

In more than one instance, we broke with Democratic praxis and intervened in primaries when one candidate was clearly a better fit than the others. In Virginia, Jim Webb fit like a glove. He was equally comfortable in the D.C. suburbs in the north and the Scotch-Irish redoubts in the southwest of the state. The bloggers spied Webb early on and got behind his candidacy. When he faced a primary against Harris Miller—a fine man, but someone who would not have fit as well with Virginia—we followed the bloggers' lead by intervening to support Webb. In Minnesota, it was clear from the first look that Amy Klobuchar is as Minnesota as they come. She got into her race early but had three opponents in the primary—we again broke with tradition and backed her.

In Missouri, we had the opposite problem. No one was running, but Claire McCaskill was right for Missouri and could win. I spent months and months trying to persuade her to enter the race. When I learned that our family vacations to London overlapped, I found out where her family was staying and invited them to dinner. Iris, the girls and I had a lovely time with Claire, Joe and their kids—and we showed them that being in the Senate wouldn't foreclose a family life.

Of all the things Harry Reid and I discussed the day I took the DSCC job, I believe that aggressive candidate selection—through both recruitment and intervention in primaries—contributed to winning the Senate majority more than any other (even more than our fundraising advantage, which was significant, to be sure).

Finally, on the point of staff, we wanted the best at the DSCC, and we were lucky enough to get them. Our four senior staffers— Executive Director J. B. Poersch, Political Director Guy Cecil, Finance Director Julianna Smoot and Communications Director Phil Singer—earned the highest compliment I can give: They're the Ruth, Gehrig, DiMaggio and Mantle of politics. They, in turn, made sure that each Senate campaign had sharp and competent teams running the show.

While I was still in Reid's office, I continued with my second condition. "Before I agree to take the job, there's one other thing. You see, there's this family, the Baileys—"

"Are they friends? Do they need help? We can get them a tour."

"No, they're imaginary. I talk to them."

For a split second, Reid's eyes widened—I'm sure he was wondering how often he'd have to visit me in the institution—and then his calm look returned.

"To me, they represent the middle class. And I don't think Democrats talk to them enough. If I'm DSCC chairman, I want to have an official leadership post in the Senate. I want to help shape our platform, our values and our message. We can't win without a message that appeals to all the different Baileys around the country, and I don't want to be at the mercy of a message that ignores them."

"By Baileys you mean—you're talking about regular people?"

"I'm talking about talking to regular people—the middle class. Harry, we forget them all too often; we can't afford to anymore."

Reid broke into a relieved smile. "Chuck, I wouldn't want it any other way."

CHAPTER 5

TRUST

THE HUNAN DYNASTY, a Chinese restaurant on Capitol Hill, serves as my late-night office and dinner spot when I'm in Washington. Photos of Washington politicians adorn the staircase leading to the second-floor restaurant, which always has the faint smell of disinfectant (on that wall, I'm younger and thinner and have more hair). A huge freshwater fish tank separates the host station from the dining area. I have eaten more meals there over the past twenty-four years than at any other place outside of my Brooklyn apartment. The food is good and it's not very expensive—a combination I look for in a restaurant.

When Hillary was first elected to the Senate, we decided that we should dine out together once a month for a while to get to know each other better and to figure out ways to avoid the typical back-stabbing that occurs between senators of the same party and same state. Hillary chose the first restaurant—a quiet place in Georgetown. The service was meticulous, fellow diners were polite and the meal was impeccable. She picked up the tab.

For our second dinner, I decided to take her to the Hunan Dynasty. I wanted to open her up to my world of cheap Chinese takeout, overly bright lighting and tropical fish decor. I wasn't sure if my choice of restaurant had amused or alarmed her chief of staff, Tamera Luzzatto. "The Hunan Dynasty?" she had laughed. "Whatever Chuck wants."

We had barely sat down when the restaurant erupted in stares and whispers. Heads craned to catch a glimpse of her. Staffers got on their cell phones. Seasoned politicians and veteran lobbyists snuck glances, betraying their feigned disinterest that the former First Lady was in their midst. Many patrons openly admired her; a few gave her looks of disdain.

Moments later, the entire kitchen and wait staff filed over with cameras. I had no idea so many people worked at the Hunan Dynasty. Hillary gamely smiled as each one had a photo taken with her. I waited patiently, sipping Chinese tea and eating fried wonton noodles with duck sauce. Eventually we ordered and ate, she seemingly oblivious to the stares and commotion around her.

For as long as I have been going to the Hunan Dynasty the owner has given me a free almond cookie after every meal, and that night was no exception. Hillary politely refused so he handed the extra cookie to me.

In trying to introduce her to my life, I got a taste of hers. For all I knew, she might rather eat a Happy Meal than dine on filet mignon, but at upscale restaurants she was a whole lot more likely to be left alone while at the Hunan Dynasty she was mobbed by restaurant staff and ogled by patrons. We are both senators from New York, but our realities are very different. It was a revelation for me: Hillary was able to garner instantaneous press coverage on the issues she talked about, but now I realized it came with a price. For me, given a choice between straitjacket stardom and that free almond cookie—I'll take the almond cookie every time.

On this particular late November night in 2004, shortly after Harry Reid and I agreed on our five principles, I was dining alone. I wanted to figure out why the presidential election, and so many Senate races, had gone so badly. Spread out before me to my left was a stack of charts showing details gleaned from exit polls from the '04 debacle. To my right were a bowl of hot and sour soup, cold sesame noodles, spicy Szechuan shrimp, and string beans in black bean sauce.

When I opted to stay in the Senate, the reason was that I felt I could do more from Washington than from Albany. I wanted to use what I had learned to make the Democratic Party the majority party again. Now, as I was picking through my Szechuan shrimp, I knew that my chance was beginning.

Tomorrow I would make my first visit to the Democratic Senatorial Campaign Committee headquarters as its incoming chairman.

I was about to take the reins of an organization that had suffered two consecutive losing election cycles, in a city controlled at every turn by Republicans, with an electorate that had become polarized and angry and among a caucus of Senate Democrats whose numbers were at their lowest total since Herbert Hoover.

In the month since the election, the usual harping, finger-pointing and recriminations commonplace after a tight loss ensued. The liberal wing of the party blamed the centrists for diluting the Democratic message and suppressing voter turnout among our base. The centrist wing castigated the liberal wing for nominating a "Massachusetts liberal" as president and for scaring away moderate voters based on cultural and national security issues. Everyone blamed John Kerry.

Kerry didn't win, but he could not be held responsible for Tom Daschle's loss in South Dakota or Erskine Bowles's defeat in North Carolina. And whether it was liberals blaming moderates, moderates blaming liberals or everyone blaming Kerry—the finger-pointing was having the debilitating effect of excusing us from confronting the difficult question about whether and how Democrats needed to change.

(In 2006, the danger is the converse—satisfaction with our victory could keep us from confronting the questions we must address to improve the long-term prospects of our party.)

On the surface, in 2004 Democrats were competitive among middle-class voters. That was the message from the first chart on the pile to my left. Among middle-class voters, Bush beat Kerry by six points and congressional Republicans topped congressional Democrats by a slender three points. It would have been easy to delude and console ourselves into a false sense of electoral competitiveness. A better message here, stronger turnout there—we could reverse those numbers. That was what a lot of Democrat activists and officeholders were saying.

"We're not that far away," a colleague said to me after learning that I had taken the job of DSCC chair. Not far away, but not close either.

When it was broken down (as was later shown by Third Way, a moderate think tank), a different picture emerged. We were competitive among the middle class—voters with household incomes between $30,000 and $75,000—only because of near-unanimous support among middle-class African-American voters. Meanwhile, among white middle-class voters—a third of the electorate—Bush beat Kerry by twenty-two points. Twenty-two points! Congressional Republicans won the white middle class by nineteen points.

In other words, Democrats came close with the middle class because we had an eighty-point advantage among African-Americans. But the overwhelming support for Democrats by African-American voters at all economic levels has a lot more to do with three decades of the Republican Party's exploiting white racism to win elections than it does with any great Democratic Party achievements. If Republicans were able to convince an additional 10% of African-American voters to turn away from a Democratic Party that too often fails to earn their loyalty, Democrats would be finished. We would essentially cease to exist in large swaths of the country and would be unable to compete on the national stage. Two things were clear: We needed to do a better job of reaching the middle class, regardless of ethnicity, and, whatever we did, we could never ignore African-American voters.

The next page illustrated an economic tipping point—the income level at which a white voter was more likely to pull the lever for a Republican than a Democrat. *It was $23,700 in household income*— only slightly more than the poverty level for a family of four!

That froze me in my seat.

I'm a numbers person. I read polls; I love analyzing data. Like most Senate Democrats, I periodically get briefings on the state of the electorate and the party. Despite all that, these numbers shocked me. For years, I had known that my party could do a better job of focusing on the middle class, but I had no idea it was this bad—we were in deep, deep trouble.

The next few charts dealt with the Hispanic vote. Hispanics were expected to be a saving grace for the Democratic Party: one of our few aces in the hole. In 1996, Bill Clinton scored a fifty-point landslide win among Hispanic voters. We knew the Hispanic population was growing, particularly in key states like Arizona, Colorado, New Mexico and Florida. For years, Democrats had been counting on a rising Hispanic tide to lift candidates to victory.

By 2004, the Hispanic voting population had doubled as expected, but the Democratic margins contracted. Kerry squeaked by with an eleven-point win and congressional Democrats fared only a hair better.

As the next chart explained, along with the doubling of Hispanic voter rolls—and the waning of the Democratic advantage—had come an explosion in Hispanic voter incomes. Between 1996 and 2004, Hispanic incomes increased faster than any other ethnic group and at twice the rate of whites and African-Americans.

Whenever income begins to rise among an immigrant group, it creates more Baileys—be they Kims, Salims or Popovs. In this case, they could be Jose and Maria Ramirez. The Ramirezes are middle class, proud of what they have achieved, connected to their ancestry but proudly American, optimistic, upwardly mobile and living in the suburbs. They still occasionally feel the sting of discrimination but are confident they will overcome it. They are not scarred by the political and civil rights battles of the 1960s because their family came to this country afterward. They are no longer working to survive, but striving to excel. Their communities are not beset by strife, but buoyed by hope. They are looking less for government to protect them, and more for government to propel them. In many places, they are the Baileys.

Democrats fared best among a handful of voting blocs, each of which was drawn to our party despite the lack of a specific middle-class appeal—unmarried women, those with graduate degrees, African-Americans and those who never attend religious services.

Two years later, in the 2006 election, Democrats did better among middle-class voters (those with incomes between $30,000 and $75,000): We won by about seven points. We improved, in part because our advantage among Hispanic voters grew by nearly thirty points, probably in reaction to Republican fear-mongering on immigration. And, we continued to have an eighty-point advantage among African-Americans. We also did better with middle-class whites than we had in 2004. But even with the improvement, we again lost this group. Without our enormous margins among minorities at every income level—which, again, are more a result of the Republicans' negative message than our positive one—2006 would have been a very different story. It should be sobering that in a year when everything was going well for Democrats we still lost middle-class whites by approximately six points.

Two lessons are as true in 2006 as they were in 2004. First, we have to do a better job of reaching the middle class in general. Second, we must strengthen a platform and champion policies that work for the largest and most supportive group in our coalition—minority voters. In the '60s and '70s, Democrats earned the trust of minority voters by truly working on their behalf. It is a proud legacy that we must never forget. To me, the numbers and the moral imperative lead to the same conclusion: The Democratic Party must reaffirm its commitment to protecting civil rights, speaking for the voiceless and protecting the downtrodden and, at the same time, we must broaden our message to address the needs of the middle class, whatever the ethnicity or background of its members. The two are not mutually exclusive; in fact, accomplishing both is the only way for Democrats to gain a majority that will last for a generation.

I packed up the remaining noodles, string beans and Szechuan shrimp into to-go cartons and stuffed the election charts into my briefcase. The owner handed me a free almond cookie, and I walked out into the chilly December air.

Capitol Hill was empty at that time of year. Congress was out of session and the restaurants and bars along this two-block strip of Pennsylvania Avenue catered mainly to staffers and House members. Most of them were home with their families. Normally I would be home in Brooklyn, but my new duties as DSCC chairman brought me to the Capitol during the desolate evenings when Congress was not in session. A police cruiser slowly motored by. A homeless man braced himself against the wind at an ATM machine.

As I walked home, my mind was on the couple who had carried me through the dark days of my first statewide run. In 1998, Joe and Eileen had taken a chance on me. In 2004, they were with me all the way. But they had also voted for Bush over Kerry, Thune over Daschle, Martinez over Castor and Coburn over Carson.

In 2006, they were more likely to vote for Webb over Allen, Tester over Burns and McCaskill over Talent, but too many still voted against Democrats. The middle class had hardly become committed to the Democratic Party.

I thought of my election to the Senate in 1998. My campaign against D'Amato had started with a speech on the night of my primary election victory. I had opened with a simple declaration:

> *This election—the next seven weeks—comes down to one word: trust.*

I equated trust with asking voters who would fight for the issues that mattered to them.

As I walked along, the street was still. The only sound was my shoes hitting the pavement. Who do the Baileys trust to defend this nation against a heartless and fanatical foreign enemy? Who do they trust to keep America on top in this new global economy and to fight for their jobs? And who do they trust to protect their families against the cultural forces that mock their traditional ways of life?

In 2004, the Baileys had given their answer: Republicans.

Even now, two years later, in 2006, as our party basks in the glow of victory, I know that Joe and Eileen are not yet ready to answer: Democrats.

CHAPTER 6

BRAVE NEW WORLD

BACK AT MY APARTMENT, I put the Chinese in the fridge and tossed some old leftover cartons into the trash. My roommates were back in their home states. The place felt empty. I debated calling home but decided against waking my family. I flicked on the television and caught the last moments of *The Daily Show* and then turned it back off again. My mind was racing.

In 2004, the Baileys had trusted Bush and the Republicans over the Democrats. Fifty years ago, it was a different story.

When I was growing up, all my friends' parents were Democrats. This was partially because New York was a one-party town. But it was true all over the country. Oklahoma was as Democratic as New York. Democrats were the party of the middle class.

For anyone who lived through the New Deal, it wasn't even a question. In the 1930s and 1940s, people desperately needed government to step up; the Democrats, led by Franklin Delano Roosevelt, answered the call. When FDR took office, laissez-faire policies had failed at home. Within a decade, it was clear that a foreign policy governed by narrow self-interest would fail abroad.

Faced with two of our nation's darkest hours—first the Depression and then Pearl Harbor—FDR articulated a vision of the future. He saw that government could be more than a patronage mill. He understood that protecting Americans required a broad definition of national interest. He created a government that was more involved in citizens' lives—provided more and demanded more—than any that had come before. When Americans faced hardship, worry or danger, his message was clear. For the first time, FDR created a government that said to the average person, "We can help."

There is no doubt that FDR's marshalling of the government to lead our country out of the Depression and through World War II is his greatest legacy. But his ability to create a coalition of diverse, and often divergent, groups may have been his greatest genius. FDR's Democratic Party included blue-collar white ethnics (the Irish, Italians and Jews who shared my block on East Twenty-Seventh Street), liberals, rural southern whites and African-Americans. The Work Projects Administration, collective bargaining and the GI Bill appealed to blue-collar workers and unions; the expansion of the electrical grid benefited Southern white farmers; even modest advances in civil rights earned the support of African-Americans and Jews; a humanistic intellectualism brought liberals into the fold.

FDR had envisioned a government that could do good for all Americans; he made his vision a reality by creating a government that offered something to each constituent group as well. Through it all, the basic vision provided coherence to his programs. Some, like Social Security, benefited everyone, regardless of group identity. But it was the coalition of interests, including Joe and Eileen's middle-class parents, that made the Democratic Party the dominant political force for a generation. FDR's coalition held together after we got out of the Depression, after we vanquished Hitler and after the man himself, the architect of it all, died. It held through Harry S. Truman's throwing down of the gauntlet against communism. It lasted despite Dwight D. "Ike" Eisenhower's two terms. The same coalition of groups carried the first Catholic into the Oval Office and then, shaken by his assassination, voted to keep his Texan vice president there.

During this period, the Joe and Eileen Baileys of the day (Joe Sr. and Dorothy) were staunch Democrats. Everyone, Democrat and Republican alike, understood that if you were middle class, you were a Democrat. Republicans had pockets of support; they were the party of elites, isolationists, small-town and suburban conservatives and, by the 1960s, closeted segregationists. But because we had the middle class, Democratic control of national politics was unassailable. With the exception of two terms, we held continuous control of the House and Senate. The one Republican president during this period, Ike Eisenhower, managed to be successful by defining himself more by his earlier military career than by his membership in the Republican Party. Eisenhower represented the then-strong moderate wing of the Republican Party.

Sometime in the 1960s, the seeds of an incipient change were sown. Everyone has a theory about the seminal moment. Some peg it on Barry Goldwater's nomination as the Republican candidate for president in 1964. Some say it was Robert Kennedy's assassination in 1968. I've even heard an argument that it was the shootings at Kent State in 1970. The precise moment isn't important.

The point is that when Lyndon Johnson was elected to his one full term in 1964, there were two descriptions of the Democratic Party that were not debatable. We were the party of the middle class. And we were the party of the majority.

Sixteen years later, when Ronald Reagan proved the pundits wrong and beat Jimmy Carter by winning 45 states, neither description still held true. By then, too often, Democrats could be cast as the party of welfare, wimps and, to quote President Carter, malaise.

Three major shifts weakened the Democratic Party over the years. The first, and most important, was the remarkable success of Democratic governance. By the 1960s, Democrats had lifted much of America into middle-class prosperity. Since the '30s, a huge percentage of the country had become comfortable and secure. There's a dialectic at work in that. The success people experienced made them forget the role government had played in facilitating that success. High taxes were fine in the '30s—most people had no money to pay them anyway. By the '60s, the successes of government had allowed more people to have considerably more money—of course, they were now also bothered by high taxes and didn't need such an active government. If the New Deal had failed—if rampant poverty and unemployment had persisted—Democratic precepts may have resonated for longer.

The second shift was the great homogenization of the country. Ethnic, geographic and cultural groups stopped meaning as much. In 1932, we were made up of distinct nations unified by a flag. Southern Mississippi and North Philadelphia were totally different places—the people in one place had nothing in common with those in the other.

By 1980, people in Southern Mississippi and North Philly were much more bound together than they had been forty years earlier.

They were working for the same companies, watching the same TV shows, driving the same cars and vacationing in the same places. Wherever they lived, Americans were more likely to move to the suburbs than to the city or the country. The expansion of the middle class had something to do with the great homogenization. But the real binding force was technology.

Between 1932 and 1980, the telephone, telegraph and television spread to every corner of the country. Meanwhile, the interstate system and jet travel made our transportation network efficient and seamless. These advances created a national economy and fostered a national culture. Consumer products and jobs went national. The national distribution of television shows, movies, record albums and print media obliterated regional differences in culture. With economic and cultural similarity, more and more people identified first and last as Americans. The Democratic appeal to people as groups—Italian-Americans, rural white Southerners, etc.—became less and less effective as people felt increasingly a part of the whole.

The one group that maintained a primary identity was African-Americans. Legal barriers against African-Americans were not lifted until the 1960s, and even in the years since, racism has often been a predominant force. So, as Irish and Jewish immigrants, union members and rural Southerners started to feel more and more similar, many African-Americans were persistently forced into group definitions. Not coincidentally, even as the New Deal coalition broke down, African-Americans continued to be the mainstay of the Democratic Party. This is not a reflection of any great work that the Democratic Party has done for African-Americans; it is largely because Republicans have too often profited by wooing bigots. But, as racism hopefully recedes, African-American group identity will become secondary, as well. This will be a great thing for our country. And, it will require Democrats to dramatically adjust to the new reality.

There's a third shift. In the '30s people had more tolerance for those who were strongly critical of our system than they did forty years later. As America worked better for more people, many lost their enthusiasm for criticism of the American system. The suffering brought about by the Great Depression caused people to doubt the country. They were unsure about democratic capitalism. In the

1930s, Americans might have been more offended by Enron-type abuses than by flag burning. By the end of the '60s, the middle class had changed; capitalism had worked for most Americans. Flag burning overtook corporate abuses on the list of offensive activities.

The driving forces of the 1960s—for civil rights and against the war—were great causes. They moved the nation because they were right and because they included the middle class. Even if the Baileys weren't marching, they understood that morality was on the side of the protesters. But starting in the late '60s, when those protesters cursed the returning veterans and Stokely Carmichael advocated armed resistance against the "white ruling class," the Baileys were lost. Watching positive, peaceful protest transform itself into antiestablishment diatribes turned them off.

I understand their feelings because I went through them myself. Shortly after I got to Harvard in 1967, I was faced with what Alexander Hamilton called *mobocracy*. In my freshman year, I joined the College Dems to support the McCarthy Crusade. I spent every weekend in New Hampshire, trying to help McCarthy beat LBJ in the primary. The College Dems were against the war and for civil rights, but we believed in working within the system, not against it. The Students for a Democratic Society (SDS) had a different idea. They were vehemently antiestablishment. Some of their rhetoric sounded positively anti-American. They were so sure they were morally right that they could justify taking over buildings, shouting down speakers and rejecting electoral politics.

I would argue with them. "If we're right about the war, our job is to knock on doors, help on campaigns and convince the rest of the country of our position." They would have none of that. They thought it meant being a sellout and disdained those of us who worked within the system.

At protests, SDS members would go over to police officers. They would get nose to nose with them, almost daring the cops to hit them, and scream in their faces, "Pig! Fascist pig!"

It sickened me. The police weren't pigs. They were the people I'd grown up with. They were my neighbors. My friends. They were the Baileys. Weren't we supposed to be supporting working people? What did these prep school–graduate Harvard kids think regular people did for a living—write papers?

My most vivid memory of SDS is from 1969. By then they were called SDS-PLP (Progressive Labor Party), having at Harvard been infiltrated by a group with decidedly Maoist leanings. The medical school wanted to build a new lab on a muddy lot by a pond. SDS opposed this "imperialist theft of the workers' land." Bewildered, a gentle professor named Wilson agreed to have a public debate on the issue.

Wilson opened with a plea: "A few years before you were born, every time a young child got a cold in the summer, his mother worried that her dearest would get polio and never walk again. Now, because of buildings like the one we want to build, she does not have to worry anymore. In this new building we may have a chance to eradicate heart disease or cancer, as we have eradicated polio. Why don't you want us to build it?" There was a pained and confused look on his face. This sincere and brilliant man was utterly flummoxed by the opposition.

The SDS leader stood and cleared his throat. He spit on the floor at Professor Wilson's feet. I was disgusted. Whether the muddy land by the pond deserved to be saved or not (it didn't), this man deserved respect. SDS was not fighting to protect the muddy land or workers' rights. They were so angry, they seemed to want to tear down every part of the American system. Even medical research ran afoul of their goals.

Though Democrats held power, in the late '60s and early '70s the party came to be seen as tolerant of groups like this. Republicans, including presidential candidates Richard Nixon and Ronald Reagan, attacked these groups relentlessly for being antiestablishment and anti-American; Democrats, for the most part, did not. As a result, in the Baileys' minds, Democrats became connected to them.

Punishing Democrats for the radical fringe may not seem fair. The Democratic Party, after all, never endorsed these groups. But it's how the world works. For years, Democrats denounced Republicans for refusing to denounce racist or sexist institutions. "Look at their friends," we would cry. "How can you trust them?" It is only fair that the same test be applied to us. In politics, you have to either defend or denounce what your friends say. If you don't, people start to wonder what you really believe.

By the late '70s, the Baileys did not trust the Democrats anymore, and the Democrats weren't listening to the Baileys. After fifty years of governing, we had lost touch. Democrats in D.C. had forgotten what regular voters cared about. Things had changed, but the party didn't realize it. In the 1930s, the Baileys may not have seen America as a success story. Forty years later, they did. They felt like part of the success. It started with FDR, but the prosperity of the '50s and '60s cemented it. The electorate had shifted in the three ways described above: People no longer felt as dependent on government to help them succeed, were not as responsive to group appeals and were more dubious of candidates who tolerated those who vitriolically criticized the system. Democrats, ensconced in Washington and for too long almost guaranteed reelection, seemed oblivious to these changes.

As the world moved on and new issues came to the fore, the party didn't adapt. Instead, Washington Democrats too often took their cues from interest groups without considering the needs of the average person. Group identities around the country were less important, but those claiming to represent group interests in Washington were stronger than ever. Democrats had lost touch with their base—the middle class.

This hit home when I first got to Congress. I was elected on the same day Reagan was: November 4, 1980. I was one of seven freshman representatives from New York—six Republicans and me. That year, the biggest issue for my constituents was crime. Crime was tearing apart our neighborhoods. Property values were plummeting. People of all backgrounds, ethnicities and races were losing everything because they had to sell their houses to flee crime.

Even as an assemblyman, I'd experienced it. Each night, I would park my car on the street. And many mornings, the windows of every third car on the street would be smashed. Every now and again, I'd wake up and not be able to go to work. I'd have to go to a local glazier to replace the window.

So, the first thing I'd do when I woke up was throw on my khakis and run downstairs. Every morning I'd check my car to see if I could drive to work that day. Night after night, week after week this went on. It was brazen lawlessness and the police seemed powerless to stop it. (We eventually learned that a local glazier had hired a gang of kids to break the windows; at $160 a pop to fix each window, he'd done pretty well for himself. And, because the system was broken, he knew the risk of being caught or punished was small.)

Crime was hurting people, scaring them and causing them to lose their property. But just as bad as the crimes themselves, or maybe worse, was the government's seeming inability to deal with the problem. Everyone agrees that protecting the public from crime is one of the basic reasons men and women came together thousands of years ago to create governments. If government failed at this most basic task, what was the point of it at all?

When I was elected to Congress, I vowed to do something about it; I wanted the federal government to get more involved in an issue that was tearing apart my constituents' lives. I was a thirty-year-old state assemblyman from Brooklyn with a reputation for being aggressive, press-savvy and hardworking. But I was no expert in the ways of Washington. When I got there, I was shocked. I hadn't had any idea of how out of touch my party was.

The House subcommittee on crime was chaired by a representative from the San Francisco Bay area, a former FBI agent named Don Edwards. I liked Don. He was warm, interesting and smart. He was also a total believer in the American Civil Liberties Union (ACLU). When Democrats needed crime legislation, it seemed to me that Don didn't just give the ACLU a seat at the table, he gave them a veto pen.

The ACLU deserved to be part of the discussion, but its unchecked influence was a disaster. There is a continuum in debates about criminal justice—how far do you expand defendants' rights to prevent the horror of wrongly convicting one innocent person, when it inevitably means that many guilty people will go free? In effect, the ACLU's beliefs led to a conclusion that society should let a thousand guilty people go free lest one innocent person be imprisoned. This equation may have made sense in the hallowed halls of UC Berkeley. But it was ruining communities and lives in Brooklyn and Queens. Democrats didn't seem to understand. After so many years in power, their perspective was warped. You don't get a good view of the nation from inside the Capital Beltway; Democrats had forgotten what the country looked like from the other side.

Democrats didn't only lose touch with large, crime-ridden Northeastern cities. It was happening everywhere. On a family vacation out west, the full extent of our failure hit me like ton of bricks.

We were driving in the isolated northeastern corner of Arizona, on our way to Monument Valley. It's not a national park because it lies entirely within the Navajo Nation Tribal Park, but Monument Valley is one of the most beautiful sites in our country—you should be sure to visit. It was a clear, sunny morning. The road was flat and straight. There was not another car in sight. Suddenly I glanced at the speedometer. I'd inched upward to 95 mph! Not wanting to break the law, I immediately put on the brakes. I slowed to 85 . . . 75 . . . 65 . . . finally down to 55 mph.

As you may remember, that was the speed limit. Some very reasonable and learned advocates in Washington had convinced Congress that the solution to the oil crisis was a national speed limit. Fifty-five miles an hour, they said, is the optimal speed for fuel efficiency. Lawmakers had decided the advocates were right. So, the national speed limit was set at 55 mph.

Driving 55 mph in northeastern Arizona on that unending, unbending and uninhabited road was excruciating. It felt like we weren't moving at all. Fifty-five was good for the Beltway—it saved lives and reduced gas consumption—but it sure didn't make sense on this road. That morning was a revelation. Westerners had the same feeling about speed limits that I had about crime laws. I felt Westerners' anger at the pointless encroachment of government as palpably as I felt my constituents' anger at government's inability to tackle crime. Democrats were still good-hearted and well meaning, but from coast to coast, we had lost touch.

Now I understood on a gut level why Reagan was elected; I felt the frustration that he had been talking about. In many ways, the federal government *was* too big and too intrusive. It was out of touch. After three hours of driving at fifty-five, I turned to Iris. She was as annoyed as I was. Then she smiled.

"Chuck," she joked. "I want the government out of my life."

I pulled the leftover Chinese out of the fridge and sat back down on the couch.

When the Democratic Party was a successful majority party, it forged an alliance between the middle class, the poor and minorities. While Democrats were advancing civil rights, they were also bringing electricity to rural areas. While Democrats were pledging to improve public education for the poor, they passed the GI Bill to guarantee a college education for middle-class soldiers returning home. While Democrats were fighting to feed the hungry, President John F. Kennedy challenged the nation to land a man on the Moon within a decade. Sometime in the 1970s, that alliance shifted.

Beginning with Reagan, the Republican Party forged a new alliance between the middle class and the rich and leisure classes. While Republicans were fighting to reduce taxes on the very wealthy, they fought to lower crime. While Republicans sought to eliminate the estate tax, they campaigned to eliminate the marriage penalty in the tax code. While Republicans were waging a battle against corporate regulation, they stood up to protect the American flag from the incendiary impulses of the occasional left-wing fanatic.

Bill Clinton did not break this mold; no one could have. He wisely adapted the party to fit it. Eisenhower, the two-term Republican president of the Democratic era, had delivered a Democratic message with a Republican's voice. Clinton, the two-term Democratic president of the Republican era, built his success by adapting Republican issues to jibe with Democratic values. And it worked for all of us. We had some great successes during the Clinton years. Thanks to his leadership, I was finally able to get passed the crime bill I had spent 14 years fighting for. We called it tough on punishment, smart on prevention. One of the proudest days of my Congressional career occurred when a majority of the Congressional Black Caucus and a large number of Republicans voted for the bill— a federal solution to this most contentious issue, which had ripped apart the country a decade earlier. Welfare reform and deficit reduction were also landmark achievements that represented a synergy of Reagan Republicanism and Clinton's "New Democrat" values.

The Clinton message was so successful that Karl Rove appropriated it for George W. Bush in 2000. "Compassionate conservatism" is the Republican mirror image of Clinton's "third way." The great irony of the 2000 race is that Al Gore, the vice president, ran away from Clinton's legacy and W, the son of the man whom Clinton had defeated, got into the White House by imitating it.

But by 2004, the world was entirely different than it had been when Reagan won in 1980, and even different than it was in 1992, when Clinton had to succeed in a landscape still fundamentally defined by the Reaganites. That's because since the early 1990s, technology has so revolutionized the landscape that the Republican answer of twenty-five years ago—strangle the government—no longer works. In the quarter century since Reagan's ascendance, technology has completely changed...everything.

It is a brave new world.

The ability to transfer huge amounts of information quickly and at virtually no cost, and to access that information from anywhere in the world, has created a whole new playing field economically, socially and politically. Technological advances have spurred vast changes that are beginning to unsettle Joe and Eileen's world. As a result, as in 1932 and 1980, the political loyalty of the middle class is once again up for grabs.

The change has been lightning quick. Cell phones were invented in 1973. The first commercial fiber optic cable was laid in 1977. The IBM PC was released in 1981. The World Wide Web as we know it was created in 1990! Together, these advances have revolutionized information and communication. Products that most of us had never considered in 1980 have become as ubiquitous as lightbulbs and cars. Twenty-five years ago, most of us had never heard of these things. Through the '80s, these technological advances were the subject of the occasional newspaper article, but their effect on all of us was still minimal.

In the 1990s, technology exploded. Technological advances that had seemed like science fiction in the '80s were suddenly everywhere. They unleashed powerful new global forces. Through the '90s, they swept across the world. It was so fast and so dramatic that we are still trying to figure out what happened—is happening.

The scale and speed of the changes we are experiencing today are unprecedented. In the past, new technology replaced our muscles and our bones. From the Stone Age through the Reagan revolution, machines made humans bigger, stronger and faster. The advances of the last two decades are different. They are changing how we think, who we are. Today, technology changes our brains. Factories and machines increased how much we could make; cars and airplanes increased how much we could travel; computers and the Internet are increasing how much we can know. And while it took many generations for previous advances to change daily life, this time the change has happened in less than one. The effect on Joe and Eileen has gone from zero to sixty in the blink of an eye.

The challenges are huge. Issues that ten years ago were on the back burner now dominate. Think about terrorism. Fifteen years ago, it seemed like something that occasionally happened somewhere else; now it has become the dominant foreign policy issue of our time. Technological advances have transformed terrorism by turning even small numbers of bad people into a dire threat. You could be in a cave in Afghanistan and, through a satellite link to your PC, learn as much about America as an American university professor knows. The sad fact of the matter is that if two hundred people were injected with an evil virus that would cause them to spend five years fanatically trying to figure out how to hurt America, the odds are too great that they could succeed. Today, the primary terrorist threat in the United States comes from Al Qaeda. Tomorrow it could just as easily be Chechens, Colombian drug lords or even homegrown radicals from our country.

There have always been groups of bad people, but technology has made it feasible for them to attack us in our homeland. When the vaunted Japanese military wanted to hurt us in 1941, they could only get as far as Pearl Harbor. Today, a small group of terrorists could do severe damage in Abilene or Peoria if they wanted to.

Technology has also radically changed our economy and job market. The worldwide spread of broadband is forging a single global labor market. As Thomas Friedman has written, the ability to transmit information cheaply and quickly means that every job that does not require face-to-face contact is now up for grabs—not regionally or nationally, but globally. It's more than factory and call center jobs. It includes computer programmers, administrators, consultants, investment bankers, lawyers (other than courtroom litigators), even doctors.

Yes, doctors! While internists are safe because they have to examine patients in person, radiologists, whose job does not depend on physical contact with patients, are not. The possibility of outsourcing physicians' services represents how enormous this change is.

Technology has also allowed us to live longer and be healthier. This profoundly affects government as Medicare and Social Security costs balloon. More important, the extension of our life span has changed the cycle of our lives. People marry, have kids and settle into careers later than ever before, creating a new category of young, single, job-hopping adults. On the other end of a career, retirement now lasts longer than ever before, expanding the ranks of the leisure class.

Technology has changed our homes into offices and libraries. It's changed parenting by increasing the ability to monitor and be in contact with our kids. At the same time, it's made it harder to protect our kids from inappropriate and damaging forces, such as pornography. Technology has also changed what childhood means, as children spend less time outside and without physical activity than ever before.

Beyond these, there are other, less concrete but equally profound effects. Technology has contributed to the refining and ever-expanding reach of commercialism—the strain of capitalism that's focused on exciting our desires to encourage acquisition and consumption. New technology has made commercialism ever more successful. Those who sell products have far more sophisticated ways to identify, excite and capture customers than in the past. In the old days, you couldn't do better than an ad in *Time Magazine*. Today, you can create a multimedia and product placement blitz specifically targeted to, say, aardvark enthusiasts (useful if you're selling aardvark paraphernalia).

It's a little like HAL, the anthropomorphic supercomputer in the 1968 Stanley Kubrick movie *2001: A Space Odyssey*. If you haven't seen it, you really should. The movie is a classic look at man versus machines. It opens on prehistoric apes using a bone to create the first crude tool. It then cuts, brilliantly, to the twenty-first century—a world in which the complexity of machines has overtaken that of humans. The supercomputer HAL epitomizes this incredible refinement. In HAL, we see that machines have become too powerful, almost too perfect.

That's what's happened to commercialism. Almost from birth, it targets, tracks and excites our desires with near perfection. It makes us feel like there's always something else we need—however much we can buy, we always want more. This is one reason that the middle class feels like it's slipping. Since there's an ever-growing list of things to want, we are ever less happy with what we have. This perfectly manipulated desire drives more and more people into debt. In twenty years, the national savings rate, the percent of income that an average household saves, has gone from almost 8% to less than zero. Average household savings have decreased even while disposable income has increased. People want more and spend more, regardless of how much they have to spend. It affects our savings rate, our budget deficit and people's overall happiness and contentment.

Technology has also changed the relationship that corporations have to our country. In the past, large American corporations were committed to America's future. They had invested so heavily here that their future was tied to the country's. They were American forces, working for America. Today, large corporations have much less interest in this country. In the '60s it used to be said that what was good for General Motors was good for America. Back then, it was mostly true. Today, to say that what's good for General Electric is good for America still has some truth, but not nearly as much. As companies have internationalized their business interests, they have become international forces.

By their very nature, corporations are not sentimental or patriotic; rather, they are the sum of their capital. In the globalized world, they are doing exactly what they should—increasing returns for shareholders. Still, it's undeniable that internationalizing diminishes the overlap between business interests and our national interest. It's ironic that in a period when corporate interests and the interests of our country have diverged more than ever, the Bush administration has offered unprecedented influence and policy benefits for corporations.

Without a doubt, technological changes are mostly positive. The advances are wonderful. When I visited China to investigate the effect of their currency manipulation on American workers, I was able to call my daughter's cell phone, in Boston, from mine, in Beijing. My family sends pictures to my parents by e-mail. Even writing this book, accomplished using a word processing program that catches spelling errors before I can, would be unthinkably more difficult without computers.

We are more efficient. We are more connected. We live longer and healthier lives. There are very few twenty-first-century Luddites who reject technology—and for good reason. The world is a better place because of the innovations we've made.

Even for those who might not think so, the question is moot. It's not whether we like technology or not. Even if we wanted to slow down the pace of change, we couldn't. Water always flows downhill.

The important point is that life has changed for the Baileys. When that happens, government must adapt to meet their needs. Technology has done a world of good, but it has also created new problems that our government, and our political parties, must address.

Whenever human advances catalyze dramatic change, citizens demand that government respond. There were major advances in knowledge and technology in the eighteenth century, the age of the Enlightenment. The advances strained the old structures and rendered obsolete the concept of an infallible government ruled by a divinely chosen monarch. The revolutions at the end of the eighteenth century—first our own and then that of the French—resulted, at least in part, from the new societies that technology and increased trade created.

About a hundred years later, technology did it again. Between 1870 and 1910, electricity, the internal combustion engine, the telephone and film all traveled the road from invention to near-ubiquity. Democracy is a more flexible system than monarchy, but the changes were again dramatic. As society's basic structure was altered, government was forced to adapt. The Progressive Era was the first step. But it was not until the New Deal—after transatlantic phones, air travel and radio had all accelerated the transformation—that we finally understood how to govern in the reshaped world. The New Deal wasn't implemented for thirty years after the birth of the Progressives; this time, the solution can't wait that long.

Neither all good nor all bad, the changes wrought by technology are all-encompassing. Technology provides an opportunity and poses a threat. We don't yet know the ultimate consequences of interconnectedness, shared knowledge and diffuse power. All we know for sure is that it's a new world for everyone—individuals and governments alike.

As I sat on my couch in the empty apartment, I picked at the last remnants of Chinese food. So much for leftovers. My old LCD alarm clock read 2 a.m. I had to be up in four hours to catch the early shuttle to LaGuardia.

I did what I often do with vexing questions. I thought of the Baileys. In their gut, Joe and Eileen understand the scale of the transformation wrought by technology. Some, they have experienced. Others, they just sense. From terrorism and the global economy, to maintaining their values, paying for a longer life and holding the line against rampant commercialism—they no longer feel fully in control of the influences that affect their lives and enter their homes. Deep down, they know it's a totally changed world.

In 1980, the Baileys wanted the federal government's hand out of their wallets and their lives—they wanted Washington to impose fewer taxes, let cops fight crime and stop regulating every facet of life. Today, life has changed. The Baileys would welcome a helping hand, as long as their individual accomplishments and choices are unimpeded, they are not condescended to and the help that's offered is efficient and productive.

Today, the Baileys are looking for support and solutions in a way that they weren't twenty-five, or even ten, years ago.

For the first time in years, government is back in style.

CHAPTER 7

EIGHT WORDS

I AM BLESSED. I love my job. I wake up every Monday morning excited about the week ahead. The one downside is how consuming it is. I don't have much time for leisure activities. Sure, I'll try to catch the Yankees or the Giants when I can, but I mostly follow my teams through the morning papers. In general, there are two ways I like to spend time when I'm not working: either with my family or on my bike. (As you've no doubt deduced by now, I also love eating; luckily, I can enjoy this pleasure while working, spending time with my family or exploring a new neighborhood by bike.)

When I ride my bike, I like to be alone. With my helmet and sunglasses on, I'm not recognized. Anonymously, I ride through New York City. I don't think there's a neighborhood in the five boroughs that I haven't biked in (including in Staten Island, though the Verrazano-Narrows Bridge still doesn't have a bike path). It's a beautiful way to see people and places. It's also a great time to noodle on difficult problems.

About a year after my November 2004 trip to Hunan Dynasty, I got a chance to enjoy the rarest of all pleasures: a weekday afternoon bike ride. Late fall is a great time to bicycle in New York. The bike lanes aren't crowded like they are in the summer. And the air is dry and just cold enough to feel it cooling you with each breath. As you bike along, you are enveloped in gold—the setting sun glowing off car windows and along the cornices of the brownstones, the golden leaves precipitously clinging to their branches and skipping down the curb.

As I started my ride on that crisp afternoon about halfway between the 2004 and 2006 elections, I was still bothered by the same concern that had been gnawing at me for the last year: the uncertain future of my party. From the Great Depression through the 1960s, the Democrats were the party of the majority and the party of the middle class. We won by talking about the social safety net, neglected groups and a stronger federal government. In 1980, the Reagan revolution shifted that mantle to Republicans. The old New Deal ideas didn't work anymore. The country was focused on crime, taxes and America's place in the world. For twenty-odd years, the Republican worldview dominated public policy. But technology had changed things again. The shrinking-government message of the Reagan revolution was no more relevant to the Baileys than LBJ's Great Society had been to them in 1980.

Yet, in 2004 the Baileys were still voting for Bush in droves. The data were unequivocal. The white middle class preferred Bush by twenty-two points. Moreover, the Democratic advantage among Hispanics had diminished enormously. In 2006, we did better with both groups, but our improvement was driven more by animosity toward Bush than by a great connection having been forged with Democrats—and, even with it, we still lost the white middle class.

I turned down Eastern Parkway, heading for Queens. Whenever I bike down Eastern Parkway, I am struck by how much the neighborhoods have changed. Sutter Avenue in East New York, Brooklyn, is my favorite. Just about every storefront on Sutter used to be boarded up. Today you can feel the difference. Stores are open, people are out walking. I like to coast down the street, enjoying the rhythm of a neighborhood that's come back to life. The rebirth of Sutter is part of New York's incredible renaissance, which began as crime receded. In East New York, a lot of credit is also due to the Reverend Johnny Ray Youngblood, one of the great spiritual and community leaders, and East Brooklyn Congregations, perhaps the leading disciples of Saul Alinsky's theory on how to build neighborhoods.

I made the right turn back onto Eastern and returned to the issue at hand. If Republicans were no longer winning with the message of the Reagan revolution, what message were they using? And why was it so competitive?

Starting in the '80s, but particularly in the '90s, two groups within the Republican Party formed an alliance. Today they form the backbone of the party and drive its ideology. The first group I call the theocrats. Theocrats are people of faith, though the vast majority of people of faith are not theocrats. I have been to enough houses of worship—inner-city black churches, rural Methodist congregations, working-class Roman Catholic parishes, orthodox Jewish shuls—to know that faith is a gift. I am a person of faith myself. For me and many others, faith in a higher power infuses life with a higher purpose.

Theocrats have a different agenda. They are not just the faithful; they are the narrow band of the faithful who want to take their faith and impose it on government. And that, in a word, is un-American. It is directly at odds with our Constitution. Government involving itself in personal faith is exactly why many of the founding fathers put down their plows and picked up their muskets to fight.

The theocrats share control of the Republican Party with a smaller, more insidious and more powerful group. I call them the economic royalists. These are people of enormous wealth, mostly self-made. They are concentrated in the South and Southwest of the country, but small numbers of them live in every state. They hate government because it gets in the way of what they want as capitalists, landowners and holders of vast wealth. They are the spiritual inheritors of the robber barons; they would like to go back to the 1880s or even the salad days before the French Revolution, when their class was free to do whatever it wanted.

To describe this group, I like to imagine the following scene, which I can see taking place regularly at a country club in a wealthy Houston suburb whenever their conservative congressman comes home to press the flesh. (This is only my imagination. I've never been there—they might not even let me in.)

Within five minutes of walking in, the representative would be accosted.

"Congressman, Congressman," a constituent would stalk up, filled with self-righteous anger. "*I'm* a self-made businessman, *I've* made all *my* money *my*self. How dare *your* government take it from *me*? It's *my* money. *I* shouldn't have to pay taxes to *your* government!"

Shortly thereafter, someone else would accost him. "Congressman, Congressman," would come the furious complaint. "*I* bought those 10,000 acres in central Texas with *my* money. It's *my* land.

How dare *your* government tell *me* what *I* can put in *my* air and *my* water? *I*'ve bought all *my* land with *my* money. *I* should be allowed do whatever *I* want."

Moments later, he would be approached again. "Congressman, Congressman," a golf partner would growl. "*I*'m a self-made businessman. *I* built *my* business with *my* hands. *Your* government didn't help *me*—it's *my* business. How dare *your* government tell *me* how much *I* have to pay *my* workers, how *I* have to treat *my* workers, and which workers *I* have to hire? It's *my* company. They're *my* workers. If *I* want to pay them below minimum wage or not hire blacks or women or gays, that's *my* right. Get *your* government out of *my* business!"

There are two words that define this group: narrow greed. They care only about doing what they want, regardless of the consequences. Even the most stringent free-market economists believe that externalities—uncaptured external costs and benefits to society—must be part of any economic model and temper a purely Adam Smith–type system. To economic royalists, externalities are irrelevant. The government is nothing more than a barrier to unfettered property rights and free will—almost an insult to their economic manhood.

The economic royalists are worse than the theocrats. The theocrats exhibit a self-righteous moral superiority, an attitude that is, in truth, not unknown in certain quarters on the left of the political spectrum. But at least the theocrats and those on the left are sincere in their convictions. The royalists, however, are driven purely by greed, which is far more odious than honest, albeit dogmatic, conviction.

The royalists and the theocrats have a stranglehold on the Republican Party. They have tremendous influence; even many Republicans who do not agree with them have been forced to go along with their doctrinaire views. They have had their greatest influence during the Bush administration. Despite what happened in 2006, you can be sure they will be back with a vengeance in 2008.

These two groups do not represent anywhere near a majority of Americans. Yet they have had tremendous electoral success. Why? Their success is largely because of four critical techniques that they have developed and implemented with uncanny skill.

The first is a sophisticated soup-to-nuts message machine. The royalists have spent a generation funding and perfecting their machine. The machine includes think tanks and university professors. It includes pollsters and wordsmiths. And it includes an extensive network of partisan media outlets. Together, these components of the machine, working in harmony, all too often win over a large portion of America for whom the conservative ideology no longer holds substantive appeal.

The think tanks and professors have spent decades laying a patina of philosophy over the royalists' greed. They write papers. They hold conferences. They make a big show of their academic rigor. In the end though, no matter how flowery the language or elaborate the theory, their work all boils down to the same basic point: What's good for the wealthiest is always, always, *always* good for America.

The pollsters and wordsmiths have taken the arguments and branded them. Simply by labeling the tax on large estates the "death tax," they got families whose wealth was far too limited to be affected by the estate tax to fight for its repeal.

Finally, the conservative media has taken this framework of argument and branding and has broadcasted it to the nation. Editorial boards, talk radio shows and news networks propagate the message. And they are more effective than anything.

If I were running a national campaign and could draft any resource for my side, my first pick would be Fox News. No question. Almost every day, some issue—often originated by Karl Rove or someone like him—will spark on Fox News. It could be swift boats, it could be Dan Rather. They keep repeating it over and over again. They are like the electric starter on a grill. At first it's just one spark. Within a week, it will have spread; all the coals of the media grill will be sizzling with the story. Even the mainstream "liberal" media will be aflame. When it comes to cooking a partisan agenda, Fox is more effective than anything.

There is a liberal media, too, but it's different. It's not necessarily Democratic. The poster child of the liberal media, the *New York Times* editorial page, attacked Bill Clinton with relentless vigor for his transgressions. On the other hand, much of the right-wing media *is* out-and-out Republican. It will hew to the party line above all else, including its own ideological convictions. The *Wall*

Street Journal's editorial page used to be libertarian, far more aligned with economic royalists than theocrats. No more. For the sake of all-important partisan unity, it has acquiesced to the theocrats on many issues.

Furthermore this right-wing media specializes in personal attacks, tearing people down with mean-spirited mockery. They are far more ruthless than pundits and commentators from anywhere else on the political spectrum.

The Republican message machine is one reason for the Republicans' success; the way they choose candidates is another. One of the most brilliant moves made by the theocrat–royalist alliance was backing George W. Bush for president. They knew if they backed someone who was one of them, who had an ideological smell about him and talked openly about their ideas, they could never win. In Bush, they found a man who wasn't one of them, but who let them do just about anything they wanted. He's someone you'd like to have a beer with—a down-to-earth, decent guy. Not an ideologue, not even that interested in politics, he's exactly the type of person who appeals to the Baileys.

Yet he gives his party's fringe what they want, tempered only occasionally by Karl Rove's instinct for political expediency (the Medicare prescription drug bill, for example). Bush got elected by being himself. Because he's not that interested in governing, he gave the radicals, particularly Dick Cheney, the keys to the store. Bush is out there as the everyman while the rest of the administration sticks to its core governing philosophy—he tells the middle class he'll cut their taxes, then they pass tax cuts focused on the very rich.

It's like a monster with two heads. The ideologues, with the help of Dick Cheney, run the show; Cheney's brain controls the body. His approval ratings—in the low twenties—reflect the popularity of the theocratic and royalist ideologies he oversees. Meanwhile, George Bush is the likeable face and voice. His affable head is attached to the same body as the ideological one, yet during much of his administration, his approval ratings hovered around the forties. For years, Bush's regular-guy charm was a shield for the unpopular actions of his government. Democrats too often fail to choose someone with the easy affability of a George W. Bush as our candidate for president; Bill Clinton was a rare exception. You can be sure that the theocrat-royalist alliance will look for another candidate with strong, likeable attributes in 2008.

The third reason for the continued Republican success is their willingness to practice a politics of fear and division instead of forthrightly defending their positions. They create trumped-up bogeymen and relentlessly hammer the country with them. In 2002, Georgia Senator Max Cleland, a war hero who sacrificed three of his limbs in service to our country, was turned into a symbol of weakness in the face of America's enemies. In 2004, gay marriage and disingenuous claims about Kerry's military record became a mortal threat to our society's existence. In each case, Republicans screamed and screamed until the danger seemed real. Of course, without their message machine, these issues would never have taken hold. In 2006, Republicans tried to make illegal immigrants, affirmative action and gay marriage the enemies within. Although this time these fictional bogeymen were overwhelmed by the all too real issues of Iraq and the economy, there is no question that Republicans will resort to them again in 2008 and beyond, and that their message machine will again to have the tools and self-discipline to make them effective.

The fourth and final reason for Republican success is more important than the others. Republicans are incredibly skillful at identifying clear issues that connect to their values, then simply and repeatedly returning to them. This reason is different and more legitimate than the other three. Those are based on producing and delivering bogeymen; this is based on the concrete, consistent and crystal-clear portrayal of deeper values.

Republicans are not afraid to take sides on certain issues. They figure out issues that connect to the deeply held values they stand for, define themselves clearly by those issues and then stand by them unequivocally. Republicans put their money where their mouth is— they tell voters what they mean, repeat it over and over again and trust that enough will agree to put them over the top.

In 2004, they did it with eight words:

War in Iraq. Cut taxes. No gay marriage.

These eight words sum up the reasons for Bush's reelection. They are not a slogan. They represent real things. Each of the ideas was something concrete that the Baileys could hold on to. Each represented a larger value that the Republican Party had stood behind for forty years. *The war in Iraq* represented a strong and interventionist foreign policy. *Cut taxes* meant limited government. *No gay marriage* was about traditional values. Bush's reelection hinged on these ideas. He risked his political life by boldly betting all his chips on them.

In 2004, they offered a meaningful contrast with Democrats. Even if these eight words were simplistic or divisive, they represented concrete ideas that attached to a larger value. They spoke directly to the Baileys—particularly since Democrats offered no comparable alternative.

The summer before Bush's reelection, I saw the power of his eight words at the Corn Hill Festival in Rochester. I was there during the same week that Bush was pushing for the constitutional amendment on gay marriage. Corn Hill is one of Rochester's biggest events, snaking through the city's cultural heart. Within minutes of my arrival, a nice couple came over to me. They were from the part of Rochester where the suburban and rural meet, the exurbs that *New York Times* columnist David Brooks has written about.

The couple greeted me politely, but I could see deep worry in their eyes. "Please oppose gay marriage," they pleaded. "If you let it happen, our society—our way of life—will collapse." They were nice people. Not angry. Just afraid. These were not ideologues. They were the Baileys of Rochester. Although they couldn't articulate a logical argument connecting the marriage of a gay couple in Massachusetts to danger to their own lives, you could see that fear had been instilled in them.

At least twenty-five people came up to me that day, each with a variation on the same theme.

After three hours, we left Corn Hill, sun-soaked and full of roasted corn. Joe Hamm, my Rochester director since I was first elected to the Senate, was driving. Whenever I travel in New York State, my staff member for the region drives me in a personal car. (I have a dedicated and astute team in offices across the state—one of the chief reasons for my success.) It's cheaper and easier than getting a fancy rental car or a state trooper to take me around. And each car says something about the staffer's personality. Joe drives a perfectly clean Buick. This is in keeping with his precise and mild-mannered appearance—more government bureaucrat than heavy-hitting politico. But knowing Joe, I bet that Buick has a turbo engine under its hood. He can be tough, sharp and funny, with a wit as crisp as the blazers he keeps on a hanger in the backseat. "What do you think, Joe?" I asked.

"Well, Chuck," his cadence was measured. "I think they've got their bogeyman. And there's nothing we can do about it."

He was right. With the help of their media machine far outgunning whatever passes for ours, they kept the focus on the simple issues they wanted to talk about. It was those eight words, all the time. Nothing else. Even though the popularity of their ideas has faded, four advantages—a forceful message machine, brilliant candidate selection, fear politics and, most important, the distillation of deep values into clear issues—kept the middle class voting for them.

In 2006, Democrats did better with the middle class. The message that won for us basically boils down to our own eight words:

No war in Iraq. No corruption. Bad economy.

In a midterm election, after six years in which we had not held power, this message was enough to put us over the top. But it is not self-sustaining. Our eight words did not describe our own vision; they were the negative image of the Republican message. They worked in 2006, but we will need to explain our own broad values and specific policies if we hope to win the presidential campaign in 2008, govern effectively and convince the next generation—which is now up for grabs—to trust the Democratic Party.

In 2002 and 2004, the Republicans were successful—though not by as wide a margin as triumphalist Republicans and cannibalistic Democrats sometimes claim. In 2006, we were successful—though not by as wide a margin as triumphalist Democrats and cannibalistic Republicans have recently claimed.

The truth is that as we head toward the 2008 election season, the competition between the parties is very close. There is no longer a dominant party. The Republican strategies have worked to get them elected more frequently, but that's largely because Republicans have an easier task than we do. The middle class has been voting for

Republican candidates, or ideas, for twenty-five years. In the absence of a good reason to switch, voters will stick with them; inertia is a powerful force. When neither party is satisfying the Baileys, they are more likely to support the party they have been supporting, even while their disgust with both parties grows.

But as we saw in 2006, over time it gets harder for the leopard to hide his spots. Today, the two interests with control of the Republican Party are not in step with the Baileys. Our increasingly diverse population is ever less responsive to the theocrats' message of a government that represents only one tradition. Polling data show that younger voters, who have more daily contact with science and technology, are becoming ever more skeptical of theocrats' desire to impose rigid, literalist scriptural interpretations on our government. And, at a time when radical fundamentalism abroad poses the most obvious threat to our country, imposing fundamentalism on our government at home is ever harder to swallow.

The economic royalists, meanwhile, are stuck in the past. In 1980, their message jibed with the feelings of the Baileys. Today, it no longer does. The increased aggressiveness of their message machine is proof that the core ideology—get government out of your life—no longer sells itself. If the message were still self-supporting, conservatives wouldn't need to so dramatically ratchet up the intensity of their message machine.

So, Republicans really are in trouble. Like Democrats in the 1970s, they have come to value ideological purity—adherence to the wishes of the theocrats and the royalists—over the needs of the middle class. It took close to fifty years for us to fall out of touch; they did it in twenty. (I wish I could claim this had to do with the intrinsic nature of each party, but more likely it's because the world now moves so much more quickly than it did a half-century ago.) A party in power will always make the same mistake: It will lose touch with its constituency and listen instead to the siren song of special interests.

Ronald Reagan didn't need Fox News to be elected—in 1980, News Corporation was but a babe. His much purer and more honest message moved the Baileys on its own. The Republican Party of 2007 is quite different from the Republican Party of 1980. Reagan was honest in his ideology. He relished debate. He loved arguing about welfare, the rolling back of communism and trickle-down economics. Theocrats and particularly economic royalists don't like honest debate. They realize that their ideological clock has run out. So, they would rather attack the messenger than debate the message.

It was inevitable that the eight words would lose their potency.

Consider the first three: *War in Iraq*. In 2004, the war in Iraq still looked like a good idea to the Baileys; it was a satisfying answer to the question of how to deal with terrorism. By 2006, the administration's duplicity and mismanagement had neutralized that argument. At the last Democratic Convention, Bill Clinton brilliantly skewered the administration's bellicose foreign policy. "Strength and wisdom are not opposing values," Clinton said. Today, Clinton's words sum up the Baileys' dissatisfaction.

But the fact that the Republicans are in trouble does not mean that the Democrats are ready to fill the breach. Neither party has yet developed a successful construct for how to deal with the war on terror. In all honesty, it's not so simple. Today's terrorist threat, with its lack of geographical boundaries and nihilism, is brand new and has complex ramifications. It's new and it's changing; we may not yet know all of its parameters. It is incumbent upon Democrats to come up with a construct. But in the meantime, one thing is certain: Bush's shibboleth—go it alone, invade and conquer—is losing its luster, substantively and politically. The grand theoretical ambitions of the neocons, who viewed Iraq as the perfect petri dish for the post–Cold War goal of unfettered American hegemony, has slowly but startlingly run aground on a fundamental and inescapable truth: In the age of terror, the war has not made us safer. *War in Iraq* worked in 2004. *No war in Iraq* worked in 2006. Neither is likely to work in 2008 and beyond.

The second message, *no gay marriage*, is a great example of what politicos call a wedge issue—so-called because it drives a wedge between voters, dividing them into two entrenched camps. I can see why it's so polarizing. Having been involved in many battles in support of gay rights, I know what this means to the community. After years of discrimination, the thirst to be fully recognized *now* is intense.

And, having been at the Corn Hill festival, I understand why so many voters respond differently. For some, prejudice is at the core, but for a huge portion, including many I saw that day, it is not. They don't hate homosexuals—according to the polls, while a majority of people oppose gay marriage, a larger majority support nondiscrimination laws. Many oppose gay marriage because, to them, the issue holds totemic, rather than rational, significance. However unfairly, it's about Britney Spears and pornography and teenage sex as much as it is about a fear of gay rights. If pornography, rampant sexuality in pop culture, extramarital relationships and divorce did not appear so prominent everywhere they turned, they would be much less fearful of gay marriage. Erroneously, they fear that a loosened definition of marriage will be another step down the road of ever-loosening morals, which they see as a threat to their way of life. More than anything, opposition to gay marriage is about a fear that society's moral standards are under siege. This irrationally echoes the same fear of the unknown, albeit not rationally, that the Baileys feel in relation to the technological and information revolution that is so dramatically transforming their world.

But this issue won't hold either, because the wedge is shrinking. In 2004, when the issue first gained national prominence in the wake of actions by the Massachusetts supreme court and San Francisco's mayor, it was easy for the Republican message machine to instill fear—"allow gay marriage and civilization will come crashing down." By 2006, while there were no legislative changes at the national level the Massachusetts decision was still law, civilization had not crashed—in fact, it was proceeding pretty much as it had been. The ability to stoke fear had subsided. In 2006, the issue seemed to provide little bump to Republican candidates in states with anti-gay marriage initiatives on their ballots. (Additionally, Republican claims of protecting "traditional values" were marred by their mishandling of the Mark Foley scandal.)

In future elections, since the Baileys' opposition to gay marriage is not about the specific issue, but rather about values in general, the issue will no longer resonate as long as Democrats step up—in a less divisive way than Bush did—in the fight to recover a sense of shared moral standards. If Democrats don't, the promotion of values issues that prey on people's fears will almost certainly rear their ugly head again, in one form or another

The Republicans' cornerstone argument among the eight words was *cut taxes*. And this position—which represents shrinking government and has been at the core of the Republican Party's platform for forty years—is also fading inexorably. Sure, tax cuts sound alluring at first; they are a perennial favorite for pollsters. But the days of wielding tax cuts as a cudgel to shrink government (to quote Republican activist Grover Norquist, "drown it in the bathtub") are passing. The argument is losing its potency year by year—it was less powerful in 2006 than 2004, and will be less powerful in 2008 than it was in 2006. As it becomes increasingly obvious that most tax cuts benefit the very wealthy, the Baileys become ever more skeptical when Republicans promise to cut their taxes.

More important, all things being equal, while Joe and Eileen would still prefer tax cuts, lower taxes are no longer their chief demand of the government. Certainly, they do not want to return to the bloated government of the 1970s; that the government be lean and mean is as important as ever to them. But the technological changes that are transforming their world mean that now, more so than even ten years ago, they want a government that is on their side. They want a government that can help them deal with new demands—fighting terrorism, preparing for the global economy, maintaining their values, paying for a longer life and holding the line against rampant commercialism—which they know they cannot manage all alone. In 1980, when government seemed out of touch and irrelevant, tax cuts trumped all other domestic issues; now, while tax cuts still resonate, they must share the field with a set of new, and very real, needs.

That leaves the economic royalists, the ideological core of the Republican Party, increasingly out in the cold.

I got back on my bike after a pit stop for polpo (grilled octopus) at my favorite restaurant in Queens. As I turned toward home, I felt like I'd gotten somewhere.

The success that Republicans had had from 2001 to 2004 was not sustainable. Their success was based on factors we could overcome: The personality of a man whose approval ratings were sinking, an anachronistic ideology, and a disingenuousness that the Baileys would happily reject, if only Democrats gave them a reason. *If only Democrats gave them a reason.*

In 2002 and 2004 we didn't. Bush's eight words were not rebuffed by anything Democrats offered. You couldn't describe the Democratic rationale in eight words or eighty. You probably could have done it in eight hundred, but only because that's enough words to let you say nothing. In 2006 we did give the Baileys a reason, but only because we countered the Republicans' eight words with the opposite—not what we would do, but what we wouldn't. In 2008 and beyond, that will no longer be enough.

But recent election history does point to one overwhelming fact: The Baileys, who have spent most of the last seventy-five years closely aligned with one party or the other, are up for grabs.

When it comes to reaching the Baileys, Republicans have four advantages and, as we've seen, they ride them for all they're worth. Democrats, I believe, have advantages as well.

First, we know we're out of touch—we talk about it all the time. Most Democrats have accepted that we need to change; the few who misread 2006 do so at our party's peril. Most Republicans, however, don't accept that they need to make a fundamental change; their special interests are too powerful to allow for soul-searching. They will flail around for five more years, trying to succeed with the cynical techniques they've used for the last few cycles, before they'll make a change.

Second, although it will take us a while, tactically we are getting better. Fully implementing our tactical improvements will take years. A Democratically controlled news network probably won't spontaneously appear tomorrow. But Democrats are more aware of tactics than ever before. We are creating think tanks, developing a media network and paying more attention to messaging. The disdain that so many in the party used to have for these sharpened tactics has dissipated.

In some areas, we have even gained the tactical advantage. Perhaps the most important is the extensive Democratic and left-leaning "netroots." They are a new and hugely significant advantage for Democrats—we saw the benefit they provide in 2006. They helped identify and encourage viable candidates, like Jim Webb and Jon Tester, in the early stages of their races. Their success with fundraising and field organizing contributed enormously to just about all of our victories. In many close elections, their contribution made the difference.

Certainly, we're not yet there in every medium. But, with the help of the online community, after years of neglect we are finally building the message machine that we need.

Third, an era in which the Baileys are starting to look to the government plays to our strengths. While neither party has yet come up with a paradigm for the changed world, it's more likely that Democrats will successfully do so. Republicans are great at crippling government when it gets too strong. Democrats are great at making it work when it's not doing enough. Reaching out, expanding opportunity, moderating the risks inherent in our system—that's what the Democratic Party does best. If we learn from what the Republicans have done in terms of tactics and clarity of message, we will be successful. Our values fit with the Baileys' better than the values of the theocrats or the economic royalists.

The Baileys need help dealing with the tectonic shifts that technology has caused; they need help dealing with forces beyond their control that are changing their lives. They don't want to return to the super-size government of the 1970s, and they certainly don't want to be condescended to, because they're proud of what they've accomplished, but they need a hand. Neither the New Deal, the Reagan Revolution, nor a hybrid offers the paradigm that will win the loyalty of the Baileys in the changed world.

FDR's forceful and creative reaction to a changed world in the '30s made the Democratic Party dominant. Reagan's identification of changes in his day established dominance for Republicans. The party that figures out how to reach the Baileys in our dramatically altered world will be the dominant party for a generation to come.

Now, all Democrats need is eight words.

PART 2
THE 50% SOLUTION

CHAPTER 8

THE KITCHEN TABLE COMPACT

SO YOU'VE SHELLED OUT TWENTY BUCKS OR SO, read a hundred pages and now you're ready for the payoff. "Hurry up, Schumer!" you're thinking. "What are the eight words that will save the Democratic Party?"

I don't want to keep you in suspense any longer. It's time to tell you. The answer is simple: I don't know.

Sorry.

The fact is, they are extremely difficult to generate. The eight words are more elusive than you could imagine. It's almost like the search for the political Holy Grail. Believe me. I've spent two years trying. I've asked advisors, colleagues, experts, political consultants and my family. Slogans are easy. Empty promises are easy. Phrases like "better health care," "the party of change," "good-paying jobs" and "a more secure America" are not hard to string together.

But they don't stand for anything—to Joe and Eileen they're typical political b.s. Anyone, of any political stripe, can proclaim them without standing for anything concrete.

As I've said, Bush's eight words were different. They represented specific policies tied to a larger value system for which he was willing to risk his political life. *Cut taxes* represented a shrinking government. *War in Iraq* represented strength against terrorism. And *no gay marriage* represented traditional values

After two years of trying, and asking countless others, I'm convinced that Democrats are not ready to have our own eight words. It's not possible, right now, for the Democratic Party to generate a series of concrete phrases that describe specific policies that relate to our core values. That's not a knock on Democrats. It took Republicans thirty years, at least fifteen of which were spent in the wilderness, to develop theirs.

If you don't believe me, try it. Let me know if you come up with something (www.positivelyamericanbook.com). A word of warning: Strong believers in a single issue often think that their issue will do it—*end global warming* is an example. But the truth is, as important as they may be, these issues are rarely targeted at the middle class—they will work for the choir, not the Baileys. And, frequently they do not describe a larger value. *Leave Iraq* is a concrete and potentially popular policy, but it does not, in and of itself, connect to a broad Democratic worldview. *Universal health care*, on the other hand, does describe a Democratic worldview, but it doesn't tie to a specific policy that we are ready to implement.

It's not possible to generate our own eight words right now, because the words themselves are the last step in creating a successful platform, not the first. To work, they must be pulled from a larger and more detailed tapestry of principles, policies and ideas. While we Democrats know what our broad values are—economic fairness, equality of opportunity, respect for the individual and, most of all, a government that works to help people—the party does not yet know what our tapestry should look like.

This book is not about selecting eight words or declaring my vision of comprehensive principles for the new millennium. Instead, the following chapters lay out eleven concrete yet ambitious goals and delineate specific policies to achieve them. Each chapter offers context and anecdotes to explain why I believe the middle class will respond to the goals described.

The difference between having eight defining words and the ideas in this book is based on the difference between deductive and inductive reasoning. In the context of politics, deductive reasoning means starting with general principles and developing detailed ideas from them. Deductive reasoning takes the principle of a *strong foreign policy* and arrives at *war in Iraq*, for example. Inductive reasoning is the opposite. It requires beginning with a set of specific ideas and then trying to describe more general principles based on them.

I'm using inductive reasoning because I believe that our most important task is to start with average people and figure out what they really need. What are the problems in their lives? How can the

Democratic philosophy of government as an efficient, accountable and adaptable force for good lead to concrete policies that make their lives better? Once we've done that, we can work upward from there.

Some may say that politics should not start with pleasing the average person. I strongly disagree. Pleasing regular people—if it means making government work to improve their lives—is what democracy and Democrats are all about. It is right and appropriate to start with Joe and Eileen's lives and let the rest follow from that.

This section presents eleven goals to be achieved within ten years that would make the lives of the middle class and those struggling to get there significantly better. Certainly, not every one of the eleven will speak to every Joe or Eileen. I like these, but there may be others that will resonate more with others. The point is not whether these goals are the only ones, or even the very best ones.

The point is to start with the Baileys.

If we do that, and then set off in the direction they send us, our own eight (or five or fifteen) words will sure enough follow. When they do—when our basic values represent clear and simple principles that, in turn, represent specific policies—that's when we'll become the dominant party.

It will take time—it could take a year; it could take five. The ideas in this book are an initial set of goals, undergirded by our fundamental values—an active and efficient government that seeks economic fairness, equality of opportunity, and respect for the individual. From these eleven goals and others like them, we should agree on a clear and simple set of principles. Once we have those principles, specific ideas—maybe the ones presented here, maybe others—will follow. That's when we will have our eight words.

Of course, we will need our own machine, as well. We will need our own intellectuals, wordsmiths and commentators to be the vehicles that will spread our words, once they are ready

There are two dominant themes that course through these chapters. They are the same themes that defined the first section of the book. They are not Democratic or Republican. Rather, they are the themes that any successful political movement must address.

The first is the middle class, as personified by the Bailey family. As I said at the outset, throughout the book the needs of the middle class and those struggling to make it trump any ideological political strategy. That's why I have framed each idea around a 50% solution. In the absence of eight words, the 50% solution is a concrete and realistic promise that gives middle-class voters something to grasp. It's a lot more specific and believable to say "increase reading and math scores by 50%" than to say "fix schools." And, because most of the ideas are quantifiable, it creates a system of accountability—even if we don't get all the way there, the Baileys will be able to measure our progress.

The idea of 50% squares with the Baileys' worldview. They're not 100% unhappy with their world or the government today—they're not looking for a revolution. What they want is for us to work toward specific goals that will give them more support in an unsettlingly changed world.

Which brings me to the second theme: technology. Over the next decade or so both parties are going to have to adapt to the dramatic changes that technology has brought. The upheavals caused by technological change most acutely affect those who are gaining the least economically—the middle class and the poor. The goals outlined in this book are designed to address the changes they are experiencing. You may not agree with the solutions I suggest for facing technology's new challenges, but you can be sure that new solutions are required.

Finally, I want to be crystal clear: This is not an all-enveloping legislative platform. It is not a comprehensive solution for every problem the country faces. And each policy may not be the perfect silver bullet for the problem it addresses. These goals and policies are not intended to define the Democratic Party as an institution for the next century. They will not provide a full quiver of principles and specific policies; they are a way of thinking that is intended to help the Democratic Party on its road back to being an enduring national force.

That road is not paved with tactical decisions. The dispute over whether it is best to target specific congressional races or focus on party building in fifty states is beside the point; neither choice by itself will bring us to a majority. The road to a majority is paved with good ideas that are based on an understanding of the voters we want to reach. Once the road is laid, smart tactics will be a lot easier to agree on.

Tactics are important, but they can never answer the number one question asked of Democrats: "What do you stand for?"

The ideas in this book will make it clear what we stand for. Not in eight words, but they will do it. They define both our broad principles and our specific goals. They separate us from Republicans. Above all, they speak to what average people care about. They are not a platform, but they form a basis from which we can inductively build a platform.

A conversation with the Baileys is the only long-term antidote to Republican electoral success. Sure, we may win an election here and there without it, but if we don't talk to the Baileys, we will never win back the middle-class majority.

I've told you how this approach has worked for me; what follows is my suggestion for how we can do it together on a larger scale.

Before you continue, I have one request. As you read the following chapters, think about Joe and Eileen Bailey sitting around their kitchen table some Friday night talking about their lives—their hopes and their fears, their dreams and their aspirations for themselves and for their children. Think about them talking about their jobs, about their kids' school and their huge property tax bill. Talking about the cost of college and filling up the gas tank, about their kids' health and their parents' health. Think about them talking about September 11th, pop culture, values.

As you read, think about the Baileys sitting around their kitchen table, wishing someone would listen.

The 50% Solution is for all the Baileys in America. It is our kitchen table compact with them.

CHAPTER 9

INCREASE READING AND MATH SCORES BY 50%

☆ TRIPLE FEDERAL EDUCATION SPENDING TO AN
AVERAGE OF $2,800 PER STUDENT.

☆ ASSESS SCHOOLS ON ONE CONSISTENT FEDERAL
STANDARD.

☆ AFTER FOUR YEARS, MAKE INCREASED FEDERAL
DOLLARS DEPENDENT ON ACHIEVEMENT AND
FUND SCHOOLS THAT ARE SUBPAR ONLY IF
THEY ENACT PRESCRIBED REQUIREMENTS AND
PROGRAMS.

☆ OFFER FEDERAL SALARY STIPENDS TO HIGHLY
QUALIFIED MATH AND SCIENCE TEACHERS.

THERE ARE EUREKA MOMENTS in life. Little things that, for whatever reason, make the lightbulb go on. In a moment you get something that you just hadn't gotten before. You see it, hiding in plain sight. And you're amazed you ever could have missed it. A few years ago, I had one. I haven't looked at the world the same way since.

Bear Stearns is one of New York's big investment banks. Companies like Bear Stearns are the lifeblood of our state. So you can imagine my reaction when I woke up a few years ago to the rumor that Bear was moving hundreds of jobs to India. I was on the phone with Jim Cayne, Bear's CEO, before I'd finished my bowl of Frosted Mini-Wheats. He told me it was true.

"You already outsourced," I said. "You moved jobs offshore a couple of years ago."

"Not these jobs," he said. "We're phasing out our computer folks. Software engineers."

"What?!" Frosted Mini-Wheats flew across the room.

He told me that the people who designed the programs were staying here, but the jobs of the next level of people—sophisticated, advanced programmers who make around $150,000 a year—were being sent to India. I pleaded with him to reconsider. He told me he couldn't. In India, he could get an employee with relatively similar skills for $20,000 a year. It would be a dereliction of duty to his shareholders not to outsource the jobs.

When I hung up, I was shaking. I couldn't finish my cereal. Software engineers. People making $150,000 a year. These were good-paying jobs. Not lower-tier stuff. This wasn't how globalization was supposed to work. It wasn't supposed to lead to a wholesale exodus of jobs from our country to the developing world. No one thought jobs like these would go. *I* never did.

The news was devastating—for someone who cares about New York and our country, it was truly devastating.

During the week after I heard about Bear, I was at the Oyster Festival. The festival's held on the waterfront every October in Oyster Bay, of Billy Joel fame. The hamlet of Oyster Bay is on the north shore of Long Island, north of Massapequa,* which is on the south shore. They have oysters cooked a dozen or more ways and some of the best roasted corn I've ever tasted. It's a great festival, full of people like the Baileys. These are, after all, the people on whom Joe and Eileen were originally based.

While I was at the Oyster Festival, jawing with constituents, a guy came up to me. His wife was a couple of steps behind, pushing a stroller and holding a girl's hand.

"Great to see you," I extended my hand.

"Chuck Schumer!" We shook. He held on. "You've got to help me."

*For a small place, Massapequa has been home to a lot of famous people. Alec Baldwin and his brothers, Peggy Noonan, Joey Buttafuoco, Steve Guttenberg, Stuttering John, Jessica Hahn, Marvin Hamlisch, Fox News's Brian Kilmeade (whom I met when our daughters played soccer in the same league), Carlo Gambino, and Jerry Seinfeld (who has joked that Massapequa is Native American for "by the mall") all could have lived on the same street as the Baileys.

"I'll try."

"Please. I'm a software engineer. I work for an investment bank in the city. They're sending my job to India."

A chill went up my spine. "What bank?"

"Bear Stearns."

"Oh no."

"Yeah." He motioned to his wife. "I've got my wife, three kids."

I looked over. A third child, his oldest, was planted behind her mother's legs.

"I never thought this would happen to me. Not now," he said. "I worked my way up. Been there my whole career. Early on, I knew anything could happen. But I'm a senior guy now."

His wife stepped forward. "We've got a mortgage," she said. "We bought a nice house. He doesn't do customer service—he writes their technology! No one ever talked about outsourcing skilled jobs!"

I nodded.

"They gave me three months." He glanced at his eldest, peering from behind her mother's legs. When he spoke again, his voice was quiet. "I don't know what to do. Please help me."

"I'll try."

I tend to be an optimist. I can have a temper, but it's hard to sink me. I just don't have time for despair. Still, I was really troubled by this. Seeing that family brought it home. When I had heard about the jobs the week before, I had known intellectually how serious it was. But talking to the family—that really socked it to me.

As I drove home from Long Island, I was about as close to despair as I ever get. I have always believed in the concept of free trade as long as environmental and labor protections are included; suddenly, I wasn't so sure. As I thought about it, I began to doubt if the whole theory really worked.

I spent months doing research. What jobs are being outsourced? Why? How do companies that outsource perform against those that don't? Which jobs aren't getting outsourced yet? Which probably never will?

I spoke to Senator Debbie Stabenow of Michigan, whose state has probably been harder hit than any other. We shared our anxieties about the future.

Paul Craig Roberts, an assistant treasury secretary under President Reagan, was eager to talk. Paul is an old-school conservative's conservative. He and I agree about almost nothing, which is one reason I was so interested to hear his thoughts on globalization.

Paul had started to doubt David Ricardo's early 1800s theory of "comparative advantage"—the gospel of free trade. The idea of comparative advantage is that each country should focus on the goods that it produces most efficiently, relative to all others. If Portugal is best at producing wine and England is best at producing cloth, Portugal should send wine to England and England should send cloth to Portugal. If countries focus on their strengths and fill in the gaps through free trade, overall production will be maximized. The rising tide of productivity will benefit everyone. But the theory is based on a limiting factor. Ricardo assumed that Portuguese vintners—and their labor and capital—couldn't pick up and go to England, just as English manufacturers couldn't pick up and go to Portugal.

Together with Paul, I wrote a *New York Times* op-ed. We did not try to offer solutions. Instead we used the opportunity to ask questions about the theory of comparative advantage. The financial world was shocked.

Paul and I argued that the world had changed in the last decade and a half. The most important change is technological. Thanks to the spread of high-speed Internet and broadband around the globe, we can now instantaneously transfer huge amounts of information almost anywhere on earth. The global transfer of any type of information or data is cheap and immediate. When it comes to doing a job, close and far are no longer meaningful distinctions. All that matters is *in person* or *not*. If a job requires direct contact with people or materials—restaurant workers, clinicians, salespeople—it will never be outsourced. If it does not—most other jobs—it can be done from anywhere in the world.

Think again about radiologists, the experts who make diagnoses from x-rays, MRIs and all sorts of cutting-edge technology. Radiologists are among the highest paid of all doctors. Their job takes an incredible amount of technical knowledge and supremely good judgment. The only thing the job does not require is face-to-face contact with patients. If you hurt your hand and go to an emergency room,

ER doctors and nurses will take a look and check your vital signs. Then a medical technician will x-ray your hand. Twenty years ago, the film would be developed and a radiologist would come by to make a diagnosis. If you went to a doctor's office instead of a hospital, the film could be messengered to a radiologist across town. Today, it's totally different. A digital rendering of your x-ray can be immediately and cheaply uploaded onto a network. Anywhere in the world, it's possible to sign onto the network, pull up your x-ray and make a diagnosis. Radiologists can just as easily be in India as across town or upstairs. As long as they have a high-speed data connection, they can work from anywhere in the world. It is estimated that a quarter of radiological examinations will be sent to India in the next decade. Internists have to examine people in person, so they're safe. Radiologists deal with data (mostly in the form of images), so they aren't.

Because of technology, globalization does not only affect low-end jobs. Anyone whose job doesn't require face-to-face contact—from a customer service representative to a radiologist to the software engineer in Oyster Bay, Long Island—is competing against the rest of the world. Low-tech jobs can be outsourced because it's cheap and easy to move materials around the globe. High-tech jobs can be outsourced because it's equally cheap and easy to move information; it is *because* these jobs are so high-tech that they can migrate. Think about all of the jobs that used to be geographically limited but no longer are. For many jobs, both high-end and low-end, there is one world labor market. The new graduates of Shanghai University or the University of Mumbai were never considered by Ricardo. Today they are in direct competition with graduates of the University of Pennsylvania.

In addition to broadband, another, secondary change has catalyzed globalization. Twenty years ago, the world was bifurcated. The battles of the Cold War were being fought in the developing world. The fear of instability, nationalization or simple incompatibility made huge capital investments in much of the world, including India and China, highly risky. Today, there are no such barriers. In a world no longer split by superpowers, capital (as well as labor) can flow based on cost alone. Investors all over the world can now search for the absolute lowest cost, no matter what country it's in. People who would never have considered India or China twenty years ago now pour in billions of dollars without a second thought. Even the spate of regional instability in the Middle East cuts off only a tiny fraction of the world.

Paul and I did not argue that free trade was wrong; rather, we argued that its fundamental premise should be looked at anew in light of the technological revolution. If capital and labor can flow around the world unfettered, the lifting of all boats that Ricardo had posited would occur with comparative advantage had to be given a second thought. In a world where so much can be moved so quickly, countries may no longer maintain immutable characteristics or maintain comparative advantages. I had not given up on free trade, but I wanted to continue the conversation and see where it led.

The op-ed created quite a firestorm. Economists from left, right and center railed against us as protectionists, or worse. It was not until Nobel Prize winner Paul Samuelson and a couple of other eminent economists publicly echoed the essential point that the fury quieted down—somewhat.

The maelstrom aside, I was increasingly distraught. I've always believed that America would stay number one not just for my generation, but for my children and grandchildren too. For America to turn into a nation like we imagine Sweden to be, where everyone is taken care of but the nation no longer strives to be the best, is untenable. In math, there are postulates—things that can be proven or disproven—and axioms—facts that are taken as givens. For the United States, being first is not a postulate, it's an axiom.

Worst of all, if Paul Craig Roberts and I were right—if China and India could outcompete us not just on widgets, but on everything—there was no solution. Building walls and halting the flow of labor and capital (i.e., protectionism) would not work. Building walls would mean our companies would only be able to sell to 300 million people, not three billion. It would mean that our consumers would only have access to products that were more expensive and less varied. Protectionism would leave our companies and our labor force behind; it would push us right out of our global leadership role. Our economy and our country would wither. For a time, it seemed to me that our options were a quick death at the hands of protectionism as the world left us behind or a slow death at the mercy of free trade as our power slowly eroded and we perhaps became a large Sweden.

I couldn't accept it. I continued to seek out the people I most respected to discuss this challenge. For years, I had been having regular lunches with the chairman of the Federal Reserve. When I was elected to Congress, Paul Volcker was the chairman. I knew him from New York, so he invited me to lunch; after a couple of meetings, we made it a regular thing. At the time, the structure of the Fed and its independence were under attack from a lot of Democrats. Our lunches worked for both of us: He taught me a heck of a lot and, because I thought the Fed's critics were wrong, I defended the institution.

When Alan Greenspan was appointed, Volcker told him to keep meeting with this mid-level congressman. Greenspan agreed. We had our first meal when he had been on the job for about three months.

"How's the new job?" I asked.

"I love it." His face lit up.

"What do you like best?"

The newly appointed most powerful banker in the world leaned across the table toward me, an eager look on his face. His eyes were bright; his hands were excitedly rubbing together. I thought he might be about to tell me about a stash of dirty magazines that Volcker had left in the bowels of the Fed's basement library.

"Know what I like best?" he whispered with a conspiratorial smile.

I didn't want to guess.

"The data!"

He paused, probably for effect, and then continued.

"When I was in the private sector I knew our balance sheets. Now, I know our competitors' as well."

From that moment forward, I always trusted his judgment. Economists who depend on data are becoming all too rare.

In early 2004, shortly after writing the op-ed, I was able to sit with Greenspan. I brought up my concerns about globalization. The chairman nodded. I could tell he had struggled with many of the same concerns. "Our economy has completely transformed," he said. "We used to add value by *making* things, today we add value by *thinking* things. When you think things, it can be done anywhere in the world."

I told him about the software engineer.

He nodded empathetically. "We will lose some jobs," he admitted. "But that software engineer will be fine. Someone of his skill level is in high demand. Globalization will work for us." He did not deny that many of the assumptions underpinning comparative advantage had shifted. But he was adamant that those changes did not have to turn globalization into a losing proposition for the United States. "Look at the data," he said.

Americans who have college degrees have seen their salaries increase over the last twenty-five years. You do fine with a college degree. The average hourly wage for college graduates grew by 25% from 1980 to 2003; the average hourly wage for someone who stopped at high school grew by a mere 3%. In every five-year period between 1980 and 2000, the average hourly wage for workers with a college degree increased; only during the torrid economy of the late 1990s did the average wage for high school graduates increase— and not by much. Over those five years, college graduates' wages grew almost twice as fast as those of high school graduates.

It's simple supply and demand, Greenspan told me. India, China and scores of other developing countries have billions of workers who are functionally literate and have only rudimentary math skills—*literally* billions. Meanwhile, there are fewer and fewer jobs for which that is enough. The supply of nominally educated workers far outstrips the demand. For the less well educated, the future is murky.

On the other hand, there are more and more jobs that demand a top-rate education—the kind of education that America's best high schools and colleges provide. Many of these jobs may go to India and China; many more will stay in America. It's not a zero-sum equation. As we've already seen, globalization does create growth. In the new world economy, there may be less stability. But there will continue to be great demand. And the supply of workers with a top-notch education does not come close to meeting the demand. Despite outsourcing, over the next century Americans who are well educated will have their pick of jobs. Americans who are less educated will not. In the global ideas economy, education means success, and hence, rising wages for Americans who have a college degree.

This was my second epiphany, and it ran counter to the first. We could succeed. We could continue to thrive. But it depended on our maintaining the best-educated population in the world.

My despair in Oyster Bay was cautionary. It showed that the competition from India and China is even greater than we had realized. But it is not a harbinger of collapse. It would have been cold comfort for that young family, but when I met with Greenspan a couple of months after the Oyster Festival, the unemployment rate for software engineers was hovering around 3%—barely more than half of what it was for the general workforce. Bear Stearns may have outsourced, but there were other jobs out there for that software engineer. I never met him again, but the odds are very high that he was able to find a job as good as the one he lost.

Greenspan didn't talk about it (perhaps because it's not data based!), but America starts with another advantage. We have the best system in the world. We harness people's talents better than any other country. We encourage creativity. We are entrepreneurial. Only in America does a poor person grow up believing that she can become a multimillionaire. Only in America are we blessed with immigrants who feel they are part of the system and infuse new energy into every generation. While other countries have immigrants, nowhere else are they so quickly integrated into the social fabric of the country as they are here. It is easy to get caught up in focusing on our trade deficit. Let's not forget about our immigrant surplus: more people want to come here than we are able to take. Americans are not moving to China or India to make a better life for their families. Among the best that China and India have are moving here, or want to.

Even before the heightened globalization of the last decade and a half, there were some industries in which we competed globally. Although we slipped in some areas, such as automobiles, we always filled the gap—think of the computer revolution. American innovation and entrepreneurialism make us uniquely able to adapt to a changing world.

We have a great system, one that is open, resilient, innovative. That will help.

I breathed a sigh of relief. There can be a future for us. I am once again optimistic about America.

There is only one thing that can prevent us from staying number one, that will stop the pie from continuing to grow.

We will not stay on top with mediocre schools. In this new world, Americans need the kind of knowledge that comes from getting a great formal education.

So, my optimism is tempered by a new sense of urgency. I've always believed in education, but Greenspan made it clear: Our future depends on it. To survive, our educational system needs to be more than decent, better than adequate. For America to prosper, it must be number one. Not number ten. Not even number two. For us to prosper, it must be the best—as it once was.

There is great irony in this debate. Globalization has been part of our political debate for the last ten years. Free traders and protectionists have been battling it out on the narrow field of trade policy. The irony is that the solution has little to do with trade policy.

The solution is education.

Joe and Eileen Bailey know that their children need the very best. They see that we are competing with China and India. They understand that the old jobs are not there. They realize that education is the future. That's why they pay huge property taxes. That's why they live where they live. Some of the biggest choices in their lives are defined by this issue. Deep in the pit of their stomach they know: the only way we will keep up is by having the premier educational system in the world.

Today, we do not. According to the Organization for Economic Co-operation and Development (OECD), our schools are not the best. The OECD, an international organization made up of thirty market-based democracies, including the United States, periodically ranks member nations. In both math and problem solving, we place toward the bottom of the OECD's rankings. In math, we are tied with Poland, Hungary and Spain at twenty-first among fifteen-year-olds. In problem solving, we are even worse. Tied with four countries at twenty-third, we were ahead of only Greece, Turkey and Mexico.

The state of our schools and our resulting slippage in the world is a national crisis that dwarfs all others. *All others.* If we lose our knowledge advantage, we will lose our place in the world. If we maintain it, the price of labor in India and China won't matter—the best jobs in the world will still be in America.

So, education must be our major thrust. Without top-notch schools, we won't be able to afford any of the other things that are also critically important and we so badly need—a strong defense, better health care, a fair Social Security system. We will stagnate. For the first time in our history, the pie will stop growing. If that happens, we are in trouble. When the pie's not growing, people fight over the pieces. Class warfare starts. People drop out. Societies decline. This will be particularly true in our country, which is used to continuous growth. It will be an angry, sullen, depressed America if the pie isn't growing.

We have to focus on this issue like no other. Everything depends on it—health care, Social Security, even the military depends on a strong economy with a growing pie. This is a necessity—not a whim, not a hope. We *need* our education to be great. When we hear that we are twenty-third in the world, we should be shivering, not shrugging our shoulders.

We must improve education. Joe and Eileen know it. There are two issues at play. The problems in kindergarten through twelfth grade (K–12) and college are somewhat different. Our K–12 system has gotten mediocre. Our college system is still very good, but it's becoming too expensive for too many people. And, as any college dean will tell you, too many kids are showing up for freshman year unprepared for school. K–12 is more of a quality problem. College is more of an affordability problem. (College is discussed in more detail in Chapter 11, Increase the Number of College Graduates by 50%).

When we try to fix K–12 education, too often our focus is wrong. Today, the top 10% and bottom 10% of schools get almost all the focus. We ignore the 80% in the middle. That middle 80% is where the real decline is occurring.

The top 10% of schools, which get a disproportionate share of the dollars, are excellent and will stay excellent. These are private schools and public schools in the wealthiest areas. Places like Scarsdale, New York; Lake Forest, Illinois; and Highland Park, Texas.

The bottom 10%, which get such a lion's share of the focus, are in terrible shape. But their problems are bigger; they go beyond education policy. Before the first day of kindergarten, many of the students in these schools have vast challenges. These schools need more money, but more importantly, they need to do a job that schools traditionally don't do. They need to fill the void of structure and values that a twenty-one-year-old drug-addicted mother leaves in a six-year-old's life. The solution for these kids is very different from the solution for kids in other schools; they need more attention and focused resources. In New York, the Institute for Student Achievement has had great success with creating support systems at schools with disadvantaged students. Programs like this must be expanded because it's good for our country and because it's the right thing to do. But that's a separate discussion.

The 80% of schools in the middle are responsible for much of the decline in the OECD numbers. These schools are our future—they educate most of our children—and they have largely been ignored as we focus our time and attention on the bottom and top 10%. To have a chance in the future, we have to make the schools in the middle excellent.

This is a call to action. The crisis in those 80% of schools demands it.

The time has come to revamp large parts of public education, and we need the federal government to be far more involved in solving this problem. We should not change the structure of our schools, or make our country's six million teachers and administrators employees of the federal government. I don't want to abolish the country's 15,000-plus school boards.

Instead, the federal government needs to take control in three ways that really matter: standards, money, and teachers. The federal government should create a rigorous national standard by which every school is judged, triple the amount of federal money for schools that agree to certain conditions, and enhance the salaries of qualified teachers in the most critical subjects, like math and science.

Under this plan, all school districts would be assessed on a consistent national standard. Federal education spending would more than triple—instead of getting an average of about $860 per student from the federal government, school districts that chose to participate in the program would get an average of more than $2,800. Furthermore, qualified teachers in very needed subjects, like science and math, would get federal salary enhancements. All districts that signed up would get the money for four years and have to develop their own programs to meet the federal standards. After four years, schools that weren't meeting the standard—or showing improvement toward meeting it—would be required to adopt proven educational strategies to get better.

In addition to meeting a federal standard or accepting federally defined strategies to improve, districts that participated would need to make one more promise: They'd have to freeze property taxes that go to education, so that in effect property taxes are cut by 50% within ten years. Tying education funding to property tax reductions will create a coalition between families with children who are focused on education and all those—older couples, younger couples and singles without children—who are burdened by high property taxes. Together, they will put wind into the sails of this plan. I'll talk more about this in Chapter 10, Reduce Property Taxes That Fund Education by 50%, but suffice it to say that if education is our highest priority, it must no longer be chained to our most hated tax.

Local school boards would continue to play an important role, as they should. I know many school board members and administrators. They do admirable work. But they are the first to admit that they are caught in a vise. They are asked to improve schools without being given the tools and resources to do it. Under this plan, we will provide better tools and better oversight.

This is a national imperative. We wouldn't ask fifteen thousand localities, or even fifty states, to be responsible for national defense— and then underfund them! Improving our K–12 educational system is at least as important to our country's future as maintaining our world's best military. We cannot leave education in the hands of thousands of disparate localities operating under tremendous strain. To start out, we will give the localities increased resources and control. We'll give them a chance. If they get it done, God bless them. But if they can't do the job, we must.

There are those who will claim that education is not the federal government's responsibility. My response? When we are talking about saving the American way of life, it's a national imperative—we have no choice.

Ever since New York State created the nation's first Board of Regents in 1784, the federal government's role in education has evolved to meet the demands of a changing world. From the outset, Thomas Jefferson dreamed of a "general education" that would "enable every man to judge for himself what will secure or endanger his freedom." Despite Jefferson's aspirations, for half a century education was left to a hodgepodge of private and religious schools. By the second half of the nineteenth century, the Industrial Revolution demanded that an increasingly urban population enter the workforce with a basic formal education. Largely in response to this economic imperative, states began to adopt compulsory education laws and a federal office was established. By World War I, federal subsidies were needed to improve vocational programs in local schools. Since then, the federal government has gotten involved when the educational system has failed to keep pace with our nation's needs. From enforcing civil rights, to performing groundbreaking research such as the 1983 Department of Education report *A Nation at Risk*, to enacting the No Child Left Behind Act, the federal government has played an ever more prominent role in the well-being of our schools. In the face of the speed of change caused by technology and the Internet, we can no longer afford a gradually evolving educational policy.

It is time for the next step. To compete in today's world, we need the federal government to be even more involved. England, France, Japan and South Korea all have a single national school system. They all have another similarity, too. They're ranked higher in educational quality than we are by the OECD. That fact is more important than anyone's ideological opposition to national education.

Economic royalists would prefer us not to be in the business of education at all. They don't want any additional money to go toward funding public schools. They try to turn the debate away from improving public schools and toward privatizing them. Their arguments have nothing to do with education and everything to do with ideology and keeping taxes down.

In schools all over the world it has been shown that well-spent money makes a difference, whether the schools are public or private. Data recently compiled by the Bush administration itself show that charter schools and public schools tend to have similar results. For those of us who thought that the privatization argument was a shibboleth, the data confirmed our hunch. Having sufficient resources and spending them well is much more important than whether a school is publicly or privately run. The Baileys certainly don't care about the public-private distinction. All they want is something that works.

I sometimes wonder who the ideologues work for. I've been hired by Joe and Eileen Bailey of Everytown, USA. They have given me their trust. Their future is at stake. Our country's future is at stake. It is up to us to do everything we can to make sure that we, and our children, have a future that is positively American.

Real National Standards

Given the crisis we face, it's surreal that we have not agreed on the basic knowledge and skills that all Americans should possess. We have agreed on a national standard in almost every other walk of life. When it comes to education, however, we've somehow flinched. If we are going to improve education, we'd better establish a consistent system of accountability for every school in the country.

Every student in America should be tested on basic knowledge in a standardized way, every year. That's how we'll know what kids are learning and how well schools are teaching. This part of the plan is not voluntary. Each year, every student in the country will have to take a national test. This test will replace, not augment, all of the state tests that are now administered. In addition to being the gold standard for student achievement, the test results will be available to states, districts and schools that want to use them diagnostically.

The kernel of this idea is not new. It is in the No Child Left Behind Act (NCLB) passed by the Bush administration. In fact, that kernel was so good that it earned the support of no less than Ted Kennedy—the Democrats' leader on education for decades. The basic concept was to create standards and then help local school boards meet those standards. But, like most other things done by the Bush administration, it was never allowed to take root. It was implemented half-heartedly, administered poorly and deprived of the dollars it needed. The parts of NCLB that are focused on the poorest-performing schools are the one success of the final bill. They should be kept in place. As for the rest, this plan takes that little seed and nurtures it. If properly handled, it may yet grow into the mighty tree that it could, and should, have been.

Standards are one of many areas in which NCLB had a good concept, but screwed up the details. Instead of imposing a single national standard, it got too complicated. It created a hodgepodge; school boards don't like that. And, thanks to the Bush administration's knee-jerk hatred of anything federal, there is not a single national test—each state is allowed to design and score its own tests. Some states have exploited this power to create tests that offer the illusion of proficiency. Other states have decent tests, but are a bureaucratic mess. There's no reason for there to be fifty different standards in fifty different states. It's the federal government's job to impose consistency, rationality and competence. There are not fifty ways to read or fifty ways to do algebra.

We need to take these kernels and create a national test for every student, one that measures every school on a national standard. These new national standards should be developed and overseen by a new National Commission on Education. The commission will be charged with all aspects of setting and monitoring national standards. It will write tests and determine their scoring. It will be responsible for creating policies to help subpar districts improve. The commission will have access to the resources of the federal Department of Education to help it carry out its mission, but it must be independent of any president or party. Even more than the Securities and Exchange Commission or the Federal Communications Commission, it is critical that the commission be completely above politics. It should be made up of a nonpartisan group of experts in all facets of educational policy, including testing and achievement in all subjects and at all grade levels. When it comes to national standards, the commission must be the first and last word.

There are shades of this idea in the National Assessment of Educational Progress, the only current national assessment tool. But it is not administered to every student or used for accountability; it basically exists to identify broad trends. That's a fine idea, but it's not the same thing as a national standard.

Sometimes people complain about "teaching to the test." They say that standardized tests replace creativity with multiple-choice questions. In truth, though, it's a false opposition. Standards and creativity are not in conflict. For most students, standards should be the beginning of their education, not the end. If students are struggling and a teacher must choose between focusing on the national test and something else, the primary goal *should* be to teach the basic skills and knowledge that are on the test. Teaching to standardized tests isn't perfect, but it's a whole lot better than teaching mush.

The key is to have good tests. If the test is irrelevant or poorly written, it might be worse than nothing. I'd choose a good teacher's lesson plan over the contents of a shoddy test any day.

But that is not an argument against a national standard; in fact, it's one of the best arguments for it. With better resources and more sustained public focus, a single national test will be more relevant and better written than much of what's used today. A good national test will be what it's supposed to be—an afterthought for high-performing districts and a catalyst for low-performing ones.

Triple Federal Education Funding

We don't stand a chance of dramatically improving our schools unless we substantially increase our investment in them. We should triple the federal investment in education, from about $860 per student to more than $2,800. That, along with the other parts of this proposal, could mean as much as $100 billion in increased federal education spending. If every district accepts the money, it will increase total average per-pupil spending by more than 25%, pushing it above the $10,000 mark.

School districts will have the option of accepting or forgoing the new money. If they accept it, the deal will be very simple. Initially, all they will have to do is freeze the amount of property tax that funds education so that it's cut in half within ten years (again, more on this in Chapter 10). If districts take the deal, they will receive the new federal money for four years with no further mandates. The money will be distributed to all participating districts based on a simple per-student formula and will be unrestricted.

After four years, we'll look at test scores. If students are meeting federal achievement standards, or have been improving toward them, the money will keep coming. It will continue to rise with inflation and flow without restrictions—no new mandates, no new requirements. But if students in a participating district are not at, or improving toward, federal standards, the district will have to adopt federally defined best practices to solve their achievement problems.

The best practices solutions will be defined by the new National Commission on Education (NCE). In addition to setting and supervising standards, the commission's experts in pedagogy and learning will design the achievement programs for participating districts that do not meet standards. The programs will have some general requirements and some requirements that are focused on each specific district's strengths and weaknesses. The type of federal best practices program put in place in each failing district will vary; the NCE will tailor a different program to meet each district's needs and address its failures. The commission's prescribed programs will ensure that the substantially increased federal investment in education is being spent efficiently and with expertise.

As an added resource, the commission will be authorized to award up to $1 billion over its first five years to fund new independent research into standards and pedagogy. This research will help the NCE create standards and define solutions for districts that accept the new money.

For school districts, it will work a little like the deal with federal highway money. States are not required to set the drinking age at 21. But if they don't, they lose their transportation dollars. Similarly, school districts will not be required to accept the new federal money. If they don't, they won't be required to freeze the amount of property tax that funds education or be subject to federally defined best practices. It's their choice.

Not all districts will accept the deal. I expect that many of the districts in the top 10% will opt out. If they're doing well, that's fine. Some communities are already spending so much more per student than the federal government would offer with this plan that the extra money wouldn't mean much to them. Because the districts are overwhelmingly affluent, the property tax burden, and the impetus to freeze it, is decidedly lower than in middle-class districts. If so, God bless them. Any district can reject the deal and continue as it has been.

Of course, the program will be costly. If 75% of school districts take the deal and get an average of about $2,800 per student—three and a quarter times the average federal expenditure today—this new program will cost the federal government about $70 billion a year. It's expensive, but consider this: Even after tripling our per-student investment, the federal government will budget somewhere around

$150 billion a year for education. Compare this with the Department of Defense, which spends $440 billion a year, or Health and Human Services, which spends $640 billion, including entitlements, or the entire federal budget, which is $2.25 *trillion*. National defense, Medicaid and Medicare are all critical to our future. It's time we get serious about the fact that education is, too.

There are some who will oppose the new spending. For years, conservative groups, funded by economic royalists, have not only argued for privatization, they have also argued that spending more money on education does not increase student achievement. They trot out examples of schools with high per-capita spending and low achievement. Or they point out that as overall education funding has increased, overall quality has remained stagnant or declined.

"You see!" they gleefully proclaim. "Money for schools doesn't matter! Cut the funding!"

However, as with so many policy disagreements, the most common argument against increasing funding for public education ends up being the best case for it. The studies have a basic flaw. They assume that all spending is created equal. Waste and efficiency are not parsed. Nor are proven and unproven programs. It is like claiming that there are no qualified pilots because the average person can't fly a plane. They use the occasional high-achievement district that doesn't spend a lot and the poorly performing district that spends a fortune to try to claim that money makes no difference. They ignore the fact that, in general, better-funded schools have higher-achieving students than less well-funded schools do. And they ignore the lesson that we learned with NCLB—imposing new standards on school districts without providing the resources to meet them doesn't work.

Their basic claim—that unlike in every other human endeavor, increased investment in education has no effect—makes little sense.

Despite this, the antifunding studies do make one good point: The way you spend your money is as important as the amount you spend. Quality *and* quantity are important. That's why standards must be part of the solution. It's why it's critical that the National Commission on Education oversee the program to guarantee that the money is spent well.

So, sure, money alone is not the answer. But money plus standards—that is.

Salary Stipends for Highly Qualified Math and Science Teachers

Under this education plan, in addition to the funding described above, the federal government will make an immediate investment in recruiting and retaining talented teachers in math and science, where they are most needed. Teachers with subject matter mastery and demonstrated teaching skills will get an annual increase in salary of up to $20,000 a year paid for by the federal government. The equation is simple: If salaries are higher for qualified teachers, more qualified people will choose to teach and continue to teach.

More than anything, our schools depend on high-quality teachers. Other than the values that are taught to children at home, teacher quality is the most important factor in student achievement. A troublesome family situation can't be solved in schools. Teacher quality can.

Study after study shows that the most important factor in student performance is teacher quality (defined as some combination of educational background, literacy level, years of experience, subject matter knowledge and teaching skill). One large-scale example is a study of the entire Illinois high school class of 2002, which found that teacher quality was the most important factor in students' college readiness. Even more striking, it found that students in low-level math classes taught by high-quality teachers did better than students in high-level math classes taught by low-quality teachers.

On the other hand, while it's a popular rallying cry, there is less evidence that class size has an effect on student achievement after third grade. Great schools usually don't have the most teachers; they have the best teachers. While it would be great to both lower class size and have great teachers, if I could choose between a great teacher with twenty-five kids in a class and a mediocre teacher with seventeen, I'd take the former every time.

There are lots of incredible teachers in our schools, but overall, teacher quality has declined in the last generation. In 1964, more than one in five high schoolers who scored in the top 10% on their achievement tests went on to become teachers. Between 1971 and 1974, almost a quarter of those in the top 10% went on to teach. By 2000, that number had declined to about one in ten. In other words, top achievers are less than half as likely to choose teaching today as they were thirty years ago.

This is because choosing and staying in teaching involves a huge financial sacrifice. As a result, many excellent candidates do not become teachers. I know this from my own experience. I was brought up in a home where we always had to be careful about money; my parents wanted me to be free of that. They urged me to be a doctor or a lawyer because those were esteemed and lucrative professions. Instead, I rebelled and ran for the Assembly at age twenty-three.

During my first year in the Assembly, I was regularly asked to teach for an afternoon at schools in my district. I taught history classes at my alma mater, Madison High School. I taught social studies classes at Cunningham Junior High. From the first time that I did it, I loved it. I found it fulfilling and compelling. I said to myself, "I could spend my whole life doing this." In 1998, I decided that if I lost to D'Amato, I'd teach. I knew that if I was ever finished with politics, it was the thing I would most want to do.

But because the salary was so low, when I was in college and law school, teaching didn't register on my radar; no one encouraged me to teach. To choose teaching takes commitment and devotion—it is a higher calling—yet because of the pay, it also involves a huge sacrifice.

The starting salary for teachers in 2003 was estimated to be about $30,000. Low teacher pay is one of our society's most egregious failures.

Low teacher pay is particularly damaging in math and science. When you can make $70,000 in the private sector with a math or science degree, it is very hard to go be a teacher. That's why so few math and science teachers today are trained in the fields they teach; according to a 2002 report, 69% of math teachers and 57% of science teachers neither majored nor are certified in the subject they are teaching. Among new teachers, the percentage trained in the field they are beginning to teach is even lower. To attract more qualified applicants to teaching, and to keep the many qualified teachers from leaving, we need to make the sacrifice less acute.

Teachers' pay has never been great, so why the sudden decline in numbers? It's largely because in the past there were always specific groups who would go into teaching regardless of the salary. These can be described in three cohorts that, until a couple of decades ago, made up the lion's share of teachers.

The first cohort was made up of people raised during the Depression. They had felt the sting of unemployment and of not being able to feed their families. They wanted security above all and were willing to take lower salary in return for that security. A civil service job seemed to be the answer. In the 1940s, '50s and '60s, a huge number of postal workers, cops, firefighters and teachers came from this group.

The brilliant teacher who employed me part-time to run his mimeo machine during high school was from this group. Before he overcame his fear of private enterprise, Stanley Kaplan had chosen teaching because of the Depression. He was a great teacher, and there were more like him. But most who were drawn to teaching by the Depression retired from our schools by the 1970s.

The second cohort willing to teach despite low pay was women. That was because so many other doors were closed to them. Until a generation ago, most bright women had two options: nurse or teacher, and that was it. It amazed me to learn that when Sandra Day O'Connor graduated third in her class from Stanford Law School in 1952, she couldn't find a job in a law firm. Meanwhile the man who graduated just ahead of her, William Rehnquist, had no trouble getting hired.

The glass ceiling holding down women was unjust. It was also why I had the good fortune to be taught by teachers like Mrs. Wagner for social studies; Mrs. Roberts for astronomy; Mrs. Chivvas for fifth grade (who had us write a play called *We Believe* to honor General Douglas MacArthur on the tenth anniversary of his ouster by President Truman) and my favorite, Mrs. McGowan, for sixth grade. She had each of us pledge never to buy Czechoslovakian tennis balls—I guess the teachers at PS 197 in Brooklyn were overwhelmingly conservative.

Today, thank God, the glass ceiling has been shattered (or at least raised much higher); women can and should do everything. More than half of all students in colleges and professional schools are women. The number of women enrolled in higher education is one of the most important developments of my lifetime. It's a great change in society, but it depletes the pool of excellent teachers.

The third cohort who once went into teaching is the smallest, and it is often overlooked. It is made up of the Vietnam War generation. A lot of my contemporaries became teachers so they could avoid the draft. By the time the draft ended, they had been bitten by the bug; they discovered they loved teaching and made it their career. My kids were taught by a slew of these men in Brooklyn public schools. Now, after thirty or thirty-five years, these men are disappearing, as well.

With these cohorts gone, and with salaries as low as they are, too many people who might otherwise teach, don't. And many who are excellent teachers are forced to leave the profession.

If we are going to raise salaries, we have to spend the money where it's most needed. Let's face the facts. Gym teachers, particularly considering today's growing childhood obesity problem, are important. But the supply of those who are willing and able to be effective gym teachers is far greater than the supply of those who are willing and able to be effective math teachers.

My friend Jim Simons has come up with the solution. Jim is one of the country's true geniuses. He started out as a mathematician and professor, winning one of the field's most prestigious prizes for his work, which was important in the development of string theory. He also worked for the government as a code breaker. For years, he was the best they had. In the late 1980s, he began one of the most successful hedge funds in the world.

Jim and I met in 1998. Our shared love of Brookhaven National Laboratory, on Long Island, brought us together, During my Senate race, D'Amato said he wanted to close Brookhaven. One day, out of the blue, a reporter asked me if I agreed.

"No way! That's five thousand New York jobs!" I answered off the cuff.

The next day I got a call from Jim. He told me he was on the board of Brookhaven. "I saw what you said about the lab," he offered. "Thank you."

"We have to save those jobs." I could tell he was a kindred spirit.

"Yes! And the Relativistic Heavy Ion Collider!"

"Um, sure."

Over the years, we have learned a lot from each other. Today, we're good friends.

Even with all of Jim's accomplishments, first and foremost he is still a teacher. The idea that so few math and science teachers are trained in their subjects infuriates him. "How can you teach someone else something if you haven't learned it yourself?" he used to ask me.

True to form, he did not just identify the problem; he figured out a solution too. Jim's idea is called Math for America. He started it as a pilot program in New York City schools. Now, it's ready to go national.

Here's how it will work. Prospective and current teachers in math and science will have to take two National Commission on Education–approved tests. The first will be a test of knowledge in their subject area to make sure they know their stuff. The second will be a test of pedagogical skill, to make sure they know how to teach that stuff to students. Teachers who pass both tests and commit to teaching for five years will be part of a national corps of teaching fellows. This will come with a significant federal salary enhancement—more for experienced teachers than for new ones. Depending on the subject matter and other factors, the stipend will be between $11,000 and $20,000 a year. After five years, teaching fellows will have to take both tests again. If they fail, they're out of the program. If they pass, they get another five years.

Initially, this program—which I call the Math and Science Teaching Corps (MSTC)—will include math and science teachers. If 50% of all math and science teachers in the country participate, it will cost around $4 billion a year. If it works for math and science, we should expand it to all subjects in which there is a shortage of high-quality teachers with the requisite expertise (computer science and foreign languages jump to mind).

To those who are jaded by years of education policy fights, this proposal may sound DOA. It's not. My legislation to create the program, the Math and Science Teaching Corps Act of 2006, garnered interest from both sides of the aisle. Even more significant, the second largest teacher's union in the country, the American Federation of Teachers (AFT), has sent a letter of support.

It is popular in some circles to bash the teacher's union, to claim that they stand in the way of progress. Well, when Jim created Math for America, I met with the head of New York's teachers, Randi Weingarten. She is known as a vigorous advocate for her members' rights. But she sees the role of her union, the United Federation of Teachers (a local chapter of the AFT), as more than that. When I mentioned Math for America to her, she was enthusiastic.

She told me that one of the lions of the teacher's union, Al Shanker, had told her that teachers needed two things. The first was to be organized—to negotiate together. The second, as important as the first, was to maintain high professional standards. He knew that his members played a special role in society and understood that with that role came a unique responsibility for the greater good. Living up to Al Shanker's legacy, Randi signed on to Jim's board and was instrumental in securing the AFT's support for the MSTC legislation. Randi and I respect each other. And we agree that good teachers are good for everyone.

The key here is quality, not quantity. There has been a lot of focus on our teacher shortage; the more critical issue is the shortage of highly qualified teachers trained in the subject areas that they teach. There will always be some who are willing to teach but are underqualified. That's not acceptable. There will also always be an inspired few—excellent teachers who would teach no matter what. Today, we ask this group to sacrifice too much.

In the twenty-first century, teaching should be an exalted profession, just as medicine and law were in the second half of the twentieth century. When the starting salary is $30,000, it sends the opposite message. It suggests that teaching is a compromise, not an esteemed calling. For those with choices, today's salaries make teaching too hard a choice to make. Teachers deserve more and students deserve better.

America is built on the promise that each generation will stand on the shoulders of the one that came before it. For more than two centuries, that promise has held us on the crest of the wave as progress has roared ahead. To carry that promise into the future, we must improve our nation's schools. To do so will require a national commitment to education unlike any we have made before.

It's worth it.

At the end of the day, the promise of a brighter future depends on a dramatically improved education system. The promise of a brighter future is a pact that America has always made with the Baileys, and the Montoyas, and the Kims and Coopers and Salims. It is a promise made to the entire country.

It is the promise on which our past has been built. And it is the promise on which our future depends.

CHAPTER 10

REDUCE PROPERTY TAXES THAT FUND EDUCATION BY 50%

☆ ENCOURAGE LOCALITIES TO CUT PROPERTY
TAXES THAT FUND EDUCATION BY 50% OVER
TEN YEARS BY FREEZING THEM NOW.

☆ IF UNFORESEEN CIRCUMSTANCES ARISE,
RESTORE THE HIGHEST–INCOME TAX BRACKET
TO MID–1990S LEVELS BEFORE TAKING AWAY
THE PROPERTY TAX REDUCTION.

EVERY YEAR, I go to as many fairs, festivals and parades as I can. I like meeting people and it's a whole lot cheaper than polling. After three hours at the Taste of Buffalo, the State Fair in Syracuse or the Lilac Festival in Rochester, I know what people are thinking better than a pollster sitting in a fancy office ever could. It's how I stay in touch with the Baileys of the world.

When you become senator of a big state, it takes a couple of years to learn about all of the events that go on around the state. I first heard about the St. Patrick's Day Parade in Rocky Point, way out on the eastern end of Long Island, in 2001. Ever since, I've tried not to miss it. Of all the events I go to, that parade is my toughest fit. Rocky Point is an exurb sixty-five miles from the New York City border. The folks out there are pro-gun, Republican and struggling to stay middle class. The parade crowd is well to the right of the Baileys. It's with voters like the Rocky Point parade-goers that George W. Bush won the election in 2004.

At my first appearance at Rocky Point's St. Patrick's Day Parade I got screamed at the moment I started walking. "Give us back our guns," came first; it was a reference to my passage of the Brady Bill.

As I walked along, that complaint was drowned out by another: "Hey, Schumer! Lower my taxes! Support Bush!"

"Schumer, get the government out of our pocketbooks! Cut taxes! Get with Bush!"

"Cut our taxes!"

It seemed like every third person was yelling the same thing. This was March of 2001, before anyone knew for sure how the newly elected President Bush's tax cuts would play. But walking in that parade, I knew. "Wow," I said to myself. "This issue's gonna have weight."

The next year, I was back in Rocky Point. The largest number of comments was about the tragedy of September 11th. A close second was the now familiar refrain "Hey, Schumer, cut our taxes!"

Bush was on to round two of the tax cuts.

About two-thirds of the way through the parade, I experienced a bit of serendipity. One of the floats up ahead stalled. The parade came to a halt. I was stopped in front of the largest group of hecklers. Unable to keep walking and waving, I went over to them.

"Schumer," they yelled. "Get with Bush! *Cut our taxes!!!*"

"I hear you," I said.

"I just got my $3,000 bill for the half-year."

"On income tax?" I asked.

"Hell no, the property tax!"

Property tax—of course. It hurts the middle class like nothing else does. Sales tax is incremental—a couple of dollars on top of most purchases. For most people income tax is incremental too, because it's withheld from the paycheck every two weeks. Meanwhile, property tax is a once- or twice-a-year burden that hits the middle class more than anyone else. For a lot of families, the day that their property tax bill is due is their defining interaction with the government each year.

I nodded sympathetically. "Love to, but it's not a federal tax. It's local."

"I don't care what it is. It's killing us. Lower our taxes!"

In that moment, I understood why Bush's tax cuts were popular even though they were not aimed at Joe and Eileen Bailey.

Republicans were talking about lowering taxes. Middle-class people felt overtaxed—particularly because of the property tax—so they were buying it. The fact that Republican tax cuts were basically for the wealthy didn't seem to matter. Economic royalists and their message machine had manipulated the issue carefully and calculatedly to blur the distinctions. The Republican claim was simple: "Your taxes are too high, so we'll cut taxes." The question of whose taxes actually got cut was lost in the shuffle. To the average family, Bush was talking about trying to lower their property tax.

The success of the Republican strategy really hit home with me a few months later. I was running late for a flight. The clerk at the American Airlines check-in counter recognized me immediately. From the look on his face, I could tell he wasn't going to hurry. He tortuously checked my ID and searched for a seat assignment. I tried to be friendly, hoping to speed him up. He wasn't having it. After an eternity, he finally printed my ticket. Less than five minutes from missing my plane, I grabbed for it.

He pulled it back, out of reach. "Before you go, Senator," he said. "I have to make a request. Get rid of the death tax. Taxes are already too high. Don't hit us when we're dead too!"

I grabbed my ticket and sprinted for the gate. I didn't get the chance to tell him that the death, er, estate tax almost certainly won't affect him or anyone in his family. It's only for big estates—those in the millions. Here was a guy making probably around $40,000 a year who thought that the estate tax was the greatest injustice in this country. All the ads paid for by groups funded by economic royalists that talk about getting rid of the death tax pretend that it affects everyone. It's another way the Republican spin machine works: Deliberate deception.

I thought a lot about that moment in the airport. It encapsulated what economic royalists have done with taxes. The pattern repeats infinitely. Republicans, following the royalists' script, say, "We are going to cut your taxes." They never talk about whose taxes will be cut—their message machine makes it seem like it will be everyone's.

Democrats oppose deficits and believe government has a positive role to play. So we say, "No."

It's a pattern that's bad for Democrats and bad for America. The government cuts taxes for the rich and does relatively little for the middle class, who remain frustrated. Meanwhile, Democrats come off as pro-tax, Republicans as friends of the middle class.

We have to break through. It is not good enough to tell the Baileys that tax cuts aren't responsible. We have to show them that we understand; we have to give them a plan. While Republicans try to cut taxes for the very rich, we should focus on the tax the Baileys truly hate. Republicans can be the party of tax breaks for the very wealthy; Democrats will be the party that unburdens the middle class of its most hated tax, the property tax.

Within ten years, we will cut property taxes that fund education in half in all localities that accept increased federal education spending. We'll do it by freezing the amount of property tax dollars that fund schools. To get the deal—significant amounts of new federal money for local schools—localities must pledge to freeze their property tax contribution to schools. Between inflation and prevented increases, this freeze will easily cut property taxes that fund education by 50% within ten years.

For the Baileys, halving property taxes that fund education— about two-thirds of all property taxes—will mean serious tax relief. It'll be a whole lot better than the little refund they got when income tax rates were cut by a couple of points. Democrats will be for tax relief that the middle class really cares about.

There are a couple of broad structural reasons to cut property taxes that fund education. First of all, it will create a groundswell of support for increasing federal education funding, which is the only way to ensure that schools get what they need. As long as education is tied to the property tax, the tax the middle class hates the most, we'll never spend what's needed.

The link between education funding and property taxes puts the Baileys between a rock and a hard place: They know they need good schools, but they hate paying the money. They will tell you that the best thing about their hometown, Massapequa, is that it's a good place to raise kids—especially because of the decent schools there. It's why they chose to live there. But the cost of those decent schools, in the form of property taxes, is the thing they like least about it.

And they worry that the schools are getting worse, because no one can afford more property tax increases.

It becomes a brutal compromise: you can have decent schools, but only if you submit to crushing property taxes. The system hurts individuals like the Baileys, but it also hurts localities. The Baileys' next-door neighbors are an older couple, the Browns, who have lived in Massapequa for thirty years. Today, their kids are grown. They are retired and fairly comfortable. They live on his pension, some savings and Social Security. The Baileys get along with their neighbors, but there is a simmering conflict between the two families. The Browns believe in good schools, but have trouble keeping up with the constant onslaught of property tax increases. Like the Baileys, they are caught in a bind—oppose new school funding or move away from their hometown. They will continue to choose the former until they are forced to do the latter.

Because of the dependence on property taxes, towns experience bitter battles over school funding. Those who have kids in school grit their teeth and support increasing school budgets and, therefore, property taxes. Those without kids in school, now a majority in virtually every older suburb and many newer ones, vote against raising property taxes and school budgets. All over the country, schools can't hire the teachers they need. New buildings are put on hold despite overcrowding. Technology becomes obsolete. Ask any school board member. It's an all too common story: Voters are compelled to reject property tax increases and the schools suffer.

But, by separating property tax from education, we can create a coalition where there is now a conflict. In fact, we can create a coalition that supports educational excellence *and* education funding. When the Browns are given the chance to have their property taxes frozen and still see the schools in the community they love improve, they'll want their local government to sign up for our education plan as much as the Baileys do—perhaps even more. Therefore, our plan will win the Baileys' support and the Browns' support. School district after school district will join the plan because of this coalition. The Baileys will support unharnessing property taxes and education because it will improve schools and give them relief. Their older neighbors will support it because they will be freed from directly funding schools to which they are no longer connected. It's a win,

win, win: Young families, older retirees and local school boards will all benefit.

But the case for lowering property taxes goes beyond school funding. There is another reason that we must act. Increasingly, wealth agglomerates at the very top of our society. It makes sense to raise a higher proportion of revenue from those who are doing the best. This is not class warfare. It's a rational update to the tax code, based on structural changes in the economy.

Joe Bailey does not want to take away the fortunes of Bill Gates, Warren Buffett, Mike Bloomberg and other self-made billionaires. He knows that they made their fortunes through good old American ingenuity. He believes they have every right to them. But he also believes in a fair system. Paying $7,500 a year to stay in his family's house, when the family's total income is $75,000, doesn't seem fair.

Once upon a time, a system of high taxation of property might have made sense. Many middle-class families did not even own their home; if they did, it had a modest value. Owning land was the privilege of the wealthy; in fact, the accumulation of wealth *meant* the accumulation of property. Of course, you do not need to be rich to own a home today. Thanks to the real estate boom of the last thirty years, you don't need to be rich for that home to have a high value and be subject to a heavy property tax. A whole lot of people today find themselves "rich" because of the increased value of their home, not how much they make. But the value of a family's home is not the same thing as liquid assets or other investments. On Long Island, for example, the average property tax bill is about $7,500 a year—that's a huge percentage of the Baileys' liquid assets. In many other areas around the country, property taxes aren't that high, but they're quickly creeping up.

Wealth is no longer as strongly based on land as it once was; it is becomingly chiefly income based. Think of it this way: CEOs live in expensive homes. An expensive home in any locality probably costs ten times more than a middle-class home. Meanwhile, CEOs regularly earn more than a hundred times more than the average middle-class family. Home values are not a reflection of real wealth; real wealth today is reflected by income, both investment and earned income.

And in the ideas economy, income is more unevenly distributed than ever before. This is not a nefarious plan. It's just how our society has evolved. When Henry Ford had his great idea for an assembly line, he needed millions of people to make it work. He needed people to build the cars, distribute the cars, sell the cars and advertise the cars. It took millions of people to take his idea and turn it into reality. Eighty years later, Bill Gates had an equally huge idea, as revolutionary as Ford's. But he only needed thousands of people to carry it out. It takes many fewer people to spread an intangible idea (like Gates's string of computer code) than it does to spread a tangible product. At the beginning of the last century, Henry Ford's idea created a million jobs at $10,000 a year. At the end of the century, Bill Gates's idea created ten thousand jobs at $1 million a year.

The nature of a globalized world is that fewer and fewer people are at the top of each industry. And the nature of technology is that fewer and fewer people are needed to support those at the top. As a result, greater wealth is concentrated among an ever smaller number of people.

This change is magnified by the synthesis of regional economies into one global economy. It used to be that every town had local businesses. Each had owners, high- and mid-level managers and wage employees. Now, national and international companies dominate business. The number of owners and high-level managers has shrunk; all that's needed are mid-level managers and wage employees. Wealth that used to be distributed among tens of thousands of local economies has become concentrated among those few at the top of the single global economy, and those few are concentrated in a few large metropolitan areas.

According to inflation-adjusted figures released by the Census Bureau, between 1975 and 2005 the mean annual income in the middle fifth of earners rose from about $37,000 to about $46,000. The income of those in the top 5% grew from almost $146,000 to more than $281,000. In other words, as middle-class incomes rose by about 25%, incomes at the top almost doubled. Over the same period, the share of total income that went to the top 5% increased by more than a third. The share that went to the middle class and below (the bottom 60th percentile of the country) went down by almost a fifth. To put that in perspective, the agglomeration of wealth means that the top 5% of earners now take in about $386 billion more per year than they would have thirty years ago, while middle and low-end earners get about $350 billion less.

And as you go up the scale, the numbers get even starker. Between 2003 and 2004, for example, the share of the nation's total income that was earned by the top 1% of families increased by almost 3 percentage points. The top *one tenth* of 1%—one family out of a thousand—accounted for more than half of that increase. By 2004, the top 1% of households earned almost 20% of all income, compared to less than 13% in 1982.

I don't believe that this income agglomeration is anyone's fault; it's the way an ideas economy works. But it is a reality that can't be ignored. As an ever higher percentage of income goes to an ever smaller number of people, it is only fair that a greater percentage of tax revenue be raised from those same people as well.

We will not have to raise taxes to fund this goal, the education goal or the other goals in this book. The revenues brought in by reducing tax evasion and avoidance by 50% (see Chapter 18) should more than do the job.

But, if we have to raise additional revenues due to circumstances unrelated to the ideas in this book, the right place to look toward would be the highest earners. If we did have to raise more revenue and did so by increasing the top income tax rate from 35% to 39.6% while still lowering property taxes, it would communicate a new message to the Baileys. Instead of believing that they will only see tax cuts for themselves when the wealthiest Americans see even bigger ones, the Baileys would understand that cutting the tax that is most onerous for them—the property tax—is independent of what the wealthiest Americans pay. Once Democrats stand for lowering the property tax, we will be able shed the middle class's perception that we are the party of high taxes.

The 1990s proved false the old myth that raising the top marginal tax rates slows down the economy. Throughout the expansion of the mid- and late 1990s, the effective rate for the top 5% of earners was between 2.5 and 3.5 percentage points higher than it was in 2003. For the top 1%, it was as much as 4.5 percentage points higher than in 2003. Yet the economy in the '90s, as you may remember, did just fine. It is counterintuitive to think that wealthy individuals will slow down their spending and investment because the top rates increase by a couple of points. The fact is that top earners try to earn as much as they can, whether the tax rate is 35% or 39.6%. The economic royalists have their think tanks and editorial boards churn out contrary positions, but the facts on the ground can't be ignored.

For those at the top, raising the top marginal rate may cut into the redistribution premium a little bit, but far from erase it entirely. For the middle class, cutting property taxes will help ease the redistribution pain enormously.

Ideologues like to dismiss the argument for lower property taxes with rigid definitions of local, state and federal roles. "Property tax is the province of local governments, with state approval," they might argue. "Federal legislators should limit their purview to the federal tax code and related statutes. Historical precedent, dating back before Edward I, holds that assessing property levies is most appropriately the role of a local authority, be that feudal landlord or representative locality."

It's a distinction about which Joe and Eileen couldn't care less. For them, the result of local, state and federal taxes is the same: less money in their pocket, more in the government's.

The Baileys and the millions of other middle-class homeowners are doing all right. But do you know what? They could use a break. That's why we have to cut their property taxes that fund education in half. Unlike Bush's tax cuts, which lower their federal taxes a little bit but inevitably lead to higher local taxes, we won't rob Peter to pay Paul. If the property tax cut must be offset, or something else comes up, the Baileys won't be stuck with the bill. Instead, we'll do what's fair: Shift the taxes to those who have worked hard and gained enormous wealth, but now can afford it more than ever before.

If you disagree with me, why don't you go to the Bailey home on some Friday night? While they sit around their kitchen table, trying to figure out how to squeeze a little more out of what they've worked so hard to get, you tell them why schools are increasingly of inconsistent quality, underfunded and declining. You tell them why they're forced give 10% of their net income away in property taxes.

You tell them why an anachronistic system that disproportionately burdens them is the best.

Or, instead, you can join me. I'll be working as hard as I possibly can to make things a little bit easier for them. To ease their biggest burdens, regardless of ideology, so that their Friday nights can be a little easier, a little more relaxed and a little bit happier.

CHAPTER 11

INCREASE THE NUMBER OF COLLEGE GRADUATES BY 50%

☆ MAKE UP TO $15,000 OF TUITION PER CHILD
  PER YEAR TAX DEDUCTIBLE FOR FAMILIES
  MAKING LESS THAN $150,000 A YEAR.

☆ GIVE COLLEGES AND UNIVERSITIES INCENTIVES
  TO KEEP TUITION HIKES AT OR BELOW THE
  RATE OF INFLATION.

☆ RESTORE PELL GRANTS AND FEDERAL LOANS
  TO LATE-1990S LEVELS, AND PEG FUTURE
  INCREASES TO THE AVERAGE COST OF COLLEGE,
  SO *EVERYONE* HAS A CHANCE.

AFTER HIGH SCHOOL, my father went straight into the army. He fought for our country in World War II. When he came home, he wanted to go to college and become an engineer. But while he was fighting in Asia, my grandfather lost his job and scraped together the pennies to start a little exterminating business. Sadly, my grandfather was too nice a guy for business. His sole accomplishment was encouraging the birth of the exterminators' union—he managed to convince his two employees to organize against him.

So after the war, my father didn't go to college. He had to save the business.

It was a small company that fed the family, but my father hated going to work. The worst memories my brother, sister and I have are of lying in bed on Sunday nights, listening to our father pace the hallway at 2 a.m. He was dreading work the next day. That's how much he hated his job—he couldn't sleep for dread of it. On those nights, I renewed the promise that I had made to myself in Stanley Kaplan's workroom. I would find a job that I looked forward to waking up for. For the last thirty years, I've been blessed with a job I love. I've worked hard and had some good luck. But I never would have made it if my parents hadn't been able to afford to put me through college.

My father was able to become a regular middle-class guy without a college degree. He did not need an education to get a decent job, a job that allowed him to support a family of five. My mother was active in the community, but she never worked full-time. She did not have to; he earned a living for all of us. Hard work, an able body and unflinching integrity were enough to ensure his career.

Most incredible, he was able to do something for all three of us that his parents had not been able to do for him: Put us through college.

Think about that. As a middle-class couple, my mother and father were able to put three children through college. They had to struggle to pay for it, but they were able to make it work. We did not graduate with crushing loans. My parents did not have to take out a second mortgage on their little house on East Twenty-Seventh Street. In today's world, the life my father provided for us wouldn't be possible. A middle-class family simply can't put their kids through college without going into serious debt.

The cost of college tuition has increased faster than inflation for *twenty-six consecutive years*. The average cost of four years of college for each of the Bailey kids will be close to $60,000. That's if they all go to a public university. For a private school, the average cost will be $120,000. For their three kids, the Baileys are facing a bill of between $150,000 and $350,000.

Look at those numbers. Read them again. Today, paying for college is harder for the average family than it was thirty years ago. College used to be a luxury, but it was priced affordably. It has become a necessity, but now it's priced like a luxury. That's not progress. We are slipping—fast.

And it's a disaster.

As Alan Greenspan told me, education, including college, is the key. We need to do a better job of preparing kids in the lower grades for college (see Chapter 9, Increase Reading and Math Scores by 50%) *and* we must increase the number who go on to finish college. Increasing the number of college graduates is as important to our future as anything else we do in education. The challenge with college is different than it is with K–12 education—it's more an issue of access than of quality—but the imperative is the same.

Joe and Eileen Bailey know this better than anyone. Paying their kids' way through college is *the* thing that keeps them up at night. More than any other financial obligation—health care, housing, even property taxes—college looms largest in their minds.

Megan, the eldest Bailey child, is sixteen. She is in her junior year of high school. Over President's Weekend, Joe and Megan are planning a trip through New York State to visit schools. They will look at Binghamton, a jewel of the State University of New York system. They also plan to see some of New York's other great public universities—probably Buffalo and Oneonta.

Joe has promised that on the trip back down the New York State Thruway, they can stop at Colgate and Hamilton, two elite, small private colleges. Megan is a good student and she will do well wherever she ends up. But she thrives when she can forge personal relationships with her teachers. Megan is keeping an open mind, but Joe and Eileen can tell that her heart is set on a smaller school.

Joe and Eileen do not want to limit her choices. The issue is particularly touchy since they already know that Abby, only in seventh grade now, will almost certainly *need* a more personal environment. She is shy and has been diagnosed with a mild learning disability. When her time to look at schools comes along, a good match will have to be the only consideration, whether the college is public or private.

The Baileys have been planning for college since before Pete, their youngest, was born. They restructured their mortgage from a thirty-year to a fifteen-year term almost ten years ago. It hurt their monthly cash flow, but even then, they knew they could never afford to pay for a mortgage and college at the same time. After Pete was born, they talked about having a fourth child. The looming cost of college was one reason they decided to stop at three.

Six months ago, Eileen mailed the final mortgage payment to the bank. The Baileys' home is now theirs. It's an open question whether they will be able to keep it that way for the next twelve years or if paying for three college educations will force them to take out a second mortgage.

If the Baileys have to, they will go back into debt. Twenty years ago, it would have seemed crazy to consider. But the calculation was different then. After high school, Eileen went to college for a year but didn't continue. Joe spent five years in school, his last two working full-time, but he got his bachelor's degree. He is among the 30% of voters who have at least a bachelor's degree.

Joe's sure glad he stuck with it. Some of the people he has worked with over the past fifteen years have bachelor's degrees. Some don't. It's never mattered much. But over the last few years, his company has hired fewer and fewer new employees who do not have a degree. Joe feels pretty secure in his job—no one's figured out how to outsource adjusters yet—but if something does happen, he knows that his college degree may be the only thing that gets him in the door at a new job.

Joe's right. As Greenspan told me, education is our future. That's how we'll save our jobs, our salaries and our prosperity. Unlike our K–12 system, America's postsecondary school system is still one of the best in the world. Workers with degrees from American colleges are in high demand.

That's the good news. What keeps me up at night is that only a quarter of twenty-five-year-olds in the United States have a college degree. One in four!

That means that up to three-quarters of young adults in this country are not adequately prepared for the changed world they are inheriting. In most cases, their job prospects will shrink over time. Instead of reaping the benefits of a growing world economy, they will mostly have access to jobs that offer flat or diminishing pay. They will not have the education necessary to compete in the new world that's dawning. Unless something changes, that will translate into a bleak future for all of us.

We used to lead the world in college graduates. According to a 2003 OECD report, between about 1958 and 1968 the United States likely had the highest college graduation rate in the world. Today, we are tied for seventh. And, compared to the rest of the world, the slippage continues. A 2006 study by the National Center for Public

Policy and Higher Education found that although the United States has historically been the leader in college education, it no longer is. In the period between 1995 and 2003, our rate of college enrollment went down relative to eighteen out of twenty countries studied.

In the age of globalization, when we are competing against the world, we must not allow the number of college graduates to slip. The bottom line is simple: The harder it is for Americans to get a degree, the worse our future will be; the easier it is, the better off we will all be. Our future can be bright. Our country has a growing number of high-paying, high-knowledge jobs. All we need to do is make it a little easier for more people to obtain the tools needed to prosper in the new economy.

It is in our national interest to make it easier for more Americans to pay for college.

The fact is that for a couple of years, we did. As I had promised when I was running against D'Amato, I proposed a law allowing families to deduct $4,000 of college tuition. In 2001, it was passed as part of the larger tax cut package. Since then, millions of families have deducted some portion of college tuition from their taxes. But as of the printing of this book, the Republican Congress has allowed it to expire.

Tuition deductibility is a tax cut! Republicans have supported just about every other tax cut! I guess since this one benefits the middle class, they're not interested.

Well, we have to bring tuition deductibility back and make it bigger. We should make up to $15,000 in college tuition and associated costs tax deductible per child per year for every family that makes less than $150,000 dollars a year. The Baileys' investment in their home was tax deductible, their investment in their children's— and our country's—future should be, too.

At $15,000 of deductibility, Joe and Eileen will save about $4,000 per child each year. In total, the Baileys will save close to $50,000 in college tuition. That makes a big difference, believe me. It's certainly worth the price tag, about $6 billion a year.

College tuition tax deductibility should have a cost of living adjustment attached to it that is indexed to average college tuition so that it keeps up with the rising costs of college. And we'd better make sure that colleges keep their costs in line. Actually, we'd better make sure their costs get back in line. Twenty-six years of beating the rate of inflation is good for Warren Buffett, but it is not acceptable for federally subsidized institutions of higher learning.

The vast majority of colleges and universities in the country, public and private, depend on federal funding. It does not make sense for us to keep pouring money into schools that are not affordable for the vast majority of our citizens. Private and public colleges whose average tuition costs (i.e., the amount students pay in tuition plus government aid and other outside contributions) increase faster than the rate of inflation over any five-year period should lose their federal funding. If a school has good reason to increase its tuition by more than the rate of inflation, it can petition to do so while keeping its federal funding intact.

Tuition deductibility and increase restraint are designed to provide a little relief for the middle class. Today, families like the Baileys desperately need it. Joe and Eileen understand that the poor also need help paying for college, but, faced with a quarter-million-dollar bill, they don't understand why they are always left out of plans for assistance.

Of course, under the Bush administration, poor families are increasingly left out too. Pell Grants, which have helped hundreds of thousands of lower-income Americans go to college, have been frozen since 2002, despite the efforts of my colleagues, including Senators Ted Kennedy, Chris Dodd and Russ Feingold. The administration has refused to increase the size of Pell Grants even as inflation and tuition increases have continued to diminish their usefulness. In the future, Pell Grants, and all other federal grants and loans, must never again be left to die a slow death by attrition; federal funding streams available for residents of each state should rise at the same rate that tuition does in that state. Cutting Pell Grants is like pulling up the ladder of opportunity. If you're toward the bottom, you won't have a chance. We can't let that happen. We must extend the ladder to the middle class and all the way to the poorest Americans. Our future depends on everyone having a chance to grab a rung and climb up.

Every time an American student is unable to go to college or cannot afford the college that best suits her, not only does she lose and not only does her family lose, but America loses.

Since our country's founding, we have always expanded citizens' opportunities. In each new generation, more and more Americans have been given good reasons to dream. Today, we are at a crossroads. If we do not do something about the cost of college, the Bailey children will be part of the first generation in American history to have less opportunity than the one that came before it. On the other hand, if we can make it easier for families to afford the cost of college, opportunity's expansion will endure. America will stay a shining beacon of hope for young people here and all over the world.

CHAPTER 12

REDUCE ILLEGAL IMMIGRATION BY AT LEAST 50% AND INCREASE LEGAL IMMIGRATION BY UP TO 50%

☆ ESTABLISH REAL ENFORCEMENT MEASURES AGAINST EMPLOYERS THAT HIRE ILLEGAL IMMIGRANTS.

☆ CREATE A BIOMETRIC EMPLOYMENT CARD.

☆ OFFER A FAIR PATH TO EARNED CITIZENSHIP FOR THOSE WHO ARE HERE.

☆ INCREASE THE NUMBER OF GREEN CARDS GRANTED A YEAR TO MAKE UP FOR THE REDUCTION IN ILLEGAL IMMIGRATION.

☆ RATIONALIZE LEGAL IMMIGRATION TO FILL HIGH-NEEDS JOBS, RETAIN THOSE WHO ARE EDUCATED HERE, INCREASE GEOGRAPHIC, ECONOMIC AND EDUCATIONAL DIVERSITY AND PROMOTE FAMILY REUNIFICATION.

TOMMY SANTINO IS a retired detective first grade in the New York Police Department. For six years, he was the head of my security detail. Tommy grew up in Greenpoint, Brooklyn. He still loves Greenpoint. Lots. If you let him, he will spend a lifetime telling you about the O.N.—the Old Neighborhood. When Tommy married, his wife made him move to Douglaston, Queens, which is one of New York's leafiest, most suburban neighborhoods. Most people who move from Greenpoint to Douglaston never look back. Not Tommy. A few years ago, he saved up and bought a little place in Greenpoint "for weekends." He is the only person I know who has a country house in North Brooklyn.

Tommy knows a lot of people. One of his buddies owns a restaurant in Queens. This guy, I'll call him Paolo, makes the best polpo salad in New York. It's to die for. Tommy and I used to stop by whenever we were in the neighborhood.

One time, when we were polishing off a dessert of cheesecake and tiramisu, Paolo came up to me. "Chuck," he whispered in my ear. "I gotta talk to you."

"Sure, Paolo," I mumbled through a mouthful of tiramisu.

Paolo motioned to the back of the restaurant. He wanted to talk alone. I stuck my fork into the last bite of cheesecake.

"I don't mean to bother you," Paolo began when we were alone. "It's just, you gotta do something about immigration."

"Immigration?" I asked. "Aren't you an immigrant?"

"Of course, but I'm a citizen now," said Paolo. "Even when I first came, I was always legal. I mean illegal immigrants." You see, Paolo was having trouble finding legal employees for his restaurant. He did not want to break the law. But, he told me, it was hard not to. The whole industry depends on cheap labor, a need often filled by illegal immigrants. A lot of restaurateurs do not even check for documentation. They hire whoever walks in off the street, no questions asked. Even guys like Paolo, who do ask for a green card or a Social Security card and a driver's license, assume that many of their employees are illegal.

Paolo told me that his employees were overwhelmingly hardworking and conscientious, but sometimes there would be a problem. When that happened, the worker would disappear without a trace. If Paolo tried to track the worker down, he would inevitably find that the name was an alias and the paperwork a forgery.

"It's no way to do business, Senator. I ask for papers, but for what?" Paolo's voice was rising. "All of us are stuck with this system, this black market. Forgeries, fake identities. No enforcement. Guys disappearing. This is supposed to be America. But this system, I'll tell you, it's a lot worse than where I come from."

I like to imagine that Paolo lives in Massapequa, on the same block as the Baileys. I like to imagine that Joe and Paolo sometimes have a beer out back on summer evenings. Joe and Paolo are about the same age. Their incomes are similar (although when Paolo's polpo gets famous, I'll bet he gets rich). They're both married and have kids. Joe works for a mid-size company; Paolo owns his own small business. They both see immigration in complicated terms.

Joe respects Paolo—in large part because he's an immigrant who made it. But Joe doesn't like illegal immigration. He plays by the rules and he thinks that everyone else should too. He believes that illegal immigrants take jobs away from Americans by working for lower pay and no benefits. This is not the number one issue on his radar—undocumented workers are not competing for his job—but when people talk about closing the borders and getting rid of illegal immigrants, it makes sense to him.

I used to share Joe's view. With so many unemployed and under-employed Americans, why would we let illegal immigrants take jobs that citizens could fill? When it came to immigration, I was tough as could be. A wealthy friend's idealistic daughter changed my mind. It was twenty years ago, when Congress was debating an immigration overhaul. The debate was not so different from what it is today. Every so often, immigration gets out of control and we have to fix it. My friend's daughter had started one of those beautiful, prosperous nurseries in Suffolk County, Long Island. You might not believe it, but Suffolk County is not only New York's most populous suburban county, it is also our biggest agricultural county, mostly because of new industries—nurseries, vineyards and the like.

Like a lot of agriculturists on Long Island, this woman hired undocumented workers at first. But, being a law-abiding citizen, she did not like it. "Why hire illegal immigrants?" she asked. "There are all these poor people on welfare. I should hire Americans so they can improve their lives." Her goal wasn't to make money. She loved flowers and she wanted to do good.

So, she built cabins and a school on the nursery's property. She even built a little church. Then she dropped leaflets all over the South Bronx announcing the deal. People would get picked up at such and such corner at a set time. She was offering double the minimum wage. The buses she had hired filled immediately. She had to turn people away.

The trouble was, after a couple of days, the backbreaking labor of picking flowers was too much. Everyone packed up and left. Even at double the minimum wage, no one stayed. They even paid their own train fare back to the Bronx.

This young woman came to me because she loved her business and she depended on her workers. She wanted to do good. "We need workers," she told me. "Americans don't want these jobs. Believe me. Immigrants do. They want to work."

This is the cry of farmers from Long Island, to the breadbasket of Missouri, to the Central Valley in California. It is the double bind that vexes many types of small business owners—farmers, restaurateurs, contractors and others—all over the country. They do not want to break the law, but to get workers they need to hire illegal immigrants. Because of their desperate need, and lax enforcement, there's not much incentive to double-check documentation.

When I talk about immigration, I always talk about my friend's daughter. "Everyone in business knows that we need immigrants," I say. "Not for your job, but for the jobs you don't want. We shouldn't always listen to business, but in this case they have a point."

There is one other story I always tell. This is the story of Napoleon Barragan. You probably have never heard of Mr. Barragan, but you have definitely heard of the company he founded: 1-800-Mattress. It employs about 1,000 people in Long Island City, Queens. It is a typical New York business—an immigrant comes, has an idea and works like crazy to make it real.

About five years ago, I visited 1-800-Mattress. In Mr. Barragan's office, there is a picture. It caught my eye immediately: A bunch of kids, barefoot and shirtless, playing on a dusty road in front of grass-roofed huts.

"What is it?" I asked.

"The picture? That's the village I was born in. It is 200 miles south of Quito, Ecuador, in the headwaters of the Amazon. Look at the kids in the picture. Of all those children, only one had the gumption to get up and come to America."

I looked more closely, trying to discover the future in one of the young faces.

"You know which one?" He pointed to a barefoot boy in the foreground. "Me. I'm the only one." He was very proud of that.

Thinking of that picture, I am struck by the beauty of our system. There is something special about every American. Each of us, or our ancestors, woke up one morning and chose to come here, or survived unimaginable hardship to get here. They may have had no money, no skill, no education, but they were still special, because in the face of poverty or persecution, they did not give up. They stood up. They dreamed of something better, maybe not for themselves, but for their children, their families, their descendants.

We are all a little like Mr. Barragan. There is something in us that is uncommonly driven. Idealistic. Hardworking. Determined. Brimming with gumption and energy. Otherwise, we never could have made it here. All Americans—whether immigrants themselves or from families that came here ten generations ago—have in their blood that gumption and determination. They or their ancestors might have been uneducated or poor or unskilled, but they all had the pluck to pick up and leave behind an impoverished or oppressed life and come here to find a better one. They or their ancestors came to find a better life when many more stayed behind.

The founding fathers never intended for America to close the door to new Americans. We did not shut the door after the Puritans, or the Revolution, or the closing of the frontier. In each generation, we have accepted the most determined and idealistic from anywhere in the world regardless of income or education. And we have always been stronger for it.

There is another beautiful aspect to American immigration. As a country, all we say to legal immigrants is, Work hard, do well for yourself and your family. The beauty of the system is that when immigrants do those things, they are doing good for America. We provide the platform and we reap the benefit. Whether it is Napoleon Barragan or a nurse from Jamaica, Ireland or the Phillipines— they help themselves and they improve us. They are a shot of energy, renewed blood, a rebirth of our nation and a return to our ideals.

Joe realizes that we are an immigrant nation. He likes that America is a melting pot. He understands the Napoleon Barragan story, just as he respects Paolo. When Joe and Eileen drive into Queens for a night out at Paolo's, he respects the busboys too. In his backyard, he complains to Paolo that they are illegal, but at the restaurant, he thanks them. He can see that they are hardworking guys.

He knows that immigration is a tradition as American as apple pie. (Apples, by the way, are "American" thanks to the immigrants who brought them here, just like they brought pizza, sushi and empanadas.) But today, for the first time, there are more illegal immigrants coming into the United States each year than legal ones. Our great tradition is being subsumed by illegality. Those who hire illegal immigrants and the immigrants themselves must avoid obeying the law at every step: by avoiding payroll taxes, ignoring labor laws, forging documents and crossing the borders. The system today is out of control. Whether you are an employer or an immigrant, breaking the law gets you ahead. Following the rules and waiting your turn hurts your chances. This culture of illegality shakes the Baileys' faith in legitimate immigration.

I want to be very clear: Joe Bailey does not oppose all immigration. (Some in this country do—those folks will never support Democrats and Democrats will never support them.) He is not a xenophobe. Parts of his family immigrated in the last century and he still holds his heritage dear.

Joe is much more worried about illegality. Irrationality. Getting a free ride. Exploitation. And, in the post-9/11 world, security. To him, these are symptoms of a system that is out of control. Ending illegal immigration is not about closing our doors. It's about enforcing the law and protecting the rights that working Americans have spent more than a hundred years fighting to win.

In many parts of the country, the Baileys are personified by recent immigrants who share that feeling. More and more, first- and second-generation Mexican-Americans, Caribbean-Americans and Asian-Americans support immigrants but oppose illegal immigration. Because for most, *illegal immigration* is not about *immigration*. It is about *illegality*. Because there are now more illegal immigrants than legal ones, the line has become obscured. Before we ask the Baileys to consider the value of immigrants, we must try to rid the system of illegality.

To do so, we need to focus on why illegal immigrants come here. The answer is very simple: They come for the jobs. Some xenophobes claim they come for the benefits, but that's just not true.

Emergency room care does not spur millions to undertake the dangerous, expensive trek across the border. Jobs do—jobs that pay twenty times what they pay at home.

Put up a fence, real or virtual, some say. It's a nice-sounding idea. And while it's better than nothing, it will never stop illegal immigration adequately. Even a $50 billion barrier would not actually close the border. We would still need commerce—trucks, boats and planes would still have to cross the fence. And after building a 2,two-thousand-mile-long barrier along the southern border, would we need to erect a three-thousand-mile-long fence along the Canadian frontier? The fact is, if you are getting paid a dollar a day in Oaxaca, Mexico, and you can make $4 dollars an hour in North Carolina, a fence may slow you down, but no brick wall or electronic sensor is going to stop you.

There is only one way to stop illegal immigration: Prevent employers from hiring illegal workers. Real enforcement is the answer. If employers knew that they would be arrested whenever an illegal immigrant was on the premises, the jobs would dry up real quick. Once the jobs dry up, the workers will stop coming.

But this administration refuses to put any onus on its friends in business. Because the economic royalists oppose all government interference, the administration protects employers over everyone else. Its prime concern is big business. That is why it prefers a fence— to avoid imposing enforcement on employers. In 2004, throughout the country, only four enforcement actions were brought against employers who hire illegally. Four! As recently as 1999, there were hundreds, although even that was too few.

Getting really tough with employers will stop illegal immigration a lot more quickly, effectively and cheaply than a fence ever could. The penalties for hiring undocumented workers should be serious: the first time, a big fine; the second time, a bigger fine; the third time, prison time. If we do that, 90% of all employers will stop hiring illegal immigrants. With 90% fewer jobs, we will have about 89.9% fewer illegal immigrants.

The problem is that we can only get tough on employers if we create an enforceable system. As Paolo knows all too well, tough penalties simply would not be fair today. Employers justifiably claim that they ask everyone for IDs. Green cards, Social Security cards and I-9s are too easily faked. We can't expect employers to verify workers themselves, especially if there are tough penalties for being wrong. That's the government's job.

Technology offers the solution. It is now possible to create a largely forgery-proof national employment card. The card would have a little chip that recorded unique biometric identifying information such as an individual's retinal or facial features. It is possible to affordably mass-produce biometric IDs that would be prohibitively expensive to counterfeit.

Every person applying for a job, citizen or not, would be required to have the employment ID card. You would only get the card if you were a citizen or authorized, based on a rational immigration system, to work in this country. The card could be checked against a national database with a simple swipe, similar to the way a credit card transaction works. All employers would be required to swipe before hiring. Employers could buy their own terminals—they would cost about the same amount as a credit card terminal—or use public ones. If the card checked out, fine—the employer would be off the hook. If an employer hired someone without a valid card— there would be big trouble.

The whole nub of the immigration problem is the jobs available to illegal immigrants. Employers get away with hiring undocumented workers because there is no enforcement; there is no enforcement because the system is unenforceable. The national employment ID card is the catalyst that will allow all the dominoes to fall—it's like the hip bone that's connected to the thigh bone. The ID will make it easy for employers to avoid undocumented workers, which will allow for tough sanctions against employers who break the law, which will lead to no jobs being available for illegal immigrants, which will stop illegal immigration.

Certain Americans and certain organizations, notably the NRA and ACLU, have opposed this kind of ID for fear that it might infringe on individual privacy. That's certainly a big concern for some, but not for the Baileys. They realize that we've had a national ID since 1936—a Social Security number. Thanks to payroll taxes, the Social Security Administration already knows who we work for and how much we make. All the national employment ID card will do is make forgery harder. Preventing forgeries is not an infringement on privacy. There is no good reason to stick with 1930s technology when it so cheap and easy to solve this problem with a twenty-first-century solution.

To those who'd still prefer a fence, I say this: Once the flow of humanity sweeping across our borders becomes a trickle, we will have a chance to close the spigot entirely. Our border patrol will have a much easier time catching a small number of stragglers than they do stopping the hundreds of thousands of people who now pour across each year. Without all the illegal workers, we will finally be able to focus on preventing drug runners, terrorists and other dangerous predators from getting in.

Stopping the flow of illegal immigrants with an employment ID has another very important benefit. The thigh bone connects to the hip bone in two other ways. Once average Americans are convinced that we will permanently stanch the flow of illegal immigration, they will be more willing to accept constructing a path toward earned citizenship for those who are already here. And they will be far more willing to increase the number of legal immigrants allowed into the country and to rationalize the system by which they are chosen. It's a complicated issue, with three distinct components— illegal immigration, legal immigration and those who are already here—but all of the pieces connect.

The question of how to handle the millions of undocumented workers who are already here has been one of the toughest to solve. On the one hand, we know that most are gainfully employed, filling jobs that no one else wants. At the same time, they are in the shadows, underpaid and exploited and, to many, representative of a system built on illegality.

Whenever we talk about letting those who are here stay, Joe and Eileen Bailey get worried, not so much about those who are here, but about a constant cycle: Every twenty years illegal immigrants will be made legal. Then more will come across the border looking for jobs and hoping that eventually they will be made legal too. That's what's happened in the past.

In 1986, Congress passed comprehensive immigration reform that was supposed to make illegal immigration disappear forever. It was heralded as the ultimate solution to the problem of illegal workers. Instead, after a brief dip in numbers, illegal immigration grew. It is a bigger problem today than it was in 1986. In fact, it is a bigger problem today than it has been at any time in our nation's history.

But with a solution that permanently solves the problem of illegal immigration, the equation changes. If we make sure that it will never happen again, the Baileys will tolerate letting some people stay. It's not that they believe illegal immigrants have a right to stay; they don't.

But above all, the Baileys are realists. They know that expelling tens of millions of people simply is not practical. So, if we stop illegal immigration for the future, they will accept a compromise in the present. Don't take my word for it. Third Way polled this issue in swing states. They found that a majority of respondents opposed a deportation strategy. What was the single greatest reason that people opposed it? They said it was impractical.

Two of my colleagues, Senators John McCain and Ted Kennedy, have crafted a realistic compromise to allow those who are here illegally to earn a path to citizenship. To earn legal status, undocumented immigrants would have to go to the back of the line behind legal immigrants, learn English, have worked here for a significant number of years and stay on the right side of the law; they would also have to pay a fine.

This is not amnesty, which I would oppose. The McCain-Kennedy plan includes a form of punishment. But, as Joe and Eileen know, practicality matters. The Baileys prefer a pragmatic solution that works to empty rhetoric, however satisfying, that fails. They will reluctantly support the McCain-Kennedy solution, as long as it's not needed again and again

Getting control of the immigration situation is not the same as being anti-immigrant. In fact it is pro-immigrant. Motivated people who are willing to leave their families and their lives behind for a chance to make it here are good for America. Legal immigrants fill gaps in our labor market, start small businesses and become Americans. Immigration is a critical source of our country's strength. In each generation, immigrants infuse our country with new energy and richness.

Getting tough on illegal immigration will be good for future legal immigration. As the number of illegal immigrants declines, we will be able to increase the number of legal immigrants. And an immigration system that is almost entirely legal will be much better than what we have today.

Across the country, we have a shortage of available workers in a number of critical areas. We are short of engineers, short of nurses, short of flower pickers. Immigrants can fill these gaps. A rational immigration system will allow us to look at our needs and welcome those who are equipped to satisfy them. Visas should be issued to ease our employment shortages, which is a far cry better than the current system that lowers salaries in many industries by allowing a glut in certain labor markets. Rational legal immigration will make our country stronger economically, as shortages of engineers or nurses or flower pickers are reduced and fewer businesses go abroad to find these workers.

A rational system would also let more people who come to the United States for their education stay and build a life here when their education is finished. It is ridiculous to provide the best education in the world to foreign Ph.D. students and then send them home. When people who are educated here want to stay, we should rejoice and figure out how to make it work, especially considering the shortage of Americans who are pursuing math, science and engineering degrees.

Additionally, the spirit of diversity is one reason we welcome immigrants—and it should be reflected among the immigrants we welcome. It is wrong for an overwhelming percentage of immigrants to come from any single country. In today's global world, there is no reason for half of all new Americans to be from any one place. Just because we share a border with Mexico does not mean that two-thirds of our immigrants should be Mexican. We should certainly take many Mexicans (particularly those who have family here), but our immigrants should not primarily be from Mexico or any other single country.

As we drastically cut the number of illegal immigrants, we can increase the number of legal immigrants, so the total number of immigrants to our country each year is no greater than today. A rationalized and *legal* immigration system would do a better job of satisfying our country's needs, as well as the needs of immigrants. It would provide workers for high-end and low-end jobs in industries that are short of them; in industries where there are already enough American workers, it would prevent the job market from being flooded. It would allow those who are educated here to make a life here and thus strengthen our economy. It would create broader diversity by representing peoples from across the spectrum in terms of nationality, geography, income and education. And, it would permit more families to be reunited legally and quickly.

Rationalizing the system would keep the total number of immigrants about steady, but it would entirely change the effect of immigration. A smart and legal system would help the American economy and protect American workers. And, while it could never win over xenophobes, it could gain the support of the Baileys and of the pro-immigrant community.

Under a rational system, we would accept a more diverse and larger group of *legal* immigrants from all over the world. More Asians, Africans, Europeans, Central and South Americans and West Indians of all economic levels would be welcomed legally.

Today's system, in which illegality predominates, does not fully meet any of our needs. But a system in which legality predominates could.

The Baileys will accept the distinction. They do not want an irrational system that contradicts the law. They do not want our borders to be a sieve. But they will accept that controlled immigration, well regulated, legal and robust, is the engine that keeps our country moving ever forward.

If we handle this issue correctly—stop illegality and rationalize the legal system so it welcomes the best from all over the world—we can recapture the Baileys' faith in a country of immigrants. Democrats should become the party that aggressively stanches the flow of illegal immigrants—and the party that welcomes a new wave of legal immigrants, who, like so many that came before them, dream of joining our great nation.

The critical first step is to decouple immigration and illegality. When it comes to the former, we must never be baited into opposition; when it comes to the latter, we should come up with a smart solution that actually works.

CHAPTER 13

REDUCE OUR DEPENDENCE ON FOREIGN OIL BY 50%

☆ SHORT-TERM: INCREASE CONSERVATION *AND* FOSSIL FUEL PRODUCTION.

> *Double CAFE standards.*
>
> *Drill in most of the eastern Gulf of Mexico.*
>
> *Encourage exploration on certain leased federal lands.*
>
> *Make existing power generation more efficient.*
>
> *Expand Energy Star to include construction. Make it a requirement for all federal projects.*

☆ LONG-TERM: END DEPENDENCE ON FOSSIL FUELS.

> *Give $10 billion a year and broad powers to a new agency to design a fossil fuel–free solution within three years and implement it over the following seven.*

ONCE UPON A TIME, in that long-ago decade known as the 1990s, energy was not the Baileys' concern. The economy was strong. Gas and electricity were cheap. As far as they could tell, there was no problem.

Sure, they remembered waiting in line during the gas shortage in the late 1970s, but that felt like ancient history. It was a peculiar symptom of a strange time—like bell-bottoms, disco and stagflation—not something that would ever come back.

They knew about OPEC and didn't much like the countries in it. They had heard about global warming; whether true or not, it didn't seem like a pressing problem. Conservation was a nice idea—for celebrities. None of it had a whole lot to do with them.

Then, gas prices began to rise out of control.

During the first few years of this century, for the first time in a decade, gas prices repeatedly spiked, each time a little higher than the last. By the end of 2002, prices were peaking at almost 50% higher than they had been only a couple of years earlier. In 2003, the average family spent 40% more on energy, including gasoline and utilities, than they had in 1990. By 2004, the average cost of filling a tank of gas had increased from $20 to $35 in three years.

The Baileys were starting to worry about gas prices.

In March of 2005, the national average price for gas again broke $2 per gallon. This time, it kept going up—to $2.30 in July, $2.50 in August. Immediately after Hurricane Katrina, the national average spiked above $3! Once the price passed $3 a gallon, the issue of energy was burned into the national consciousness—energy independence would never again be a secondary issue for the Baileys.

Now, even when gas prices dip a little lower, people know that, over time, high prices are here to stay. What started six years ago as a tickling irritation has exploded in the public's mind. Now, energy matters.

Suddenly, other problems associated with our energy policy resonate a lot more.

Energy dependence weakens us as a nation. Hundreds of billions of dollars flow out of our country each year. We are like a giant who is bleeding slowly from the wrists. For a while the giant stays strong. Then, for a while longer, he weakens slowly. Finally, the slow bleed brings him to his knees. We are a wonderful country, the strongest and wealthiest in the world. But how much longer can we continue to be dependent on foreign energy? For five more years we can probably handle it. For ten? Maybe. For twenty? I don't think so.

Worst of all, the bleeding dollars serve to strengthen those who would most like us to be weak. Among the most antagonistic of the major oil-producing countries are Iran and Venezuela. Even countries that aren't antagonistic, like Russia, Saudi Arabia and Nigeria, are needed in a way that warps our foreign policy and makes their interests too significant. Most of these countries are not enemies, nor should they be. But it's foolhardy to trust them as best friends. Today, we need those countries more than we need almost any others in the world. They hold our economy in their hands. Whatever they do, however they act, we need them. It's bad enough that they set the price of gas; it's terrifying that they often set our foreign policy, too.

The environmental consequences of foreign oil are another related problem. Hurricane Katrina—which pushed the price of gas over $3 a gallon—is the most enduring image. But global warming goes beyond the increased likelihood of disasters like Hurricane Katrina. It seems to be having other, unpredictable effects as well. A few months ago, just as winter turned into summer almost overnight, my mother called me.

"Look at this weather, Chuck!" she admonished me before I could ask how she was. "We had no spring! Last year—no fall. They're gone. The weather's gotten weird! What's next? Do something about it."

I wasn't willing to take the blame for that day's mugginess, but I couldn't disagree with the larger point. The weather has gotten weird. It's hard to know what's next, but it's all too likely that whatever it is will affect Joe and Eileen.

Foreign oil's effects on national security and global warming are in the public's consciousness like never before. Today, many believe that we might never have gone into Iraq if not for foreign oil. Many wonder if Hurricane Katrina might never have happened if not for the global warming caused by burning oil. Issues that are less immediate are part of a story that the Baileys now care about.

It's not that environmentalists have convinced them to care. Joe and Eileen now care about energy dependence because they have experienced a specific negative consequence of it. The problem feels concrete. Before, nothing they heard made them care about oil. Now, nothing will make them forget about it. Too often, Democrats try to convince people that they *should* care about things that they don't care about. It's a losing strategy—the Baileys don't need us to tell them what to care about.

But when they do care about an issue, we can help to make the critical connections. For Joe and Eileen, high gas prices are not the symptom of a problem. They *are* the problem. Democrats have to argue that energy dependence *is* high gas prices. If we solve energy dependence, we solve the price of gas.

But we have to be careful. When it comes energy independence, the Baileys reject two parts of the argument. One is hypocrisy. The other is the claim that America has to slow down and consume less.

The gas tax is a great example of the first. This idea's popular with a lot of my well-to-do friends and their favorite pundits. It seems so logical—raise the price and demand will go down. But these folks are not living in the Baileys' world. Joe and Eileen know that the only people who advocate more expensive gas prices are people for whom more expensive gas is not a big deal.

They have the same reaction when conservationists say that we're wasteful. The Baileys already watch what they spend, and they resent being told to change their lifestyle. When they look around, they see a whole lot of rich "conservationists" wasting a lot more energy than they do. Talk radio reminds them about movie stars who travel the country touting conservation—*in private planes*!

But the Baileys' concern about conservation goes beyond hypocrisy. It gets to the basic fabric of who they are and what they believe America should be. You see, they don't resent private planes. Or second homes. Or Hummers (although I do). Joe and Eileen don't think the rich should have to cut back any more than *they* should. Holding back goes against their grain and against the American grain. The Baileys don't want to say no to luxury, a bigger house or a second car. An environmentalism that says we must cut back on growth and dreams, as individuals or a nation, is an environmentalism that is doomed to fail.

The Baileys are willing to support reasonable conservation measures, but the strain in the environmental movement that says we have to do less is contrary to the basic values—hard work, ambition, opportunity—that built America. Arguing that we have to do *more* with less is fine, but pushing the Baileys to do *less* with less just won't work. They are willing to tighten their belts a little, but they won't give up their lifestyle.

We can solve this problem. In the short-term we have to break Washington out of its partisan gridlock by increasing the supply of oil and lowering demand for it. To do so, we will reduce the consumption of fossil fuels, without curbing growth, and increase domestic production. In the longer term, we need to innovate and find new ways to produce energy that is not fossil fuel based. We need to eliminate or greatly reduce our dependence on fossil fuels over time because of global warming, national security and, above all, our own economic future. Both the short-term and long-term solutions should begin today. If they do, the short-term should carry us for several years, until the long-term innovations are ready.

I know that some think we can't do this. They believe that our nation has succumbed to the need for immediate gratification. They think we've lost the ability to tackle big problems. I can see why they might think that. So far, the government has been fiddling as all that fossil fuel burns.

The Baileys have the gnawing feeling that things are out of control. They expect government leaders to look ten years into the future to identify and solve problems. It shakes their faith to see the government caught so flat-footed.

The failure to handle big problems is what makes great societies fail. They become too comfortable. They stuff their faces and fritter their time away, ignoring the challenges on the horizon. That's how Rome fell. It is how the British declined. They lost the drive and the will to identify problems and find solutions. Apathy defeated vision.

I don't believe our society is ready to fall. Our system is too strong. If we make this a national priority, the country will come with us. It's like former House speaker Tip O'Neill taught me. He loved to spend time with young representatives, and he often imparted words of wisdom.

"You know, Chuck," he began one day, plopping down next to me one slow day in the House Chamber. "I lost my first election. For Cambridge City Council."

"I didn't know that."

"Oh yeah. The next morning, I woke up and went to take out the trash. It was a gray day."

"My neighbor was an older lady. She liked sitting on her stoop, even on gray days. 'How's the mornin', Tip?' she yelled.

"'Not so good, Mary,' I yelled back. 'I lost my election. I don't know how. I worked so hard. I went to all the meetings.'

"Mary was silent. She looked skeptical.

"I looked at her. 'Mary,' I said. 'At least you voted for me?'

"Slowly, she shook her head.

"'But, Mary, I've known you my whole life. We've been to each other's christenings and weddings, we've shared our joys and sorrows, our families have been friends forever."

"'Tip,' she said. 'You never asked.'"

Joe and Eileen are ready to tackle this—ever since gasoline went to $3 a gallon, they have known it's a problem. But first, we must ask.

Short-Term

D.C. is a town known for gridlock—not just on the beltway, but in Congress as well. Of all the issues before Congress, nothing is more snarled than energy policy.

Democrats insist that the short-term solution to our energy crisis is conservation to reduce demand. This is roundly rejected by Republicans, who want to produce more, whatever it takes, to increase supply. Any suggestion of increasing supply is opposed by Democrats. Any attempt to reduce demand is attacked by Republicans. It's as if any two ideas that are different are necessarily in opposition.

Each party wants its solution and opposes all others. It's hard to understand why the two solutions contradict each other—why they can't exist side by side. After all, why couldn't we do both—increase supply and decrease demand?

Back when I got to the Senate in 1999, I had visions of a grand compromise. I'd get ten Democrats to support drilling in ANWR, the Artic National Wildlife Refuge (this was before ANWR had crystallized into the totemic issue it is today)—to increase supply—if ten Republicans would support raising fuel efficiency standards for cars (called CAFE standards)—to reduce demand. Why not both increase supply *and* reduce demand? That would get us to our goal more quickly. It wasn't long before I discovered for myself what my wife, New York City's transportation commissioner, has told me countless times: Solving gridlock isn't so simple.

I casually mentioned the idea to some of my colleagues in the cloakroom.

"Interesting . . . ," they would murmur before heading out or turning back to their papers. Their reaction wasn't great, but it didn't seem DOA either.

So I made a proposition to Senator Frank Murkowski, a salty conservative from Alaska. He wanted to drill in ANWR more than anything.

"Here's the deal," I said, cutting to the chase. Frank was not one for small talk, at least not with me. "If I get ten Democrats to vote for ANWR, will you get ten Republicans to support doubling CAFE standards?"

At first, Murkowski looked at me like I was crazy. Then he smiled. "I'll let you know."

He called me a day later. "Know what, Chuck? I'll try it if you do."

"Deal."

And he did. We both did. Turns out, we couldn't do it. Neither of us. The special interest groups on the left and right flanks of our parties were too powerful.

Special interest groups, whether you agree with their issue or not, often serve a useful function. They are better than anyone at increasing focus on an issue. Each group represents an organized and energized minority. Their engagement in the democratic process is a whole lot better than apathy. To me, the groups that derive their strength primarily from grassroots involvement, rather than from financial clout, serve a more legitimate function in our democracy; God bless the activists for being so involved and so caring.

But in government, special interest groups, however they derive their power, sometimes paralyze us because they only see their issue. They can pull the parties too far over, whatever the issue. They are so well organized, well financed and focused on their issue that they have an exaggerated influence on the process. When special interest groups are on the right and represent a narrow profit-making interest, it is easy for us to decry their influence. But when they are on the left—and we often agree with them—we must remember that they can pull us farther than we want to go.

Last year, I had a meeting with some major environmental groups in the hope of reviving my idea for a compromise. Since ANWR has become such a flashpoint, I floated the idea of opening up the eastern Gulf of Mexico instead. Their reaction was a perfect example of the special interest mindset.

"That's terrible! You can't do that," they all agreed.

"We already drill in the west Gulf," I offered. "What damage has it done?"

"The drills could disrupt ocean life!"

After my meeting with the environmental groups, I called some friends who are leaders in the environmental movement in New York. These are people I've known for years. They are die-hard environmentalists who are also generally reasonable.

"Has drilling in the west Gulf disrupted ocean life?" I asked.

"No."

"So why not drill in the east Gulf?"

"Drilling in the east Gulf is not so bad, but if we support it the floodgates will open—we'll be drilling in the Atlantic and Pacific, which would have much more serious environmental consequences. If we capitulate on one, we will lose them all."

This camel's nose in the tent argument is heard all too often in D.C. It's not that a proposal is bad; it's that allowing it could lead to something bad. The NRA used this argument against the Brady Bill. In reality, they didn't much mind most of its provisions, but were afraid that if they allowed the first step, we'd take away all their guns.

I asked my environmental friends about my compromise idea. "If I suggested drilling in the east Gulf in exchange for doubling CAFE standards, what would you say?"

There was a long pause. "Just between us?"

"Between us."

"We would accept that."

You see, it's not their fault; it's hard for special interests to ask for halfway. Their issue, which their members have sent them to Washington to protect, is the only thing and everything. That's their job. But it's not ours. Elected officials' job is to mediate.

We should listen to groups, but we can't just blindly follow them. We have to remember *all* the people whom we represent. When we follow groups too closely, we risk forgetting about the Baileys and all the families like them.

The majority of Americans don't entirely agree with the groups. Most of the time, they see both sides. They see not just civil liberties (as the ACLU does) but also protecting our nation. They see not just gun owners (as the NRA does) but also safe cities and towns. They see not just lawsuits (as the Trial Lawyers do) or just safe havens for businesses (as the Chamber of Commerce does). And with energy, it's not only supply or only demand—it can be a combination.

It's not just special interests being unwilling to compromise that holds us up. NIMBY (not in my backyard!) politics also contributes mightily to Washington gridlock. Florida will fight to the death against drilling in the east Gulf. While Republicans are generally for drilling, their party hasn't pushed drilling off the Gulf coast of Florida because Florida's governor is Jeb Bush and because it's an important swing state. Rare is the Republican—or Democratic—presidential candidate who will advocate it.

While Democrats are generally for increased efficiency, our party does not push to raise CAFE standards because the Democratic Michigan congressional delegation says it would mean death for them. While Democrats are generally for conservation, rare is the Democratic—or Republican—presidential candidate who will advocate meaningful fuel efficiency. Michigan will fight to the death against anything that affects their prized automobile companies.

Once a candidate becomes president and is supposedly able to rise above provincial interests, he is hamstrung by his campaign promises. Who would be crazy enough to alienate two of the biggest swing states? Michigan has seventeen electoral votes and Florida, which is sometimes known to have close elections, has twenty-seven.

When faced with the influence of special interest groups or NIMBY politics, politicians too often fail to mediate. Instead, they simply say yes to groups. It is a lot easier that way: When a group's issue comes before Congress, the group alerts its membership that Senator Jones, say, is against it. And the group's constituency—which might actually support a compromise that Senator Jones would prefer—thinks she is not on their side. If she votes no, Senator Jones ensures that she will be given a bad grade on the group's annual report card (such grades are generated by groups on the left and the right based exclusively on legislators' votes on a few bills each year). Even if she pushed for a well-thought-out compromise, to the constituency she will look as if she does not fully support the issue they care about. Senator Jones can spend a lot of time and effort explaining the thought that went into her proposed compromise and that she supports the issue as much as ever, but it is a difficult, time-consuming and not always successful effort. It is easier to throw up her hands and go along. Every senator, myself included, and even presidents have faced this countless times; too often, it is far easier to go along than to fight it.

So our energy policy, in a real sense, illustrates the dysfunction that is endemic in D.C. Special interests, in doing their job, take uncompromising positions and urge elected officials to adopt them. Those who would urge compromise, the millions of Baileys, are never heard from.

Add to the mix NIMBY politics—which ignores national imperatives and gives in to strongly felt but local interests—and gridlock prevails.

On issue after issue, Joe and Eileen ask why politicians can't get something reasonable done. The answer is that too often the parties let special interests and NIMBY politics prevent reasonable change from happening.

But when it comes to energy, the time has come for the grand compromise. There are three reasons why the deal that Frank Murkowski and I failed to achieve seven years ago will work today.

The first reason is that ANWR is now off the table. Instead, we will open the east Gulf, which there's little reason to oppose. In fact, in 2006, behind the leadership of Mary Landrieu, the Senate authorized opening a small portion of it.

The second is that car companies have begun to realize that improving efficiency standards will *help* them. Today low fuel efficiency is a competitive disadvantage for American automobiles around the world. Amazingly, China, which doesn't give a hoot about the environment, has higher standards than we do—they're trying to stay strong and ensure future growth, perhaps to a greater extent than we are. If Detroit doesn't improve, our companies will be locked out of the fastest growing market in the world. Even in the

United States, Detroit's low-efficiency vehicles don't align with demand. Look at Toyota's growth over the last couple of years. The Baileys would be happy to pay $1,000 more for their next car if they could save twice that in gas over the car's lifetime.

The third reason is by far the most important. The compromise will work this time because of gas prices. Joe and Eileen care a whole lot more now than they did in 1999. They will reward those who lower their costs and punish those who do nothing. There is now a counterweight to special interest and NIMBY politics.

Here's how it will work: First, we'll double CAFE standards and open up the entire east Gulf for drilling. Both are long overdue. Despite new technology and the increasing negatives associated with foreign oil, since 1990 Congress has not raised fuel efficiency requirements for cars; even for "light trucks," fuel efficiency has been raised only minimally, notwithstanding the strong efforts of Senators Maria Cantwell and Barack Obama. Increasing efficiency will lower demand—which will lower prices—without slowing growth.

Opening the east Gulf will also help with energy prices. There's believed to be more than six trillion cubic feet of natural gas in the east Gulf. Special interests and the few who live in the neighborhood should no longer be allowed to prevent the Baileys from getting a little relief on their home heating bills.

The compromise will have to go beyond that. There are federal lands in vast unpopulated parts of the western United States that we should open. We should be very careful about it—this is a short-term solution and the land is forever. National park and national monument lands, as well as other national treasures, will be completely protected.

We will open up new land in the continental United States for exploration if the areas that are already open are explored. The oil companies never talk about it, but 85% of oil and gas resources in the western United States are on federal land that's already open. The problem is that companies hold the leases without exploring the land. Lessees that don't explore should forfeit their leases and be excluded from getting leases for new areas that are opened. We have to increase domestic energy production, not give oil companies the right to prevent it.

There are other, smaller parts of the compromise as well. Today's power plants are old, dirty and inefficient. A huge number use coal and other fossil fuels. But in the short-term, they are what we've got. Let's admit that today's infrastructure must power us for the next fifteen years, but do everything possible to ensure that it is as efficient and environmentally friendly as possible. We should require old plants to become more efficient and cleaner and to increase their capacity. And we should require coal plants—whether new or refurbished—to meet strict efficiency, air quality and carbon sequestration requirements. Today, some coal plants just build huge smokestacks so that the pollution they emit will travel hundreds of miles before it comes down. Any economist will tell you that when a power plant builds a huge smokestack instead of putting in scrubbers, causing disease and asthma hundreds of miles away, it's an externality that has to be paid for. By requiring coal plants to be cleaner, we'll ensure that companies, not the government or the Baileys, are the ones paying the bill.

Despite the gridlock, there are some good projects already in place. They should be expanded. The Energy Star program, for example, allows consumer products that meet certain efficiency standards to earn an Energy Star. Consumers who shop for products with the Energy Star save energy and money. It is a win-win. I have fought to expand Energy Star for much the same reason that I created the Schumer Box on credit cards. If consumers are given good information, they will make the best choices for themselves.

We've done it with appliances, so let's expand Energy Star to the homes and offices where we live and work. The Energy Star program should include construction materials and methods. Green technology has made huge advances in the last quarter-century. Good green design can cut energy use by a quarter or more without sacrificing functionality. New construction, whether commercial or residential, should be eligible for the Energy Star program. Projects that earn it will get property tax credits. Furthermore, all federally financed or subsidized construction projects will be required to meet Energy Star standards. The nominal increases in construction costs will be more than offset by energy savings and tax credits.

Special interest groups on the left and the right may not immediately embrace the compromise. But the vast majority of Americans will welcome it.

Long-Term

On May 25, 1961, President John F. Kennedy addressed a joint session of Congress. A month earlier, the Bay of Pigs invasion in Cuba had failed and the Soviets had successfully launched Yuri Gagarin into the first manned orbit of Earth. We had been turned back in our own backyard and beaten in the first two rounds of the Space Race. Our country was reeling.

In the face of these daunting challenges, Kennedy could have blamed others. He could have offered safe, poll-tested solutions. He could have stoked the fragile nation's fears. Instead, he issued a challenge. He told Congress and the country that he wanted to get America to the Moon before the end of the decade, but only if we would come with him.

Success seemed almost impossible. "I believe we possess all the resources and talents necessary," Kennedy said. "But the facts of the matter are that we have never made the national decisions or marshaled the national resources required for such leadership. We have never specified long-range goals on an urgent time schedule, or managed our resources and our time so as to insure their fulfillment."

President Kennedy did not promise success, but he warned against the consequences of inaction. "While we cannot guarantee that we shall one day be first," he said, "we can guarantee that any failure to make this effort will make us last."

And our country followed him. Kennedy got his appropriations. We made an enormous investment in the space program. Everyone pulled together and didn't let his or her own interests get in the way. Throughout the turbulent decade, the nation followed. Two succeeding administrations, Democratic and Republican, maintained the commitment. On July 20th, 1969, Neil Armstrong planted an American flag on the lunar surface.

We had answered the call to greatness.

Our country again faces daunting challenges. From global terror, to rogue states, to Iraq, our strength is again being challenged. The threat of Communism has been replaced by that of religious extremism. In Kennedy's time we were being eclipsed in the Space Race. Today, it is no exaggeration to say we are being eclipsed in the race for energy independence.

As in 1961, the Baileys will only commit to action if they are given good reason to. Cartoonish villains and easy solutions won't cut it. A national challenge, independent of special interests, will. Contrary to the prevailing wisdom in Washington today, the Baileys still want to go to the Moon, if we ask them to.

If we invest seriously and intelligently, energy innovation will power our future. It will free us from foreign oil. It will save us from global warming. And, by allowing us to be first and best, it will strengthen, not weaken, our place in the global economy. The American economy has always been driven by American innovation. We must be the first to cross the new energy frontier.

Truely meaningful innovation will take a huge investment. Kennedy told Congress that his space proposal would cost $7.5 billion over five years. In today's dollars, that's about $10 billion a year. We should commit that amount to create a Manhattan Project for new energy. I have proposed the creation of a National Energy Efficiency Development Administration (NEEDA) to oversee this project.

NEEDA will be to energy innovation what NASA was to the Space Race. Politicians have failed to solve this problem, so let's put experts in charge and give them the funding they need. NEEDA will drive energy innovation. It will choose the technologies that have the most promise on the free market and it will figure out how the private sector should bring future technologies to the market. The agency will not spend all of its money internally. It will be responsible for core research and oversight, but much of its work will be farmed out to private enterprise. After the initial planning and research, NEEDA will turn its technological discoveries, applications and priorities over to the private sector and will operate as an oversight and coordinating agency.

The agency's initial planning stage will last three years. Every alternative to fossil fuels will be on the table for it to consider. NEEDA will be the expert, and NEEDA will make the choices. NEEDA can decide if nuclear power is needed to save the air. It can phase coal out of the economy entirely or base our future on coal gasification. If it says we need a nuclear waste dump, we will have to build it. If it says no to ethanol, we won't use ethanol. In short, NEEDA will work for Joe and Eileen Bailey, not the interest groups. Its sole goal will be to develop and bring to the market domestically sourced, environmentally sustainable energy within ten years. Green alternatives—such as solar, wind, geothermal and biomass, which have been convincingly advocated by Senators Jeff Bingaman and Tim Johnson—will finally be able to compete on equal footing, without being elbowed aside by the special interests. After three years, its plan will be unveiled for Congressional approval. In all likelihood, there will not just be one energy solution, but several.

In any case, Congress will not be able to amend it. Instead, there will be a simple up or down vote. By forcing Congress to vote on the plan exactly as it's presented, we will take the political pitfalls of our system out of the equation. Congress, which has been dominated by special interests and NIMBY politics when it comes to energy policy, won't be able to chip away at NEEDA's plan. NEEDA will be immune from pressure to spread pork in key congressional districts or to protect favored industries. It will be free of all the factors that so often screw everything up. All that will matter is what's best. You see, after the best minds in the world spend three years and billions of dollars to draft a plan for our future, and with the Baileys demanding a reduction in energy prices, it will not be in my colleagues' political interest to vote no; their only alternative will be to vote yes.

There's a major question people will ask: Why do we need NEEDA? Why can't private industry do it? They've got a point. In an ideal market, aggressive government coordination might not be required. Private competition would drive innovation. But private companies have proven they can't, or won't, do it. There are reasons for their reticence.

Energy innovation is a huge investment. The downside is much bigger than the upside. And even in the best case scenario, it wouldn't pay off for ten years. That's a long time to tie up shareholders' capital. Only a handful of companies in the world could afford that kind of massive long-term investment. And if the conditions in the energy market changed, or if, over the course of the ten years, the government made decisions that rendered the investment unprofitable, a huge expenditure would go down the drain. Few companies would take that risk.

Perhaps the only ones that could do it are the oil companies themselves. But they are fat and happy as it is. They are not interested in innovation. It was a mistake to allow big oil to merge so that only four companies, ExxonMobil, Chevron (which includes Texaco), BP (which includes Amoco and ARCO) and Shell, dominate the market. The mergers temporarily lowered gas prices, but competition is competition. Once there were so few teams, real competition precipitously declined. Competition would breed innovation; today's landscape breeds nothing but contentment with the status quo.

The problem is exacerbated by big oil's outsized clout in Washington. At a recent Senate hearing, I had the following exchange with Rex Tillerson, the head of ExxonMobil. I had been asking him about their paltry investment, about $10 million a year, in non-fossil fuels:

MR. TILLERSON: Well, Senator, I think your question is are we investing heavily in alternatives and—

ME: You're not.

MR. TILLERSON: We're not. We are investing in technology, and we are investing heavily in conventional oil and natural gas, which is the business we are in. We are not in those other businesses.

At first, I was taken aback. In effect, he was admitting that energy companies today see no advantage to investing in alternatives for tomorrow. At a hearing during which we were trying to put pressure on big oil, why would he so baldly state a position so obviously anathema to me? Then I thought about it. Rex Tillerson has no reason to try and please a senator from New York. He has the president's ear, and the ears of too many members of Congress. Whether I like the company or not, ExxonMobil feels pretty safe.

There is another justification for government involvement. To radically transform our energy landscape, a staggering number of industries will have to make significant investments and adjustments to the sources and forms of energy we use. The interconnectedness and complexity of the energy sector is mind-boggling. There are too many obstacles, too many independently moving parts, for a smooth transition to happen on its own. An example: It's hard for agribusiness to commit to ethanol if no oil company will carry it in gas stations, yet oil companies may have no interest in reducing the consumption of gasoline. NEEDA will identify and coordinate the infinite independent issues. Their bird's-eye view will ensure that all the moving parts work together.

NEEDA may be a big-government solution, but it's the only solution. Private enterprise can't do it alone—small business doesn't have the muscle and big business doesn't have the incentive. And Congress has shown time and again that special interests and NIMBY stand in the way of a gradual legislative solution. Big government didn't get in the way of landing a man on the moon and it won't get in the way of this.

In any case, giving the lead to NEEDA is not the same as giving NEEDA total control of the mission. Its role will be to choose appropriate and wisely considered energy alternatives, balance priorities, use good judgment and spur private enterprise involvement. From hydrogen, to superconductivity, to biomass, a lot of good work has been done. There are great innovators out there who NEEDA can, and should, enlist. With a little spurring and a lot of commitment, who knows which ones will revolutionize our economy.

This is a dark time in the United States when it comes to energy policy. China has higher fuel efficiency standards that we do. We depend on foreign sources of energy instead of on ourselves. For seventy-five years, domestic energy innovation has moved too slowly.

Every day that we do not figure out how to supply our own oil is another day when we are at the mercy of OPEC. Every day that we burn fossil fuels is a day when we increase the risks of global warming. Every day that we don't lower prices at the pump is a day when Joe Bailey suffers.

But every day that we work to solve these issues will be a day when America comes closer to the moon.

Chapter 14

REDUCE CANCER MORTALITY BY 50%

☆ Guarantee early-detection screenings for high-risk cancers for all Americans by requiring insurers to cover screenings and providing federal government coverage for the uninsured.

☆ Fully fund all National Cancer Institute–approved research grants.

☆ Increase research funding for new genetically based "personalized medicine."

☆ Build world-class cancer centers in the nation's top fifty population centers.

☆ Fight smoking by encouraging reduced insurance rates for nonsmokers and increasing insurance coverage of smoking cessation programs.

☆ Create a new C-DOTS program to help cancer centers electronically share information nationwide.

ON MANY WEDNESDAYS WHEN I WAS IN THIRD GRADE, a group of kids would trek over to my place. They would sneak around to the back of our house and stand on soda crates. From there, they could press

their faces against the glass and peer through the window. Within my kitchen, they beheld a curiosity—my great-grandmother.

The trek would always be inspired by a whisper that started at school, just before the last bell. The message would fly around the classroom. "Come to Schumer's after school. See the oldest woman in the world."

My great-grandmother was 82. Her skin was wizened and her back was stooped; she could barely speak. I could never blame the other kids for their curiosity. She *was* old. In the 1950s, there were very few people over 80 in our neighborhood.

Today my father is older than my great-grandmother was. Praise God, he's 83. But in just about every way, his life is different from my great-grandmother's. He plays golf three times a week. Each fall, he tries to convince my mother to drive the twenty-six hours to Florida so they don't have to pay for a flight. No one could confuse him with the oldest man in the world.

Aging has changed. People are living longer and healthier than ever. It is easy to take it for granted. The health care system gets so much criticism that we sometimes forget about this most essential victory. Think about my family. In one generation, the same age that used to be a monument to longevity now allows my father to enjoy the salad days of his retirement.

Longer life is an incredible gift. And it is incredibly expensive. As we add years to life, the health care costs continue to add up, especially now that so many of the easiest and most affordable advances have already been made. Every additional year that we extend life expectancy will come with a higher marginal cost than the previous year; we have already gotten the low-hanging fruit, as it were. As the tools become more adept at extending life, they will inevitably get more complicated and costly.

Using aggressive medical care to extend life also means enormous costs at the end of life. Today, almost a third of all Medicare spending is devoted to patients in the last six months of life. Some question this expenditure, but aggressive care to the very end is what patients and families want. Despite the costs, it's hard to argue. Who wouldn't spend every last dollar to keep a husband or wife, a parent or a child alive for an extra year? If it's possible that something can be done, most people want to try.

The problem is that as aggressive care gets more and more expensive, fewer and fewer people will have the financial ability to choose it. In 2005, 16% of Americans were not covered by health insurance. Another large chunk was covered, but not adequately. As health care costs go up, these groups will only get larger. The number of uninsured will grow and the number who have coverage that is inadequate will grow even faster.

There's an additional reason that it's hard to solve the health care conundrum. In America, everyone has an equal right to live. It's there in the Declaration of Independence, before even liberty and the pursuit of happiness. That's not something we are willing to compromise on. We are willing to say that some people will drive Chevys and some will drive Cadillacs. We are willing to have a society in which some people have a little apartment and some have a ten-thousand-square-foot mansion. But the one thing that we are never and should never be willing to say is that poor people will not have adequate health care.

It's amazing to me, and a tribute to the United States, how ingrained this sense of justice is. Mount Sinai Medical Center in Manhattan straddles two different worlds—the wealthiest neighborhood in New York to the south and one of the poorest to the north. Mount Sinai draws patients from both neighborhoods. Years ago, there was a public outcry when the New York *Daily News* reported that Mount Sinai had two maternity floors. Patients with private insurance were on one floor and patients who were uninsured or had Medicaid coverage were on another, less comfortable floor. Mount Sinai insisted that the differences had to do with the location of private rooms and the need to use staff doctors for patients who didn't have primary care physicians. Here was a system in which the very rich and the very poor were both getting top-notch care. Even so, because the services were not identical, it felt wrong; it offended an ingrained sense of fairness.

These issues bring up the fundamental health care conundrum for this century. How are we going to pay for health care that gets ever more expensive as it increases our life span? How many Americans will be able to afford the cost of extended longevity on their own? Are Americans willing to make the choice that those who can't afford adequate health care will have access to it, even as its costs increase?

Much of the debate on health care focuses on changing the delivery system. Should it be a single-payer plan or should private insurers do more? What is the balance between public and private? Should health insurance even exist?

Those are all important questions, but they are secondary. No matter what delivery system we use, adding years to life—and improving the quality of those years—for everyone in America, rich and poor alike, will require a major outlay of dollars. According to an article by David Leonhardt in the *New York Times*, between the 1950s and today, life expectancy increased by nearly ten years—from less than seventy years to nearly eighty; at the same time, in inflation-adjusted dollars, the average annual cost of each person's health care increased twelvefold—from $500 to $6,000. Over the coming decade, we should expect both life spans and costs to grow, the latter much more quickly than the former.

Five or ten years down the road, as a society we will face an enormous decision: whether we want to spend approximately another 5% of GDP on health care—which would require not spending that 5% on other things. Such a huge sum would have major implications for our economy and could require a massive tax increase. Right now, as we muddle through, we are at least five years away from that day of reckoning. But inevitably, as the numbers of uninsured and underinsured increase, it is a debate that will be forced on us. Joe and Eileen will be more willing to have our society spend that extra 5% of GDP on health care as their expenses go up and they are less able to afford the coverage they want.

There are some who say that since we already spend so much per capita on health care, the solution is for us to spend less. Increased efficiency is always welcome, but the amount we spend relative to other countries is a complex issue, one without a single silver bullet solution. For example, aggressive health care at the end of life is certainly one reason for our high per-capita costs—but it's also something that Americans want to preserve.

In the meantime, there are two ways to improve health care without a massive outlay: prevention and early detection. These are the least expensive ways to increase the quality and quantity of years we live and, at the same time, are the best chance of freeing up dollars for expanded coverage. If we focus on prevention and early detection now, it will make the difficult decisions we must make in five to ten years easier; when our health care reckoning does come, it will more likely result in a system that fully serves every American.

There are two areas in which prevention and early detection will make the biggest splash. One is obesity (see Chapter 15, Reduce Childhood Obesity by 50%), which is linked to heart disease and diabetes, two of the top causes of death in our nation. The other is cancer, our country's number-two cause of death.

Despite the incredible medical advances during my lifetime, cancer is still the one diagnosis that every single family in America dreads as much as they ever have.

Even for the healthiest among us, it looms—the unpredictable health crisis around the corner. Middle-aged men and women—Joe and Eileen's age—who have no other immediate health concerns have to be constantly vigilant. Cancer is terrifying both in the capriciousness of its onset and the seeming randomness of any treatment's success. It is the one disease that makes everyone feel vulnerable. Unlike just about all other health care concerns, cancer does not have a particular constituency. Everyone—man or woman, rich, poor or middle class—feels like it could happen to him or her.

Eileen's father, the oldest of the four Bailey grandparents, had prostate cancer a few years ago. It's not rare; one in six men are diagnosed with prostate cancer. Though the cure rate for prostate cancer is among the highest of all cancers—well over 90% when detected early—it was still terrifying for the family. With cancer, there is no guarantee.

For women, breast cancer, which has a cure rate that is not nearly as good, is an even graver problem. I don't know anyone in their fifties who has not lost at least one family member or friend to breast cancer. I have. It is devastating.

Ronald Reagan used to talk about creating a world in which children no longer went to bed worrying about nuclear annihilation. With the help of Mikhail Gorbachev, he went a long way toward making his vision a reality. With prevention, early detection and some targeted research, I believe it's possible to create a world in which people will worry much less about cancer. We won't be able to eradicate it, or even cure all the cases, but we can change what a cancer diagnosis means. We can reduce its incidence. We can increase the percentage of cases in which it's cured. We can make the care more manageable and affordable.

The key with cancer is catching it early. The earlier it's caught, the easier it is to treat. The easier it is to treat, the less it costs. It's penny wise and pound foolish to be tight with cancer screening money and then potentially have to deal with more advanced forms of the disease. Prostate cancer screening and early treatment is many times more effective, and cheaper, than treating an advanced case of the disease.

Early Detection Screenings

Despite prostate cancer's high cure rate, it is the third deadliest cancer among men. Colorectal cancer is second among men and third among women. Breast cancer is second among women. Today, there are effective and affordable lifesaving screenings for each of these killers. Unfortunately, they are not universally available. Ensuring that every adult who is at risk for these diseases gets screened for them will save lives.

Following Senator Tom Harkin's lead, I have been fighting to increase women's access to mammograms for years. With breast cancer in particular, we have already done a lot to increase awareness and access; we must do still more. With prostate and colorectal cancers, there is more to do, as well.

Insurance companies should not be deciding which cancer screening is covered; doctors should. The National Institutes of Health should set screening guidelines that all health insurance plans, private and public, are required to cover. We already require health plans to cover the costs of hospital stays for new moms, mental health parity and reconstructive surgery for mastectomy patients; dependable and cost-effective cancer screening should be on that list, too.

Even if someone's not insured, they must still have access to cancer screening. The National Breast and Cervical Cancer Early Detection Program, passed by Senator Barbara Mikulski, one of the most savvy of my colleagues, is a start. Under the program, more than 18,000 women have increased their chances of survival through diagnosis. That's a start, but it's not enough. Today, only one in five eligible women participates in the program. That means that tens of thousands of women have missed potentially lifesaving early diagnoses. The program must be expanded to give every woman in America the best possible chance of becoming a survivor.

Furthermore, its mission should be extended beyond breast and cervical cancer screening to include prostate screening for men and colorectal screening for both genders. The initial cost of ensuring that every American has access to these screenings (before factoring in the savings that would come with early detection) is $2 billion a year. And if recent developments in early detection of lung cancer, the number one cause of cancer deaths, prove medically effective, that screening should be added to the list as well.

Reducing Smoking

Early detection is good; prevention is even better. We don't know how to lower the odds of getting every type of cancer. One type we do know something about preventing is lung cancer. If fewer people smoke, fewer people will get lung cancer. Ninety percent of those who get lung cancer are current or former smokers. No other single type of cancer kills nearly as many Americans. Lung cancer causes more than 25% of all cancer deaths—one in five people who die of cancer are smokers with lung cancer.

A lot of effective work has been done to cut down on smoking in the last decade, particularly in the area of educating young people about the risks. There's still more to do. The Food and Drug Administration (FDA) should have the power to regulate tobacco as a drug. This has been proposed, and failed to pass, before. Tobacco is ingested, it interacts with the body's chemistry and it's provably addictive. If the FDA is given the power to regulate tobacco, it will change the landscape of tobacco sales. Companies will no longer be able to pawn cigarettes off as a harmless leisure activity.

Health insurers should also be part of the mix. We need to promote each insurer's right to offer reductions in premiums for non-smokers. Many already have different premiums, but a lot of large group plans make no distinction. They should. While smoking should not be outlawed, the cost of its added health risk must not be assumed by smokers and nonsmokers equally. Health insurance providers should be encouraged to have separate contribution scales for smokers and nonsmokers. If insurance costs fairly reflect the risks of smoking—just as car insurance reflects the relative risk of having an automobile in different cities—it would cut costs for nonsmokers and offer smokers another incentive to quit.

Since this should not be a punishment for those who are addicted, health insurers should be required to cover the cost of smoking cessation programs prescribed by a doctor. If the relative costs for smokers are increased, barriers to quitting must simultaneously be removed.

Fully Fund NCI-Approved Grants

Expanding existing prevention and early detection programs is critical. But we must go farther to prevent, catch and improve treatment for all cancers. The senators from California, Dianne Feinstein and Barbara Boxer, have both been beating the drum for increased funding for cancer research for years.

Each year, the National Cancer Institute (NCI) approves grants based on the research proposals that it considers promising. The problem is that it funds less than a third of the approved grants, according to a report issued by the National Cancer Legislative Action Committee a few years ago. That means that two-thirds of the promising, approved cancer research in this country never gets the money needed to move forward. Which of those two out of three projects might lead to a cure? Or a vaccine? We'll never know until we start fully funding the grants that the NCI approves.

Personalized, Genetically Targeted Medicine

NCI needs particular help when it comes to developing the next generation of treatment—personalized medicine. Also known as genetically targeted treatment, personalized medicine is one practical application of the incredible evolution in our understanding of genetics and the human genome. With personalized medicine, doctors will no longer merely target diseases in patients, they will target specific issues in each patient based on his or her genetic makeup.

This is the future of cancer treatment. It can improve diagnosis, prognosis and treatment.

Some estimate that only about 25% of breast cancer sufferers who have their tumors removed need chemotherapy. That means that 75% of women with breast cancer could be spared one of the most traumatic, and expensive, parts of the experience. Others have suggested that genetically targeted personalized medicine will allow certain tumors to be shrunk with no more side effects than today's cholesterol medications cause. All in all, funding smart and potentially money-saving research will cost about $5 billion a year.

National Cancer Centers and Data Sharing

In order to make the cutting-edge advancements in prevention, detection and treatment meaningful and accessible, we have to improve our national cancer-fighting network. Today, only a few cities have world-class cancer centers. Local hospitals everywhere else do a great job, but by their very nature, they don't specialize in cancer. Too many families are forced to choose between world-class treatment and staying close to home. Every major metropolitan area in the country should have a Memorial Sloan-Kettering or a Mayo Clinic. It would cost less than $150 million a year for ten years to create a world-class cancer center in each of the nation's top fifty population centers that does not currently have one. The expansion of the network will increase innovation, as each cancer center pursues research in consultation and competition with the others. Just as importantly, it will save families all over the country from one of the most wrenching choices that cancer foists on them.

This newly expanded network of cancer centers needs to have improved information sharing. We need to leverage our national experience against the disease. Each new center will be required to participate in a new national Cancer Data Outcome and Treatment Sharing (C-DOTS) program to, that's right, connect the dots. To continue receiving federal funds, existing centers will need to hook up to C-DOTS. The knowledge gained by experts in New York, Atlanta, Rochester and Los Angeles is not regional, it's universal. Connecting the dots will speed everyone toward the best solutions, no matter where they live.

A little more than ten years ago, the Department of Veterans Affairs (VA), which runs VA hospitals across the country, reimagined itself around many of the same precepts I've discussed here. They began focusing on prevention and data, which they shared through a national system of electronic medical records. As *New York Times* columnist Paul Krugman frequently has pointed out, by all objective measures, it's been a success. The VA has transformed itself from one of the most troubled health care providers in the country to one of the best. These changes are not a panacea, to be sure; rather, they begin to point us toward health care answers.

Like health care in general, cancer is not a problem that we can fix with a magic wand. That's okay; Joe and Eileen Bailey don't expect us to. In the short-term, we can focus our efforts on prevention, early detection and new targeted treatments to make the disease a whole lot less scary, and more affordable, than it is today. That's a great strategy for fighting cancer. It's also a model for being able to afford the rising cost of living longer, so increased longevity can be shared by all.

Cancer won't disappear tomorrow. And the health care system won't be fixed so quickly either. But, by attacking it from this angle, we can transform cancer from a condition that inspires terror to a challenge for which all Americans are prepared.

As far as Joe and Eileen are concerned, that's a pretty good start.

CHAPTER 15

REDUCE CHILDHOOD OBESITY BY 50%

☆ ADD A SURGEON GENERAL'S WARNING TO JUNK-FOOD MARKETING AND PACKAGING.

☆ TAX FAST-FOOD ADVERTISING TO FUND A NATIONAL AD CAMPAIGN TO COMBAT CHILDHOOD OBESITY.

☆ REQUIRE CHAIN RESTAURANTS TO LIST CALORIC INFORMATION ON MENUS.

☆ TEACH GOOD HEALTH IN SCHOOL.

☆ MAKE SCHOOL FOOD AND SCHOOL VENDING MACHINES LEAN AND HEALTHY.

☆ GET JUNK FOOD OUT OF THE FOOD STAMP PROGRAM.

☆ HELP LOCALITIES AND SCHOOLS ENCOURAGE KIDS TO EXERCISE.

THE SPALDEEN. THAT FAMOUS PINK RUBBER BALL—a skinned tennis ball, or so we told each other on East Twenty-Seventh Street in the 1950s. I guess today it would be an urban legend. But not back then. In those days, before every claim could be checked by a twelve-year-old with a cell phone, it was a fact.

Back then, the spaldeen cost a quarter. It was not a lot, but not a little. Enough that it hurt when you watched the pink ball roll down a storm drain or fly onto a neighbor's roof, which eventually it always would. But when you bought a new one, the possibilities were dizzying. It was like holding a whole toy store in your hand.

There must be thousands of games that can be played with the spaldeen. Stickball, of course, is the most famous. But growing up, my favorite was called slapball. We used to play slapball on East Twenty-Seventh Street, where the traffic was sporadic enough that we could go five, sometimes ten minutes without the nuisance of a car driving through.

Slapball was a four-base game owing homage, I guess, to baseball. You'd set up the bases in a tight square the width of the street. First and second base were on the east side, third and home on the west side. It was three to a team. The ball would be pitched underhand on a bounce. The batter had to try to slap the spaldeen out of the infield on the ground. It was an out if the ball left the infield on a fly. The whole thing was played at close range. It couldn't have been more than 25 feet across. You had to find the holes, or aim at a fielder's ankles, to get the spaldeen through.

Slapball was intense. It required speed and coordination. But mostly, it took continuous intensity. I loved that game.

I am not the first Brooklyn kid to write about stickball, slapball or spaldeens, and I surely won't be the last. So why add my sepia-toned memory to the bunch? I'll admit, I like remembering summer afternoons on East Twenty-Seventh, playing until even the combination of young eyes and a bright pink ball could no longer compete with the approaching night. But that's not why I bring up the spaldeen.

When I was a kid, on weekends and during the summer, you could always wander outside and find kids playing slapball, stickball, stoopball, boxball or any number of other ad hoc games. There was always something going on. That was our life. The spaldeen was our Game Boy or PS3. On school days, we couldn't wait to get home to pick up where we had been cut off by our mothers' dinner calls the evening before. On weekends and during the summer, we could always wander outside and find a game in progress.

In some ways, playing with a spaldeen is not so different from playing a video game with a group of friends. Neither is really educational. Both serve the same purpose as far as adults are concerned—they occupy our kids for hours on end so we can do what must get done.

But there is one essential difference. Playing with a spaldeen is exercise. Playing a video game is not. As it turns out, that is a very big difference, indeed.

America is fat. Nearly two-thirds of adults are overweight; almost half of those who are overweight are obese. Even worse, kids are getting fat too. Close to a third of children and adolescents are overweight and more than 15% are obese.

It has not always been like this. I tend to be sentimental, but in this case, it's true. In the 1970s, obesity among kids was one-quarter as prevalent as it is today. Obesity among adolescents was 60% less common than today. Among adults, it was half.

Let me highlight that. Kids today are four times more likely to be obese than they were thirty years ago. Adolescents are two and half times more likely. Adults are twice as likely.

Joe and Eileen Bailey have noticed. Eileen notices it on the days when she works at the elementary school and watches the kids at recess. Joe notices it among fellow tailgaters at the single Jets game he goes to each fall. They both noticed it last year when they took the kids to Disney World at spring break.

People's heaviness offends the Baileys a little bit, although it's hard for them to put their finger on why. Maybe because it seems so undisciplined. Gluttonous. When they read that lawyers were suing McDonald's for making customers obese, Joe and Eileen thought it was ridiculous—another example of people doing whatever they want and looking for someone else to deal with the consequences, they thought.

On the other hand, the Baileys understand the sense of powerlessness that many people feel about their weight. Over the last ten years, Joe has gained some pounds. And to be totally honest, Eileen never got back to her ideal weight after her last pregnancy. Joe is not too worried, although maybe he should be; it seems like most of his friends have gotten bigger as they have gotten older. Eileen, however, is among the 48% of Americans who worry about their weight. Every year, she contributes a couple of hundred dollars to the $30 billion weight-loss industry. Some diets work for a while, but nothing seems to keep the weight off.

But more than anything, Joe and Eileen are upset about Pete, their youngest son. In the last two years, he has grown. He has grown taller, sure. But he has also grown fatter. They both have theories about why he has gained weight, but neither knows what to do about it. Pete's weight does not keep them up, tossing and turning at 2 a.m., but it bothers them.

Joe and Eileen know that weight is more than just a question of vanity. Obesity, caused by diet and physical inactivity, has become the leading cause of preventable death in this country. Obesity is linked to the skyrocketing rate of diabetes, which, at $90 billion a year, is now one of the most expensive health-care problems in this country. Kids are not at risk of having heart attacks, but they do get diabetes. Many of the other medical problems that plague overweight adults also plague children. And worst of all, overweight kids are more likely to become overweight adults who, in turn, are most likely to have overweight kids.

It seems like this should be a preventable problem. With a little discipline, it should be easy to beat. What the Baileys have found, though, is that it is not easy at all. That might be the most upsetting thing. It seems so simple and yet, for both Eileen and Pete, it has been so hard to control.

Video games play a part. Eileen has cut down on the number of hours Pete is allowed to play video games and sit in front of the computer. But it does not seem like a solution. Even without video games, it is not as if he can just go outside and find a pickup game; all the other kids are cloistered in front of screens in their own houses. Pete ends up bored, or at a friend's house, where they end up playing all the Madden NFL 07 they want.

But it is not just video games and computers. There are other, larger forces contributing to our incredible fattening. Society is different than it was in the age of the spaldeen. For one thing, as I mentioned earlier, commercialism is much more perfect than it used to be. Commercialism is not, in and of itself, a bad thing. It allows those who sell products to communicate with those who buy products; it creates willing buyers for goods and services, which is essential in a capitalist system. But as commercialism is perfected, there are side effects.

Since its birth, commercialism has appealed to our most basic urges by creating or capitalizing on desire. In the last forty years, new technology, combined with the refinement of time-tested tools, has made it better at pushing our buttons (one could argue the same thing has happened with electoral politics, but that's another book).

Commercialism as we know it first appeared with the spread of industrial capitalism in the second half of the nineteenth century. Its earliest tools were direct-mail flyers and catalogs. The creation of the Sears, Roebuck catalog in 1897 was a watershed; it was not the first catalog, but it was the best.

Radio advertising helped continue the advance. But it was TV that really catapulted commercialism to HAL-like levels of effectiveness. It has been less than sixty years since the first televised White House presidential address (Harry Truman calling for "meatless Tuesdays"). In that time, television advertising has become staggeringly effective. Each new technology, from the Internet to the cell phone, has increased commercialism's reach. These new tools complement those that came before. Today, commercialism has become too adept at exciting our desire.

This is not necessarily a negative development. Marketing can be used for almost any purpose, good or bad. Its power is neutral. The Partnership for a Drug-Free America has spent years running massive, professional antidrug ad campaigns. Tracking has shown that it has had a marked effect on young people's behavior. And in the last few years, well-funded antismoking campaigns brought teen smoking to significantly lower levels. Both are examples of perfected and targeted commercialism improving society.

Commercialism is the engine that drives our system. We should not curtail it. But when the message is harmful, we must counter it.

McDonald's has an incentive to get people to eat their food. With their sophisticated commercialism, they have the advantage of knowing exactly what we'll like and how to make us crave it all the time. It's not that they revel in selling unhealthy food. If spinach were as cheap and easy to sell as french fries, they'd sell spinach. But it's not.

The sad fact is that healthy is not as profitable. That's why no large company has the incentive to encourage healthy eating.

Faced with this barrage, we have to start countering the ubiquitous and sophisticated marketing of unhealthy foods. Bad health is destructive, preventable and expensive—exactly the type of issue on which the government must take a stand.

We must use the free market, which now encourages so many unhealthy choices, to spur a couple of healthy ones.

Surgeon General's Warning for Junk Food and Fast Food

The Surgeon General should issue a report on the effect that foods that are high in calories, sugar and fat have on the health of children. Packaged foods that are found to be potentially harmful to children should carry a Surgeon General's warning. All advertising and packaging materials for those foods would be required to include a brief warning, similar to those found on alcohol and cigarette ads and packaging today.

Parents can choose for themselves what their children eat; that's not the government's job. But it is the government's job to warn parents of risks to their kids' health. Excessively eating food that's high in calories, sugar and fat poses significant health risks, not unlike the health risks posed by smoking or excessive drinking. Parents have the right to know the risks so they can make the best choices.

Packaged foods are already required to list their ingredients and nutritional information. The Surgeon General's warning will serve as a quicker and more easily understandable summary for all of us parents who don't have the time or expertise to interpret the information that's there now.

Some may argue that this is government overreaching or Big Brotherism. It's not. Big Brother would tell you what you are allowed to do; it would decree what you can eat. Instead, this will help to create a more perfect market. It will bring parents closer to what economists call *perfect knowledge*. It will ensure that everyone knows the risks of unhealthy foods, not just the benefits, which McDonald's reminds them about every day.

National Ad Campaign

The findings of the Surgeon General's report should also be the backbone of a nationwide advertising campaign.

Similar to antismoking and antidrug efforts, the campaign would teach people about good eating and smart nutrition. I'm not talking about an occasional public service announcement or a couple of highway billboards. The campaign must be sleek, sophisticated and ubiquitous. The government should hire the best that Madison Avenue has to offer. And, we must invest real money. Ads should be in magazines and on the radio. They should be all over the Saturday morning cartoons. We need to speak directly to kids.

Any marketer will tell you that kids are the best audience. They are the most impressionable. We are all familiar with disgusting examples of companies that have exploited this fact. So, why can't we talk to kids to counter it? Teaching good values or healthy living is an appropriate counter to the message beamed at them every day.

We can pay for the campaign with a surcharge on all fast-food marketing. The fast-food industry would have to contribute 10% of all their marketing expenditures to a dedicated fund that would finance the campaign. Conservatively, that would create an annual fund of $550 million. Fast-food providers can advertise as much as they want. But when they proclaim the allure of a burger and fries, we should get the chance to remind people about the importance of a balanced diet.

The Baileys believe in the free market. They know it works. But they also know that big corporations can be dishonest or manipulative. They don't mind when government counters that by telling the truth. Neither the ad campaign nor the Surgeon General's warning will limit the Baileys' freedom of choice; in fact, they'll both further it.*

Nutritional Information at Restaurants

People eat out more than they used to. Longer hours, both parents working and commercialism all contribute. A combination of factors spurs people to the drive-through or the local kid-friendly franchise.

*Of course, higher taxes on cigarettes have also contributed to the reduction in smoking. Taxes undeniably have a potent effect on consumer behavior, but they should be the last resort. In the case of obesity, it should be left to the laboratory of the states. We must be clear that they have the same prerogative to impose taxes on junk food as they do on tobacco, alcohol and consumer goods.

The problem is that people eat more and eat worse when they eat out. Kids' menus, especially, tend to offer fat in three forms: chicken fingers, french fries and hot dogs. I don't blame kids for loving that stuff—I love it, too. But at restaurants, kids often don't have any other choices. I'd always *prefer* a crispy Nathan's hot dog with a generous slathering of mustard, but blessedly, it is rarely a choice that I can, or must, make.

It should be easier for Joe and Eileen to know what they and their kids are eating. Every chain restaurant, defined as any restaurant that has more than ten locations, should be required to provide basic fat and calorie counts for its frequently served dishes right on the menu. This sounds onerous, but it is actually affordable. Getting nutritional information costs between $350 and $1,000 per menu item—a business expense that is deductible on tax returns at the end of the year. The marginal cost is minimal; certainly worth the information consumers would gain access to. It's another tool to help support individual choice.

Healthy Schools

We have to reach kids in every way we can, particularly when they *have* to listen. Schools must promote the anti-obesity message. Physical education and classes on good nutrition should be taught in every grade. When good health becomes a habit for young people, it lasts a lifetime.

Of course, we will never get kids to listen to this message if fatty foods and sweets are sold in their schools! School lunches and breakfasts must be revamped. Today, they fly in the face of a healthy message and a healthy lifestyle. Agribusiness, national food distributors and school districts push cheap and easy-to-prepare freezer-to-fryer foods. School vending machines, which are packed with sodas, chips and candy bars, are even worse.

The United States Department of Agriculture (USDA) already oversees the meals served in school cafeterias. We need to set stricter nutritional guidelines, including the maximum fat content per meal, mandate a ratio of fresh fruits and vegetables to other foods and prohibit the use of trans fats.

Congress should further expand the USDA's power and allow it to regulate all foods served in schools, including those in vending machines. Rather than deprive schools of vending machine revenue, the USDA should work with private vendors to find nutritionally appropriate foods to stock in those machines. President Clinton's Alliance for a Healthier Generation has done great work by convincing some of the nation's largest junk-food companies to stock healthier options in school vending machines. Senator Patrick Leahy's farm-to-cafeteria grant program also encourages schools to serve fresh and healthy food. Both are great initiatives, and the USDA should build on them.

Of course, some will say that the federal government should keep its hands out of local schools' cafeterias and vending machines. But, as with the ad campaign and the Surgeon General's warning, it's needed. In a world of perfect commercialism, it's appropriate for the government to take a stand and send a positive message.

When it comes to our children's health, we must not shy away from communicating honest, good and healthy values.

Food Stamp Program

For better nutrition to take hold, we must be consistent across the board. Wherever the government is, we should be healthy. We have to get rid of junk food in the food stamp program. You can't use food stamps for cigarettes or alcohol; you shouldn't be able to use them for junk food, either.

The food stamp program was created in the 1960s to combat starvation in America. That problem has now been joined by the nutritional crisis, which disproportionately affects the poorest Americans, so food stamps must become a nutrition program as well. It is not the government's job to limit poor people's—or anyone's—freedom to choose their own food. People on food stamps could still use their own money to buy whatever they wanted, just like everyone else. Taking junk food out of the program is not a punishment. It's meant to ensure that food stamps do what they were created to do: save lives. If anything, the restriction would increase options for the very poor. If convenience stores and supermarkets in poor neighborhoods could no longer get food stamp money for selling junk food they might start stocking some better options.

Our nation's weight has gotten out of control, but that does not mean it is an uncontrollable problem. Better education, a little information and an aggressive culture of health will help Joe and Eileen tip the scales right back to where they want them.

As for Pete? Well, I hear they've started making the spaldeen again.

CHAPTER 16

REDUCE ABORTIONS BY 50%

☆ ENSURE REAL AND AGE-APPROPRIATE SEX
EDUCATION IN PUBLIC SCHOOLS, INCLUDING
EDUCATION ON ABSTINENCE AND
CONTRACEPTION.

☆ MAKE CONTRACEPTIVES MORE AVAILABLE.

☆ INCREASE FUNDING FOR FEDERAL FAMILY
PLANNING PROGRAMS (TITLE X).

☆ CREATE A NATIONAL MEDIA CAMPAIGN TO
REDUCE UNWANTED PREGNANCIES.

IRIS HAD JUST TURNED 35 when she became pregnant with Alison, our youngest. The doctor recommended that we get an amniocentesis. "There are some risks," he said, "and you should have as much information as possible."

So, without much thought, we made an appointment.

At the doctor's office, they set up a sonogram, which is part of the procedure. When the nurse turned on the monitor, it was a total shock. Iris was only three months pregnant. But we could see fingers and feet. We could see our daughter-to-be sucking her thumb. Sitting in that doctor's office, looking at the image on the screen and watching the little flutter of that tiny heart, I connected with Alison. It was one of the most profound moments of my life.

That night, Iris and I talked it through. It was a short discussion. We had the same thought: If Iris got pregnant again, we would not want to have an amnio done. The test results would not matter. We would not consider an abortion, unless Iris's life or health were at stake.

Our decision that night did not shake our pro-choice beliefs. In fact, it strengthened them. I realized that our conversation, our decision, is how it ought to be. Each woman, hopefully with a supportive partner and with the help of a doctor, a minister, a priest, a rabbi or an imam, should decide for herself.

In a lot of ways, it was easy for us. We were adults. We were married. I was an elected official. Iris had a good job. Our daughter, thank God, was healthy.

For many women, it is a much more wrenching decision.

Early in my career, my district included a particular working-class neighborhood. Joe and Eileen Bailey probably lived in a similar neighborhood in Brooklyn or Queens or Staten Island when they were first married.

Most of the parents in the neighborhood sent their kids to the local parochial school. Once a week, a group of mothers would convene at a little luncheon group during the school day. Sometimes, they would invite a guest.

Over the years, I have found that luncheon groups of this sort are fairly common; I have probably attended several dozen. But this was my first time. The invitation made me a little nervous; I did not want to intrude on their group. On the other hand, I have never been one to turn down a chance to meet my constituents, especially when invited. I accepted.

When I arrived, we immediately clicked. The women talked about their husbands, their children, their problems. We all felt comfortable. It was one of those rare moments when people let their hair down. As the hostess was serving coffee, the talk turned to abortion. I told them I was pro-choice, recounted the story about Alison's amnio and asked how they felt. For whatever reason, the women were very honest. All of them knew someone—a sister, a cousin, a close friend, themselves—who had had an abortion.

None of them were happy about it, but they did not express regret. No one told them about the things they needed to know, like avoiding pregnancy, when they were teens. There was little education at school or at home. There was very little discussion at all. When they, or someone close to them, had learned about life the hard way, what were they supposed to do? They all said they would never do it again, but they believed it had prevented their lives from being ruined in the wake of a terrible mistake.

The luncheon was wrapping up when a dark-haired woman spoke for the first time. I had been wondering what she was thinking since I had sat down. I don't remember the woman's name, but when I think about Eileen Bailey, I often think of her.

"Listen to me, Chuck," this woman said. "Stay pro-choice. Just don't talk about it too much."

Over the last thirty-five years, no issue has epitomized the "culture wars" more than abortion. It has been framed as a debate between secular liberals and the religious heartland. It has been viewed as a fight between women's rights and male chauvinism. It has been seen as a battle between life and choice.

Those perceptions largely miss the mark. Or, more accurately, they define a very small percentage of people on either side. The broad middle agrees with the dark-haired woman at the luncheon: the answer is not so clear-cut. Supporting abortion's legality is not the same thing as supporting abortions. Opposing abortion is the not the same thing as imprisoning those who have them.

According to the results of an August 2005 Pew Research Center poll, in every region of the country—East, West, Midwest and South—a majority of people believe that abortion should be available in more than just extreme cases (rape, incest or risk to the mother's life). In every region, fewer than one out of every seven people wants to outlaw abortion with no exceptions. A majority of nonevangelical Christians, both Catholics and Protestants, want abortions to be available, even for cases that don't involve extreme circumstances. Surprisingly, slightly more men than women support having abortion available, and slightly more women than men oppose it entirely. Even the partisan divide is misleading: moderate Republicans are more likely than moderate Democrats to favor abortion rights beyond extreme cases and less likely to oppose abortion outright.

Sure, some trends are as you'd expect. The more religious you are, the more likely you are to think abortion should be restricted. People on the coasts are less likely to support restrictions than are those in the South. Liberal Democrats are most likely to support abortion without restriction; conservative Republicans are most likely to oppose it without exception.

Still, in general, most people agree with the dark-haired woman and disagree with both parties. They disagree when Democrats talk about preserving access to abortions without talking about reducing them as well. They disagree when Republicans say that mothers who choose abortion and doctors who perform them should be considered criminals. Unlike Democratic and Republican talking heads, most people are not ardently pro-life or pro-choice.

For many people, abortion is not just a religious fight—it is a debate about permissiveness and its consequences. Joe and Eileen are offended at the idea that abortion is a tool of liberation. They are offended at the idea that people might use abortion as a form of birth control. To them, these are symptoms of a culture that has lost its moral compass. They are turned off when people claim that every choice is as good as every other choice.

Joe and Eileen believe in a moral right and wrong. They believe that promiscuity should be avoided—by both men and women. They know that when it isn't, it can cause real pain and unhappiness. The choices that the Baileys consider immoral, whether it's underage sex or adult infidelity, have consequences. They have seen the consequences. They fear a society that ignores the morals they depend on.

Yet, they also live in the real world. They know about human frailty. They know that people make mistakes. They believe in second chances. They believe in forgiveness and redemption. They believe that when people make mistakes, they should have the right to deal with the consequences themselves, to choose how to solve their own problems without the government dictating to them.

I think that's why the dark-haired woman wanted me to stay pro-choice, but did not want me to talk about it. I think she believed that it is each person's responsibility to make decisions for him- or herself, but she did not want her elected officials to endorse behavior that she considered immoral. She knew that it is possible for people to choose the wrong path, and she wanted society to push back. If society didn't, she feared all hell would break loose.

There is a need for a societal superego to counteract our individual id. For many people, this is the role of the church, the synagogue or the mosque. The Baileys may not agree with all of their church's views—and they may not always follow its dictates—but they are glad it is saying what it is saying. Their church advocates taking responsibility and maintaining values. In a society that sometimes seems to have too little of that, they're glad for its voice, even when they disagree with it. As much as family and country, it is a critical part of their value system, their worldview and their life.

When government officials talk about abortion too much, or in a way that is morally neutral, it seems like the opposite. It comes across as an endorsement. While the Baileys don't believe abortion should be prohibited outright, they never want it to be endorsed. They believe, as Bill Clinton masterfully put it, that abortion should be "safe, legal and rare."

To be in step, Democrats need to focus not only on the "safe and legal," but also on the "rare." Too often, it doesn't seem like "rare" is very important to us. But "rare" is critical to Joe and Eileen Bailey. When faced with the Republicans' "never, never and never" cry or the Democrats' "safe and legal" mantra, they are ambivalent. The Baileys cannot in good conscience support "safe and legal" abortions without the clear understanding that they must also be "rare."

Recently, Harry Reid and Hillary Clinton, two Democratic leaders with different views on abortion, have both been pushing the party in the right direction. They have been holding the line on safe and legal *and* articulating the importance of "rare."

Safety and legality are critical. There are parts of the country where safe abortions are not available. This must change. There are states in which *Roe vs. Wade* is under assault. We must defend it. To be fair, most Americans have access to safe and legal abortions—and, of course, we must keep it that way.

On the other hand, 1.3 million abortions are performed each year in this country. That equals about one abortion for every four live births. Abortion is a long way from being "rare."

The answer is not, and never has been, criminalization. Making abortion a crime undermines its safety and creates criminals where there are none. As Democrats, we must never accept that. Instead, we should make it a top priority to reduce abortions by half *without* resorting to criminalization or government coercion. This is not as hard as one might think.

We know how to avoid abortions: reduce unwanted pregnancies. There are three million unwanted pregnancies a year. Close to half are terminated with abortions.

We know how to reduce unwanted pregnancies: education, abstinence and contraception. The 7% of women who use no contraception account for more than *50% of unwanted pregnancies*. If that small percentage used the same precautions that the other 93% of women use, unwanted pregnancies, and therefore abortions, would be cut basically in half. The logic is inexorable. To reduce abortions, we need to reduce unwanted pregnancies. To reduce unwanted pregnancies, we need to increase education, abstinence and contraception.

The problem is, we haven't done it.

First, we should call for age-appropriate sex education in public schools that is specifically designed to reduce the number of teen pregnancies and sexually transmitted infections. Kids are learning about sex at a young age—whether it's from Internet porn, late-night television, pervasive marketing or the street. More than half of all abortions are provided to women under the age of twenty-five.

We need education to counter the tide. Very few schools have good programs today; more than a third of the programs that do exist are incomplete. Many sex-ed programs are opt-in only, which makes it too easy for teens to miss out on critical knowledge without active intent.

For sex education to work, the curriculum must be complete and medically accurate. Parents who do not want their children in sex-ed classes should always have the right to explicitly opt out. For everyone else, it should be part of the school's core program.

The programs have to be good, though. Too often, sexual education, or "health," classes are too coy. Who doesn't remember dreary hours spent in pointless and uninformative health classes? They always seem to be an afterthought or a casualty of political football. No wonder many people believe they don't work.

But in reality, accurate and complete educational programs— teaching abstinence *and* contraception—do work. That's why Senator

Frank Lautenberg has been such a strong proponent of them. Such programs have been proven to delay or prevent sexual activity among young adolescents by 15% and to increase the use of contraceptives among those who are active by 22%.

Abstinence education should be a cornerstone of the effort. Just as we must communicate that we want to reduce abortions, we also must communicate that high schoolers should not be sexually active. We should make the value perfectly clear: Abstinence is preferable to sexual activity until you're an adult. Period.

Sex education programs must also include accurate information about contraceptives. We have to teach about contraceptives because, as Joe and Eileen know, you don't avoid sex by avoiding contraception. You avoid sex by teaching good values, and by making it clear that having sex has consequences. Contraceptives are not the difference between sexual activity and abstinence. They do not make teenage sex okay. But when people make bad choices, there's no question that using contraceptives is better than being infected with HIV or having an abortion.

Values and education are crucial. But once people know the facts, they need the tools to enable them to make smart choices. Contraceptives have to be available to all women in every part of the country. You don't need a prescription to buy condoms, and you shouldn't need one to buy most other contraceptives either. Most contraceptives today are no more dangerous than a slew of over-the-counter medicines. Contraception, including emergency contraception, should be moved from behind the pharmacist's counter.

The federal government must do its part to prevent unwanted pregnancies. Title X of the Public Health Service Act was passed to improve family planning at all income levels. Every year, the program provides more than five million people with abstinence counseling, contraceptives and educational services through a network of 4,600 clinics around the country. The federal Office of Family Planning estimates that the program helps women avoid more than a million unwanted pregnancies a year. Shamefully, Title X is underfunded. In inflation-adjusted dollars, it gets less than half the funding it did in 1980. We need to bring Title X funding in line with the 1980 level and peg it to inflation so it does not shrink again.

Medical insurers should be required to get on board with reducing abortions. All individual and group health plans should cover the costs of abstinence education courses and the costs of contraception, including emergency contraceptives. Families should be allowed to opt out of this coverage, in accordance with their religious beliefs.

Finally, there needs to be a sustained national media campaign to reduce unwanted pregnancy and the behavior that leads to it. Industrialized countries that have national media campaigns on this issue have teenage motherhood rates that are four to eight times lower than ours. We should take the best of their programs and use them here.

The media campaign, like all of the other solutions I've mentioned, would be about communicating values, such as responsibility and abstinence. This will, I'm sure, cause discomfort in some corners. It should not. Democrats have to become more comfortable with government leaders taking the role of the country's superego in certain limited areas related to broadly held values. Ideally, traditional transmitters of values, like family and church, are the superego, but religion is not as unified, or as universally heeded, as it once was, and for many, families are not as strong an influence as they once were. The commercial impulses of capitalism exacerbate the problem by pulling us away from the superego and toward the id.

In a democratic civil society, government leaders should not automatically refuse to take sides on important values questions. Being comfortable with the elected official's role as a *communicator* of certain widely held, nondivisive values need not mean expanding government's role as an *imposer* of values. Taking sides is not the same as criminalization or coercion, and communicating values is not the same as imposing them.

It's a distinction that I see reflected in the results of the Pew survey on abortion rights. And it's a distinction that I heard reflected at that luncheon twenty-five years ago.

If they were asked if they consider themselves pro-life or pro-choice, I can imagine how the Baileys would respond.

"Stupid question," they would snort. "We're both."

It's true. Like most Americans, the Baileys are torn. They respect life above all else, but they do not want anyone's personal morals, even their own, to dictate everyone else's choices. They believe morals are critical and they understand human weakness. Above all, they know that absolutes are almost never a good idea. They want us to expect the best from people and be prepared to deal with something less.

The good news is that most Democrats agree with the Baileys. The bad news? We have failed to communicate our values. Our failure jeopardizes abortion rights more than the right wing ever could. The best way to ensure every woman's right to a safe and legal abortion is to make it safe, legal and "rare."

CHAPTER 17

CUT CHILDREN'S ACCESS TO INTERNET PORNOGRAPHY BY AT LEAST 50%

☆ HOLD CREDIT CARD AND OTHER PAYMENT
PROCESSING COMPANIES ACCOUNTABLE FOR
SECURE AGE VERIFICATION FOR ADULT WEB
SITES.

☆ IMPOSE A 25% TAX ON PORNOGRAPHIC SITES
TO FUND REAL ENFORCEMENT OF AGE
VERIFICATION AND CAN-SPAM.

☆ CREATE A SCHUMER BOX FOR ALL CELL PHONE
AND ELECTRONIC MEDIA PLAYER CONTRACTS.

IN COLLEGE, I had a friend who was a radical. When I joined the Harvard Young Democrats, she scoffed. She did not believe in working within the system; she believed in working against it. While I was organizing letter-writing campaigns arguing against the war in Vietnam to members of Congress, she was at Walpole State Prison counseling inmates on how to run the prison when the guards went on strike.

Throughout college, we would argue all the time. Sometimes I felt like we talked for only two reasons: So she could yell at me about something I was doing or see the shock on my face when she told me about something she was doing.

From time to time, my phone would ring at 7 a.m. I would groggily answer.

"Chuck," I would hear through static. "I hitchhiked to North-field."

"You what?" I would scream.

"I'll be here a day or two. There's a poetry reading."

"Don't you have a test tomorrow?"

"I don't know. Maybe. Don't tell anyone, okay? 'Bye."

Now my old friend lives in the suburbs and has two great kids. But she is still more liberal than this old square. On many mornings I have come into my Senate office to find that she's sent me a newspaper clipping. I always hope it's an article from the local *Bee* about her life or her children or, heaven forbid, a piece about an issue I've been working on. But more often than not, I'll find an op-ed by Paul Krugman, an editorial from the *Nation* or a long academic treatise. The same note is always typed neatly at the top:

> *Chuck,*
> *DO SOMETHING ABOUT THIS!!!*
> *Hope you're well.*

Over the last couple of years, the subject of the clips has changed. She less often highlights concerns about the spotted owl or complains about violations of Title IX's gender-equity provisions. Now, one of her main causes is Internet pornography. You see, stopping the spread of pornography on the Internet has become her number one cause. Although she might not know it, for once my friend is on the same page as Joe and Eileen Bailey.

The Baileys use the Internet. Joe used it to research cars when the old Taurus finally gave out. Eileen keeps up with the kids' soccer schedules by e-mail. But the three Bailey kids spend a lot more time on the computer than either of their parents do. They send e-mails, they search the Web, they have MySpace profiles. Pete's face lights up when he finds a new Web page about magic tricks; Abby's friends from day camp stay in touch with a weekly online chat. Joe and Eileen encourage this—they know that having Internet skills will be critical as their kids get older—but it also makes them uneasy.

Because let's face it, for all the virtuous things the Internet has brought into our homes, it has also brought pornography.

The porn industry grosses roughly $12 billion per year—more than ABC, NBC and CBS combined. There are 420 million pages of Internet pornography on the Web. Nearly one out of every eight Web sites is pornographic! Today, the most frequent viewers of online pornography are kids between the ages of twelve and seventeen. The typical eleven-year-old has seen Internet pornography.

Of course, pornography has been around since people sketched figures in caves. When Joe Bailey was growing up, he probably had his first experience with it at the local malt shop. As he headed for the counter at the back of the store, he would cast a guilty glance at the dirty magazines partially shrouded on the top row of the magazine rack. Or when he was thirteen, maybe he raced through a tattered *Playboy* that a buddy found in the neighbor's trashcan.

Today, pornography has changed. With the click of a mouse, it is possible for children to be exposed to images that most adults a generation ago would not have seen throughout their whole lives. And these images are making their way into middle schools and high schools. More and more often, kids are imitating what they see.

We need to make it harder for kids to access pornographic sites. Today's blocking software is not good enough. Kids have a better chance of installing blocking software correctly—and then disabling it—than their parents do. In a lot of families, parents can't get blocking programs to work without their kids' help. The thin veil separating the Bailey children from the coarse and dark world of online porn is nothing more substantial than a simple Web search and the click of a mouse.

Iris and I learned just how big a problem online pornography is a few years ago, when we set up an AOL e-mail account for Jessica and Alison. I figured that our teenage girls would use their account to talk about homework or dissect the results of last week's CYO Basketball League game. I did have one concern—I told Iris they might use it to correspond with boys from school.

Iris laughed at me. "Yeah, Chuck, they might."

Jessica and Alison laughed at me. "Yeah, Dad, we might."

As often happens in our house, the women prevailed.

But before long, the inbox was full of notices about opportunities to invest in Nigerian oil wells, pitches about buying cheap prescription drugs (if only it were so easy!) and, to our horror, explicit advertisements for pornographic Web sites.

No one in our house had ever expressed interest in Nigerian energy futures, black-market pharmaceuticals or pornographic Web sites. All we had done was create an e-mail account that somehow got harvested by a spam e-mail ring. Through the Internet, pornography was creeping into our house. And there was nothing we could do to stop it.

That's when I started proposing legislation to do something about spam. In 2003, working with Senator Conrad Burns, Senator Ron Wyden and the Commerce Committee, we passed CAN-SPAM. CAN-SPAM is what we call the Controlling the Assault of Non-Solicited Pornography and Marketing Act—members of Congress have a weakness for acronyms.

CAN-SPAM makes it a crime to send unidentified commercial e-mails, requires clear identification of sexually explicit e-mail and mandates that all commercial e-mails have an opt-out reply option.

Mainly due to blocking software developed by e-mail providers, but partially because of CAN-SPAM, it's no longer the Wild West when it comes to spam. Quantifying the total volume of spam is difficult, but there's no question that many users have seen a marked decrease. Still, without better enforcement, the problem will not be solved.

But even more important than defeating spam is blocking kids' access to the porn sites themselves. As I've said, they're huge and they're everywhere. Their presence casts a shadow across the entire Internet. Teens know all about them and, too often, have no trouble gaining access to them.

The solution here must be smart. Many pornographers are shady, underground figures. They will happily go offshore rather than be held accountable for their sites' content. They won't cut down on kids' access to adult sites voluntarily or out of a sense of decency.

Porn purveyors, almost by definition, aren't worried about decency or discretion. They want money. If we can cut off their funding, we can force them to comply with the law, and in that way protect kids from their product.

Since porn companies often elude enforcement by going offshore and underground, we must focus on the involved parties who can't—

the credit card companies and Internet payment processing services. These are the lifelines that keep the shady world of Internet pornography afloat; the money collected by credit card companies and payment services is everything to pornographers. And, unlike Web site operators, MasterCard, Visa and American Express can't disappear. They can't go offshore.

And, unlike Web operators, they can be compelled to comply with the law.

A bill offered by Senator Blanche Lincoln of Arkansas would apply some much-needed regulation to this multibillion-dollar industry. Blanche is a wonderful mother and a wonderful senator. The Lincoln bill would hold credit card companies, banks and other Internet payment processing companies responsible for the money they collect on behalf of Internet pornographers.

It is counterproductive to regulate porn Web sites that operate within our borders but to, in effect, give carte blanche to those that go offshore. The Lincoln bill would allow us to regulate all pay pornography sites, no matter what shelter these sleazebags burrow into.

Credit card companies and payment services should be forbidden from processing transactions for any Web sites that do not comply with rules designed to make the Internet safe for children. The first rule is reliable age verification. All pornographic Web sites should require users to verify their age with a government-approved ID, such as a driver's license, that matches a credit card. The Web sites should also be required to use age-verification software that has no loopholes and has been approved by the Federal Trade Commission (FTC). Financial institutions would be allowed to take payments only for Web sites that complied. Those that didn't comply, or gave kids access to porn, would be fined an amount far more than the cost of doing business. This would significantly increase the barriers to entering a pornography site—instead of merely clicking "Yes, I am 18," perhaps dishonestly, unlawful entry would require full-fledged ID theft.

The second new regulation should be a 25% excise tax on the sale of Internet pornography. As with age-verification requirements, the onus would be on payment processors to collect these taxes. The money would be put in a trust fund and used to catch child pornographers and child predators, monitor age verification, develop better blocking software, show parents and teachers how to monitor children's online activity and truly enforce CAN-SPAM. CAN-SPAM has taught us that you need serious resources to enforce the law on the Internet. The trust fund would finally give the chronically underfunded FTC the resources it needs to track down international rings hell-bent on breaking the law.

The key here is put adult Web sites out of the reach of kids by holding financial institutions' feet to the fire. The credit card companies and payment processing services are making a significant profit through processing Internet porn. Unlike the porn providers, they are aboveground and can be forced to comply with the law. It is only fair to hold them accountable.

As with so many solutions in this book, rational enforcement to stop those who brazenly break the law is one part of the equation. Providing better information that will give the Baileys the tools they need to protect their kids and themselves is the other.

I have always believed that giving consumers more information is the key to making the market work. That's why I created the Schumer Box for credit cards—to make critical information accessible and clear. The Schumer Box pulls important fee and interest-rate information out of the small print and puts it in plain sight on every credit card contract. You used to need a corporate lawyer and a magnifying glass to know what you were getting into when you signed up for a new card. Joe and Eileen don't have the time or the money for that. But if they can see their options set out clearly, they will decide what works best for them. (See Chapter 15, Reduce Childhood Obesity by 50%, concerning a Surgeon General's warning I'd like to see on all junk food and fast food, for a related idea.)

We must give consumers the same easily accessible information on how to deal with pornography. Many parents don't realize it, but cell phones and other new gadgets also give kids access to the dark world of porn. Although CAN-SPAM made it illegal to send pornographic spam to cell phones, we must do more to stop it. Cell phone contracts should include an informational box that warns parents that their kids can access pornography and provides information on how to use blocking technology to prevent it. This requirement should apply to makers of portable entertainment devices like iPods, as well.

This sort of government intervention—prohibiting exploitative commercial activity and providing useful information to help people protect themselves—is exactly what the Baileys want. Joe and Eileen don't believe in overly restrictive regulation. If they were asked about it, they might say that they don't want all adult content to be banned; they would resent the government making their choices for them. But they want a government that can keep companies honest and that makes it easier to make informed choices. They also believe that kids don't, and shouldn't, have the same rights that adults do. When the government steps in to keep kids from accessing pornography, they applaud.

Right now, unless you're a computer expert, you have just two options: Give up the Internet or give in to its seedy underbelly. That's a choice that parents should not have to make.

For once, my old friend from college is not asking for something that's all that radical. All that she, and Joe and Eileen, need is tools that will let her control what comes into her living room. Targeted regulation, strong enforcement and clear disclosure will give us the tools we need to protect kids.

All while letting Pete Bailey find all the magic tricks a twenty-first-century kid could ever want.

CHAPTER 18

REDUCE TAX EVASION AND AVOIDANCE BY 50%

☆ RESTORE ENFORCEMENT LEVELS FOR HIGH
EARNERS AND CORPORATIONS.

☆ WITHHOLD 10% OF DIVIDEND AND CAPITAL
GAINS INCOME.

☆ INCREASE COMPLIANCE AMONG SOLE
PROPRIETORS AND THE SELF-EMPLOYED.

☆ CRACK DOWN ON ILLEGAL CORPORATE TAX
SHELTERS.

☆ REQUIRE CORPORATIONS TO REPORT PROFITS
CONSISTENTLY.

ASK JOE BAILEY, or any American, what's for sure in life and you know what they'll say.

"Death and taxes."

The two most dreaded, and seemingly inevitable, parts of life.

So far, death *is* inevitable. Technology hasn't solved that yet. But a whole lot of people have figured out how to avoid their taxes. About 15% of taxes owed are evaded or avoided. More than $300 billion a year in owed taxes go unpaid. Cutting tax evasion and avoidance by 50% could save $1.5 trillion over ten years. That's enough to pay for every project in this book, with money left over.

Put another way, the average tax return includes about $2,000 to make up the difference between those who pay the full amount they owe and those who don't. That's $2,000 a year that's in effect being stolen from regular people.

People like Joe and Eileen Bailey. The Baileys earn salaries from which taxes are withheld, they own a home and they have a few thousand dollars in mutual funds that send out 1099 worksheets at the end of the year. They take deductions for donations to the church charity, for their kids and, until they paid it off recently, for their mortgage payments. An audit would be a headache for them, and a waste of the IRS's money because they would come up as clean as could be.

It is not that the Baileys are naïve. They know that a lot of people evade taxes or figure out ways to avoid them. One reason they pay everything they owe is because of how hard it would be not to. Eileen's brother-in-law is a self-employed building contractor. They know that he shields his income from the government. They don't blame him personally.

But they do resent it—both his evasion and the system that allows it. The fact that they have to do their part when so many others—especially corporations, CEOs and huge investors—don't makes giving 30% of their hard-earned money to government a bitter pill to swallow. I'm not saying that April 15 would otherwise be a day of celebration (unless a refund would be coming), but if Joe and Eileen knew that everyone was paying what they should, they would blame Eileen's brother-in-law for shirking on his taxes, not the government for allowing him to. If it felt fair, their tax bill would not feel quite as hard to tolerate.

Before we raise taxes or put our country into even bigger debt, it is our responsibility to ensure that the taxes we do have in place reap what they should. Enforcement has to be smarter and it also has to be stronger. Senator Max Baucus has been the Senate's leading voice on this.

The IRS yields $4 for every $1 it spends on enforcement. That seems like a good investment. Yet the IRS's enforcement capacity has been cut by a whopping 25% over the last ten years. At $4 lost for every $1 saved, that's bad business, plain and simple.

The first step is to stop pretending that low and high earners are equally good targets for the IRS. In fact, in recent years it seems as if the IRS has believed that low earners are *better* targets. In 2005, those who made less than $25,000 a year were twice as likely to face an audit as those who made more than $1 million, because the IRS was obsessing about abuses of the Earned Income Tax Credit. The new IRS commissioner has claimed he will fix this, and there was some improvement last year. But this pattern illustrates that the government often gives the benefit of the doubt to the very wealthy while at the same time tending to come down hardest on those who make the least money. When you consider the potential benefits of enforcement of tax laws in different categories of earners, that doesn't make any sense.

Over the last few years, around 1% of high-income earners and corporations have been audited. Amazingly, that is only a third as many as were audited ten years ago. The IRS must, to quote *All the President's Men*, "follow the money" and refocus their enforcement efforts on high-revenue taxpayers.

The decline in enforcement has led to a marked increase in tax evasion and avoidance, because people believe they will not get caught if they cheat. This, in turn, has led to a dramatic decline in revenue—a cut in tax collection that has largely been ignored. While everyone knows that lowering tax rates for high earners has resulted in huge savings for the very rich, few realize that in terms of revenue, cutting enforcement actions against corporations and high earners has amounted to a massive tax cut, too.

This isn't an accident. It is consistent with economic royalists' true, though often obscured, ideology. It is a perfect example of their under-the-radar approach to their goals. The president can only lower taxes so much. So, in addition to the tax cuts he has passed, he has given his enormously wealthy allies another gift—pallid enforcement. This one does not garner headlines. It is a stealthy change that could well have as much effect as lowering the rates has. By weakening the IRS's enforcement mechanism, Bush has made the odds of an IRS audit of wealthy taxpayers so small that there is not enough punitive incentive for those taxpayers to pay exactly what they owe. We rely on the honor system, which works for most—though not all—taxpayers, wealthy and not.

It's particularly egregious to cut enforcement on high-income taxpayers at a time when wealth is increasingly agglomerating with that same group. It's as if the wealthiest Americans, even if they haven't asked for it, have gotten lucky. They've hit the trifecta: A larger share of the economy, lower taxes and lax enforcement. Of course, for the Baileys that translates into a one-two punch: Less money in their pocket and a government that is less able to respond to their needs. The consequences for our economy and our society are growing more and more severe.

Certainly, not every wealthy person is taking advantage of the trifecta; most don't avoid taxes. But the risk of an audit should be real enough to create a meaningful incentive for those high earners for whom the honor system isn't enough.

The resources for auditing these categories of taxpayers should be brought back to 1996 levels. In that year, there was a 3% chance of being audited, which is still low, but it would increase the incentive to comply. And, even a modest uptick in compliance among high-income earners and corporations would be a huge boon for the tax rolls.

Audits of high-income earners and corporations alone will not fill the tax gap. According to the National Taxpayer Advocate (NTA), the taxpayers' watchdog within the IRS, sole proprietors and the self-employed account for almost two-thirds of unpaid income and payroll taxes. Many in this category avoid taxes because they are not forced to declare payments their businesses receive and because those payments, which make up their income, are not subject to withholding. When the IRS requires payments to be reported, 96% of owed taxes get paid. When payments are subject to withholding, it's even better—99% of all owed taxes get paid.

To truly slash the tax gap, we need to expand reporting requirements and tax withholding for sole proprietors and the self-employed. The NTA has put a number of initiatives on the table—they include requiring companies who pay sole proprietors to withhold more frequently and mandating that large payments to sole proprietors be reported by both the provider and the recipient. Each of these actions should be considered by a new IRS office that would be dedicated to reducing underpayment in these categories. The office, similar to the "Cash Economy Program Office" suggested by the NTA, would have to meet clear tax gap reduction goals while minimizing any additional paperwork burdens.

Dividend income and capital gains should also be subject to expanded withholding. Investment companies and brokerage firms should be required to withhold 10% of all dividend payments and capital gains (only gains, not gross sales). By withholding 10%, which is less than the tax rate for investment income, losses incurred in any year will, in many cases, be offset. Any further losses could still be claimed on an investor's tax return for a refund. Withholding is not a penalty for investors any more than it is for Joe and Eileen Bailey. But it does work. And it's as fair for those who earn money through investment to be subject to withholding as it for salaried people like the Baileys. Under this system as well, every effort must be made to minimize bureaucratic and paperwork burdens.

Joe Bailey cares about cutting down on tax evasion and avoidance because he believes that today some taxpayers are getting away with murder. If you ask him who gets away with the most and pays the least, he'll tell you it is corporations. For Joe, the image of a multibillion dollar operation shielding all its profits in the Cayman Islands so that it pays less in taxes than he does is the enduring image of the system's injustice. Senator Byron Dorgan has repeatedly pointed this out. We can do more to hold corporations responsible for paying the taxes they owe. In 2004, the IRS formed an international task force to crack down on tax shelters. The task force includes Canada, Australia and the United Kingdom. That is a nice start, but we need to pressure other nations, particularly those Caribbean and Latin American nations that house the most egregious violators, to join. If they refuse to cooperate, we should cut the amount of aid we give them or impose trade penalties. If they will not help us collect the money due to us, we should stop providing free money to them.

Corporations do more than just rely on dubious tax shelters. Too many also play fast and loose in reporting their profits. They submit to the IRS one set of numbers that shows little or no profit and another to their shareholders that shows a huge profit. There are undoubtedly some instances in which this can be justified, but we must make sure it is not abused. Companies for which there is a significant difference between profits reported to shareholders and profits reported to the government should be required to explain it. The explanation should not just be submitted with companies' tax returns, as it is today, but also be made public to shareholders and online. When companies declare losses on the one hand and profits on the other, they should be accountable to the government and their shareholders. If they are forced to justify these differences, it will be much harder for them to avoid taxes.

Income taxes will never win a popularity contest. But when they are unfair, it makes them even harder to swallow; that's when the Baileys begin to reject them. When taxes are spent responsibly and administered fairly, the Baileys are willing to pay their share.

In an age when record-breaking deficits have become an annual tradition and there so many ways in which the middle class needs a little more help, the government has to figure out how to raise more money.

Over the next ten years, we may have to increase taxes for corporations and the highest-income individuals. But that would only be a second step. First, let's make sure that the system we have in place is being administered fairly. Before we raise taxes, we have to do a better job of collecting the taxes that already exist.

If we do, that's one increase in tax revenue that the Baileys might even like.

CHAPTER 19

INCREASE OUR ABILITY TO FIGHT TERRORISM BY 50%

☆ STRENGTHEN INTERNATIONAL ALLIANCES.

☆ EXPAND SPECIAL FORCES.

☆ INCREASE "HUMINT" CAPACITY.

☆ CREATE AN EFFECTIVE INTERNATIONAL FORCE TO STABILIZE HOT SPOTS.

☆ SECURE PORTS, BORDERS AND SKIES AND PREVENT BIO-, NUCLEAR AND CHEMICAL TERRORISM.

SEPTEMBER 11, 2001, was a beautiful day along the East Coast. It was one of those clear late-summer days that must have inspired the early settlers on our continent and provided a respite from their life of challenge and sacrifice.

On that morning I was in Washington, D.C., in the House of Representatives' gym. Even though I had been in the Senate for almost three years, I still worked out in the House gym. It has basketball courts, new equipment and enough TVs tuned to C-SPAN to ensure you can always get a good angle. In 1999, the Senate gym, reflecting the average age of our august body's membership, had a nice set of medicine balls.

Since then, Chris Dodd has done great work to get the Senate gym renovated, but I've stayed with the House. I am a creature of habit. Also, I like the location of my locker, just a couple down from where Tom Delay's was. Many times I postponed a shower to argue with the towel-clad then-majority leader; I was once even able to cajole tens of millions of dollars from him for New York.

On the morning of September 11th, as I was cooling off, reading the paper, Jerry Moran, a Republican from Kansas, screamed for me. "Chuck! The TV! Right away."

I ran over.

"It must have been a prop plane," someone said.

"Must have," others agreed.

"Bad accident," said the first. "No way the pilot survived."

I felt it more keenly than that. The largest office building in the largest city in my state had just been hit. But still, I thought it must have been a terrible accident—tragic for the pilots and their families, but nothing more global. I called my office. My staff agreed.

I hurried back to my locker and rushed to get dressed. I wanted to get to my office to monitor the accident. I continued to check the TV every few minutes. People were still speculating.

"I bet they lost pressure, like Payne Stewart."

"Too low for that."

"Props aren't pressurized."

"Some are. Maybe a heart attack?"

People considered the possibility. I checked the television.

And then the second plane hit. I saw it. It was no prop plane, but a large jetliner.

Someone gasped. We were silent. Fifteen politicians had lost their voice. It was clear that this was no accident. These were no prop planes. America was under attack.

I watched the screen. My mind was racing. How many people work there? Nearly 50,000. About 25,000 in each. What time is it? Just after 9:00. Early. But lots of traders—early days. What floors were hit? Above the seventieth in both. People per floor? 25,000 into 110. About 225. How long to evacuate? A minute a floor. Okay, an hour and a half or two.

Then, an alarm went off in my head: Jessica. My oldest daughter Jessica was a senior at Stuyvesant High School. Stuy is in Battery Park City, just across West Street and couple of blocks north of the World Trade Center.

But how far, I thought. How far exactly?

I ran for my locker. Got my phone.

Iris's cell was not working. I tried her office. It rang forever. Finally, she answered. "How are you?" I asked. Her office was also in Lower Manhattan, less than half a mile from the World Trade Center.

"I'm fine. I'm on with City Hall." My wife had been commissioner of the New York City Department of Transportation for exactly a year.

"Alison?"

"Called her school. They're letting them go home."

"Good. And Jessica?" I waited.

"No word," she said. "I'll call you back."

I went back to the television. The group had grown. Gym employees now stood with the congressmen. People were dumbstruck, watching the unimaginable. I have to get to my office, I thought.

I was in the car, rushing to my office, when Iris called back. She began talking as soon as I answered. "The mayor's sure it's an attack. Stuy's evacuating."

"How far is it? Stuyvesant. From the towers?" I took a breath. "If they fall." Surreal words to speak out loud.

"A few blocks. Let me see." She went to her wall map. "How tall are they?"

A hundred and seven stories. I knew, because we had been married at Windows on the World, at the top of the North Tower. "About 1,300 feet. How long is a block?"

"Two hundred and fifty feet, a little more."

I considered. "So is Stuyvesant more or less than five blocks away?"

"Hard to say. Just about four. Or five. All the blocks are screwy down here."

"Go find her," I said. "But be careful."

"You too."

I hung up and looked out the car window as we crawled through the D.C. traffic. The day was so clear. Everything was so calm.

Then I saw it. Another plane. Low and fast. I saw it going down. Then a flash of light. An explosion. It was silent at first—like a fastball to a catcher's mitt. In a moment, it reached me—a low growl of thunder across the Potomac. Then a broad band of smoke staining the blue sky. From the vicinity of the Pentagon.

This is it, I thought. World War III.

At the office, everyone was sure there were more planes coming. We got word that six more had been hijacked. Not World War III, but an attack beyond imagination.

Then, an alarm went off and a voice crackled over the PA system. The entire Capitol complex was suddenly being evacuated. We began to exit calmly. A rumor shot through the crowd. The Capitol was next.

There were screams and sobs. People sprinted for the exits. Every one of us was scared. Once we were outside, the staff reconvened. With my office off limits, we headed to my little apartment.

My apartment, which feels stuffy when all four roommates are there, was cramped and hot. The staff crowded around the small TV in the living room. Many of them were in shock; some were terrified. But on the whole, they were calm and focused, ready to do whatever was needed. It was a horrible experience, but I was proud to be with them. Frustratingly, that morning there was not much we could do but watch.

I was on the phone constantly. Talking to city, state and federal officials, staff and, of course, Iris. Cell phones were barely working, so between meetings with the mayor and local agencies, she would call. The apartment only has one phone line; half the time no one could get through.

As the minutes and then hours added up, we grew increasingly panicked. Jessica still couldn't be found. We got word that her class had successfully evacuated. She was not with them.

Around noon the president reached me from an undisclosed location. He promised to help New York. It's a promise he repeated two days later in the Oval Office, when I asked for $20 billion to help us recover. To his credit, and to New York's everlasting benefit, it is a promise he kept.

I thanked the president and told him I had to get home, to be in New York. "You'll fly with Big Country," he offered, referring to FEMA director Joe Allbaugh. The next day, Senator Clinton and I flew up in a FEMA plane with Allbaugh. We were escorted by fighter jets and helicopters. On that trip, and throughout the next months, I liked Allbaugh. With me, he always shot straight.

Finally, at around one o'clock, my phone rang. It was Iris.

"We found her," she said.

"Is she okay?"

"Perfect." I could hear tears in her voice.

I choked up, too. "Thank God," I whispered.

It turns out that Jessica, always a kind heart, had been on the ninth floor of Stuyvesant. When the evacuation began, she stayed behind to help an elderly teacher down the nine stories. The delay had separated her from her class. In the chaos outside, she had not been able to reconnect with them for those four hours.

When Iris finished the story, I was silent for a minute. I stopped pacing the kitchenette and leaned back against the fridge. I was proud of Jessica, but not yet calm. I took a deep breath. What about the thousands of Jessicas who were still missing—and the anguish of their families?

"We've got work to do," I said. "I've got to get home."

There are millions of stories from 9/11. Some are like mine, some are different. Every American has one. For the rest of our lives, we will all remember exactly what happened to us, and to our families, that day.

Individual experiences of the day are too specific for me to speculate about what might have happened to the Bailey family. What I do know is that many of those in the World Trade Center were from places like Massapequa. They were from Hicksville and Mineola and Islip, from Staten Island and the Bronx and Northern Jersey and Rockland County.

Many of the victims, not only those from the New York area, but those from Washington and Boston and Los Angeles and San Francisco, were like the Baileys in other ways. They were hardworking, middle-class people. Day traders, business travelers, restaurant workers, civil servants, flight attendants. Cops. Firefighters.

The twin towers and the Pentagon were chosen by Osama bin Laden and his evil band of fanatics for their monumental significance. They thought that attacking our symbols of capitalist and military would hurt America. But it wasn't the collapse of the towers or the damage to the Pentagon that hurt most. It was the attack on all those hardworking people, people like Joe and Eileen Bailey, that really shook our foundation. Without knowing it, they hit the heart of America.

Al Qaeda cannot understand this. For them, life is a power struggle. A jihadist battle waged for admittance to an elusive paradise. They don't understand that America's strength, our greatest monument, is the quiet heroism of regular people living regular lives. Moments shared with family and friends. A hard day's work. A weekend barbecue.

Joe and Eileen knew that their way of life, their daily life, was under attack for the first time since the end of World War II. Immediately, the only political characteristic that mattered to them was the ability to protect them and their families. Because without that protection, nothing else matters.

In the period after the cold war ended and before September 11th, national security was not a primary concern for Joe and Eileen. In the absence of the looming threat of the Soviets, the government's national security policies lost relevance—with or without government action, the Bailey children went to bed safe and secure. Just as the drop in crime pushed law and order out of the Baileys' top five most important issues, the absence of a clear antagonist took national security off the checklist of critical government functions. But 9/11 changed that. For the first time in a decade, Joe and Eileen sought the government's help and demanded its protection.

Protecting our country in today's world poses new challenges. Technology has empowered small groups of bad people, and for the first time in history they can hurt us right in our heartland. Al Qaeda was the first to discover this, but others will follow. In the future, others could follow.

After 9/11, Joe and Eileen Bailey, like the rest of the country, were unified behind the president. Their reflexive reaction was to stick with him in the war on terror. This instinct persisted over the next few years, through the 2004 election. The Baileys heard the Democrats' criticisms of the president, and sometimes they agreed with them. But they were still inclined to give the president the benefit of the doubt.

"The president's not perfect," they thought. "But at least he's trying. What would you do?"

The fact of the matter is that many Democrats have not expressed a clear vision for what should be done in the war on terror. Democrats' answers to the big questions—when would we use military strength, how much strength would we use, what would we do to disrupt terror networks—are not clear to the American people. Many think Bush and the Republicans tend to use the military too quickly. But they think Democrats wouldn't use it quickly enough. When faced with the choice, all other things being equal, they're more likely to choose Republicans.

A lot of members of my party ignore this point. Instead, they insist that we are the victims of our own complexity, a superior spin machine or both. A colleague brought this up to me a couple of years ago.

Ted Kennedy and I were in the Democratic cloakroom, an area off the Senate floor where senators relax and socialize. The cloakroom is a little like the teacher's lounge in a high school, except the food's free. Many of our country's most important decisions have been hammered out in that room.

Senator Kennedy and I were watching a Red Sox–Yankees game. This was before the Red Sox broke their streak, so I was ribbing my mentor a little. A colleague approached us. "Popcorn?" I offered.

"Chuck," said the colleague, ignoring my offer, "you're good with the press."

Kennedy guffawed, "Ayah, that he is."

"Not as good as Jeter at the plate," I shot back.

"We'll see about that," Kennedy stood and turned to go. "I have to vote. Pedro'll take care of you."

The colleague in question was not interested in baseball, but sat down anyway. "So tell me, why don't they trust us on foreign policy?"

"Us?" I asked.

"Democrats."

"They?"

"The press. The people."

I paused and considered. Jeter got a hit. I looked at my colleague. "I'm not sure they should," I said.

"Of course they should! The problem is that our positions are too complex. They can't be packaged as slickly, expressed as cleverly. People don't take the time to understand. That's why they don't trust us!"

That's the U.S. Senate for you. If a senator asks you a question, more often than not, that same senator will give you the answer.

Still, my colleague was partially right. Joe Bailey didn't lose faith in the Democrats while reading *Foreign Affairs* or weighing the comparative advantages of bilateral versus multilateral negotiation with North Korea.

On the other hand, he wasn't tricked by clever phrasing and slick packaging, either. He listened to each party's rhetoric, assessed its priorities and reacted to its ideas. In his gut, he *knew* whom he felt comfortable with. Even in the 2006 elections, with all of Bush's mistakes in Iraq, exit polls showed that the American people still trusted the Republican Party more to "make the U.S. safer from terrorism."

Gut reactions are easy to dismiss. I often don't like it when leaders invoke their gut to justify complicated public policy. But you know what? In my thirty years in politics, I've found that Joe Bailey's belly is a better barometer of political credibility and coherence than a ten-thousand-word article in *Foreign Affairs* ever could be.

For the first few years after 9/11, the president passed the belly check. The Baileys saw that Bush understood what the attacks meant and was determined to defeat our attackers. Now, because of the president's failures in Iraq, the Baileys have become disillusioned. They know that the president was neither straight nor competent in entering and fighting that war. They can see that there is no plan.

But this has not sent them running for cover under the big Democratic tent when it comes to fighting terrorism. They are disillusioned with Bush's incompetence and dishonesty, not with the general vision he laid out describing how to defend our country in the war on terror. Despite Bush's mistakes, they still believe in American strength. But unlike Bush, they understand that we need smarts too. In 2006, they voted for Democratic congressional candidates to send Republicans that message. But that alone will not give them faith in 2008 or beyond that Democrats are willing enough to use strength. Their natural inclination is still to support Republicans, Iraq aside, regarding foreign policy and terrorism (as the 2006 exit polls showed).

The truth is that Democrats and Republicans are much closer together on the use of strength than the public thinks. When we were attacked by al Qaeda, which was being shielded in Taliban-controlled Afghanistan, every Senate Democrat voted to authorize the use of force. The constant suggestion that we are against strength is false.

But the claim has credibility because it's true that we have not enunciated a clear vision; the fact that we're not weak doesn't mean that our position is strong. As the foreign policy discussion has shifted to Iraq, Democrats have correctly focused on mistakes that have been made there and on other errors in foreign policy. But we have not focused enough on our own clear vision of how to fight the war on terror. Until we do, Republicans will have no trouble pinning the security monkey to our back.

Democrats must agree, and must make clear, that we would never wait for enemies to attack us. The consequences of inaction are too severe. It used to be that there were only a few countries on earth powerful enough mount an attack on our homeland. Today, many small groups potentially have that same awful ability. If there's a threat, we must be proactive—the risks of waiting are too high.

Most Americans believe that there is a high likelihood that terrorists will be able to strike us again—even after we are out of Iraq, even after al Qaeda is defanged—and I agree. It's the reason that we as a nation, and the Democratic Party, must have a strong, realistic and farsighted foreign policy.

For a time, Bush was using President Harry Truman against us. He has made it a habit to link himself to Truman in foreign policy speeches. As far as I'm concerned, it's blasphemy. It's true that Truman presided during a period very similar to this one, when the tectonic plates of foreign policy were shifting dramatically. But unlike Bush, Truman understood the wisdom of strategic alliances and deterrence, as well as unilateral action. In Truman's day, we had just defeated the Nazis and the Japanese. Most Americans just wanted to come home and enjoy the fruits of victory. But almost immediately, it was clear that we faced the great Soviet monolith. Truman did not start another world war. He created alliances to contain the Soviet Union—alliances that eventually helped to bring it down. On Truman's watch,

America took the lead to create NATO, the United Nations, the International Monetary Fund, the World Bank and the Marshall Plan. He also implemented George Kennan's doctrine of containment to deter the spread of communism. And, when there was a need for direct, proactive action, he did not shy away from it; he deployed the military in Greece and Korea. He ordered airlifts into Berlin.

When faced with doubt, it would be wise for Democrats to do as Truman did. Where Republicans' guiding principles are preemptive war and going it alone, Democrats should focus on a Trumanesque synthesis of aggressive deterrence, strategic alliances, targeted strikes and, as a last resort when necessary, the use of all-out force.

First, we will never foreclose preemptive war, but we will consider it in the context of a wider array of possible responses. Republican preemption, as advocated by Dick Cheney, falls into an "attack first, ask questions later" trap. It is based on the belief that the only way to avert disaster is through high-stakes, large-scale war. Tough diplomacy and negotiation, economic sanctions, highly targeted military action and the threat of large-scale attack must all be employed—whenever possible in the order given—with all options always being kept on the table.

Second, we must never forget that terrorism is the primary threat to our security. And terrorism is most likely to emanate from small rogue groups, not from nations. We must keep our eye on the ball and focus on the dangerous groups. When the administration directs its energy toward grander, more diffuse issues—Islamic fascism, democratization—it spreads our resources, military and otherwise, too thin. Certainly, we should stand up for democracy and against intolerance. But for us to expend military resources to correct these wrongs when the number one threat to our nation is terrorism is a strategic mistake. We don't like the leaders of Venezuela, Cuba, Zimbabwe, Belarus or a host of other nations, and for good reason. But over-deploying finite diplomatic, economic and military resources against them—which inevitably means not doing all we can to fight terrorism—does not serve the vital security interests of the United States in 2007.

North Korea and Iran are more critical cases, not because they are two of the many human rights–abusing regimes around the globe, but because they have, or are on the path to developing, nuclear weapons. Their nuclear capability is unlikely to pose a direct threat to us—MAD (mutual assured destruction) even works against madmen. The greater danger is that one of the countries could supply weapons to shadowy terrorist groups who would not hesitate to use them against us. Meaningful action against North Korea and Iran, beginning with tough international sanctions, is required. But presently, we are stymied because of this administration's reliance on unilateralism (see "Build Stronger Alliances," on page 248).

As for Iraq, the administration's policy has clearly failed. The idealistic goal of bringing democracy to Iraq is proving impossible to implement. The war in Iraq has devolved into a civil war: It is clear that Sunnis, Shiites and Kurds hate each other more than they like the idea of any democratic central government. Furthermore, the goal of democracy building in Iraq never withstood the test of consistency. Why did we invade Iraq but not other equally cruel dictatorships? Would we eventually send troops to all of them? The weapons of mass destruction argument, which would have been legitimate if there had been a real likelihood that Saddam would have passed WMDs on to terrorists, proved to be exaggerated at best, and fabricated at worst.

Many of us, myself included, voted for the war because we believed that in a time of terrorism, when our country had been attacked, it was appropriate to give the chief executive a degree of latitude. The administration's argument at the time, as articulated to us by Secretary of State Colin Powell, was reasonable: The ability to initiate a multilateral show of force, supported by the family of nations (still possible at the time we voted), against a hostile regime that had shown sympathy to terrorists was an appropriate level of latitude to allow the president.

Today, I still believe that when our country is under attack, the chief executive deserves a degree of latitude. If, God forbid, we were attacked again, I could well vote to give it to a future president, Democrat or Republican. But given the administration's record—they have played fast and loose with the facts, failed to protect our troops and displayed a fundamental incompetence—I can't imagine ever again giving *this* president the same latitude. I also believe that if Democrats had controlled Congress, we would have operated with greater oversight and served as a more significant check on executive power.

So, Iraq has clearly become a diversion from the war on terror. The military solution, as of this writing, seems best contained in the Senate resolution crafted by Carl Levin and Jack Reed, a measure that I joined most Democrats in voting for. Under it, we would make 2007 a year of transition in Iraq. We would stop policing the civil war and significantly reduce the number of our troops in harm's way, both within and outside the country's borders. Our military effort in Iraq should redirect its focus toward four missions: Counterterrorism, to combat the only real danger we face; force protection, to greatly reduce U.S. casualties; the training of Iraqi security forces and logistics support, which together will increase the Iraqi government's ability to control the nation.

As we make 2007 a year of transition and redeployment militarily, we must also determine how Iraq can best govern itself in a lasting, stable way. One solution is to tell the Iraqis that if they can't govern themselves, we're leaving. As Senator Levin has suggested, as long as they know we're staying, they will never take on the responsibility themselves. If they know we won't stay indefinitely, they may well. For this to work, other countries, including Middle Eastern countries, will have to be part of a diplomatic solution to help maintain stability and avoid untoward outside meddling in the country. Another solution is the tripartite solution, which has been advocated by Les Gelb and Senator Biden. Because the Sunnis, the Shiites and the Kurds hate each other so much, the hope for a successful central government is dim. Instead, each group should be allowed to govern its own semiautonomous region. The Shiite and Kurdish regions, the oil-rich portions of the country, would give some reasonable compensation to the Sunnis annually. As with the Levin solution, under this one, the surrounding Middle Eastern countries would have to support this solution and desist from untoward meddling. Whichever direction we choose, the solution should be fully implemented by 2008—by which time the number of American troops in harm's way must be greatly reduced.*

The fundamental strategic flaw in the administration's Iraq policy has been to insist that unilateral military action serves us well.

*The Baker–Hamilton report, which, as of this writing, has not been issued, may endorse one of these solutions or present another; it will, I'm sure, be closely watched.

Joe Bailey was a full-throttled supporter of such policies when President Bush first pursued them. Eileen was also a supporter, though she was perhaps a bit more skeptical. But, given the casualties and the serious mistakes in Iraq, today Joe and Eileen understand, with some degree of chagrin, that our policy must change in a fundamental way.

The Baileys, and millions of Americans like them, want us to continue to protect America from terrorism with every atom of our being. But Iraq has engendered a new awareness that while strength is necessary, it is hardly sufficient. To be successful, they understand that we will need both strength and smarts. Bush's failure in Iraq creates a unique window of opportunity; millions of Americans like Joe and Eileen are much more open to Democratic solutions than they were six months ago. At this moment, it is possible to create a new, more successful paradigm in the fight against terrorism.

In short, the Democratic vision to fight terrorism should have three pillars: First, the war on terror should be focused on terrorism, not on ancillary goals. Second, while it should always be on the table, unilateral military action must be the last, not the first, resort. Third, while American resources must always be available, they must also always be used carefully, because they are precious and finite.

It is impossible to fully describe the implications of these pillars in the abstract, beyond making platitudinous exhortations (to say we'll use force when America is threatened is true, but not specific enough). On the other hand, it is possible to talk about policies that support your principles and illustrate your view of strength and smarts. That's what I've tried to do below.

Like all the ideas in this book, these proposals are not the be-all and end-all. Rather, they are concrete changes that will help show the Baileys that when it comes to strength and smarts, Democrats have the will and the way.

Build Stronger Alliances

In Brooklyn, the biggest guy in the schoolyard could out-brawl anyone head to head. If he got angry, everyone would run. But that alone was never enough to put him in charge.

The big guys who didn't make friends had a miserable time of it. They'd be in fights all the time; a group of not-quite-the-biggest kids would inevitably challenge the biggest guy's dominance. He would always win, but sometimes he'd get pretty badly bruised. Also, we twelve-year-olds generally agreed that the normal code— no ganging up—didn't apply to him. If a couple of kids wanted to jump him after school, no one would think twice about it.

On the other hand, when the biggest guy made friends—when he protected the regular kids from the not-quite-the-biggest kids and the not-quite-the-biggest-kids from each other—he did great. He could set the schoolyard rules. He never had to defend his position, because no one dared challenge it. If they did, they'd have to answer to every kid in the neighborhood. In Brooklyn, the biggest guy always had a choice to make. He could be isolated and always on edge, or he could be in charge.

In a world where small numbers of bad people can do severe damage, it is very hard for any single country, even a vastly powerful one, to defeat terrorists alone. International cooperation and support are needed to deprive them of safe havens, funding and weaponry. Though Israel is no bully, last summer's battle in Lebanon between Israel and Hezbollah is an illustration of the limits of great military power against heartless terrorists. Despite Israel's overwhelming military advantage, it was not able to score a victory. Every night, from the beginning of the conflict to the end, Hezbollah indiscriminately lobbed rockets into civilian population centers. The solution required the cooperation of Lebanon and an international force. As of this writing, it's not clear how well this solution will work. Either way, it will prove the importance of alliances—even those that might be only temporary. Israel is depending on other countries, some of whom are not very friendly, to help it deal with Hezbollah. In the eyes of Israel's military leaders, a full-scale invasion and occupation would have been far more costly and, in the long run, probably more debilitating.

Even when we need to use military force, it's much better to do it with international cooperation. We have the largest and strongest military in the world, but because we're essentially in Iraq alone, our ability to do anything anywhere else is hampered. If Iraq had been a truly international venture, we would have had much more flexibility to deal with Iran, North Korea and other gathering storms. When you are fighting terrorist groups that are more diffuse and more elusive, international cooperation is critical.

In addition, without strong alliances, our military is the only factor in the conversation. With strong alliances, not only is the threat of military force more credible, there are also increased nonmilitary options. When dealing with countries like Iran and North Korea, that's critical. Both countries know that a large-scale invasion is unlikely. They have made it clear that any major action will be countered with a horrific attack on one of our closest allies—Israel and South Korea, respectively. Strong alliances would make it a lot easier to neutralize the threat. In both cases, economic sanctions could forestall progress in their nuclear weapons programs and bring their blustery leaders to their knees. In North Korea, we would need China's complete commitment. In Iran, while we would need much of the world, Russia and France would be particularly critical. Unless we start to rebuild alliances, our options are to lose control by passing the lead to the UN, risk Tel Aviv or Seoul by attacking the countries unilaterally or do nothing but talk.

Not a great set of choices.

Alliances can be a headache. Building them requires a painstaking effort. Inevitably, they don't come for free—no strong alliance has ever been built without compromise. Look, everyone knows that the UN can be shamefully hypocritical and is often a bureaucratic nightmare to boot. The International Criminal Court can be almost as bad. The Kyoto Protocol is not as forceful as it should be and gives seemingly unfair advantages to developing nations like China and India. But the fact is, we might have to work within some of these international structures to build the alliances we need. Unfortunately, the alternatives are worse.

It's not just people like Harry Truman and Joe Biden who could see the value in strong alliances; our enemies see their value, too. Over the last year, our most hostile antagonists have been warming up to each other at an alarming rate. As we have weakened our international relationships, they have strengthened theirs. It is increasingly clear that a host of world leaders from Venezuela to Iran see a strategic advantage in allying with other antagonists—including some terrorist organizations—against our interests. If we had more positive relationships around the world, it would be much harder for these leaders to gain relevance. By alienating so much of the world, we have turned mice into tigers, or at least into barking dogs.

We must rebuild our alliances. The painstaking and sometimes painful diplomatic work to create enduring relationships is critical. As we do it, some things won't be on the table. We will not allow our military to fight under another flag. We will not allow American soldiers to be prosecuted elsewhere for their actions in service to our country. We will not negotiate with terrorists. But there are some compromises we must be open to, including considering a more accommodating stance on the UN and Kyoto, as well as working with countries to bolster other international structures.

The Baileys probably have even less faith in international structures than I do. But they know how life works. They know that small compromises sometimes produce big gains. They have been in the schoolyard. They know that it doesn't matter how big you are if you don't have any friends.

They may not like the compromises that come with alliances, but as long as they see the results, they will accept them. Our allies must ease the burden on American soldiers. They must demonstrably help to defuse international crises. They must step up themselves, not just call on us to do so. Above all, they must help us in the fight against terrorism, wherever it might appear.

Expand Special Forces

As of 2006, there were an estimated 53,000 Special Forces military personnel in the armed services. In a military that is well more than a million strong, that translates to a tiny percentage of our force strength.

This is because our military was designed to fight a land war against the Soviets, not target isolated terror cells and destabilize rogue states. We spent the forty-plus years of the cold war building infantry, airpower and massive weapons. They were the tools of containment and deterrence. And they worked.

But these tools are not effective against the new threats we face. Traditional infantry is not trained to identify and eliminate small bands of terrorists. As we learned in the 1990s, airpower alone does not do the job. And no one supports dropping a thirty-megaton nuclear bomb on a terrorist training camp.

The tools of the cold war also limit our hand in dealing with rogue states that harbor terrorists. They give us only three options: occupy, obliterate or do nothing.

Army Rangers, Navy Seals and other elite Special Forces are designed to respond to modern threats. They are teams of soldiers that can get in, strike and get out quickly. They are agile, adaptive and adept at going after small groups of terrorists without a long, debilitating occupation. They can surgically deal with a problem without requiring a major invasion or an occupying force; they excel at excising cancers, not treating the whole body. Thanks to new technology, Special Forces now carry massive firepower and communications capacity. Had more been on tap and ready to be deployed aggressively before 2001, we might well have been able to take out bin Laden before he struck the twin towers.

But don't take my word for it. The Hart–Rudman Commission, which wrote a well-respected report on terrorism, lists five capabilities that the military needs in the twenty-first century. Special Forces (the report uses the term "expeditionary capabilities") were at the top of the list. "The Defense Department should devote its *highest priority* to improving and further developing its expeditionary capabilities." (The emphasis is mine.)

This report was not released after we invaded Iraq. It was not released in response to 9/11. It was released in *February 2001*. I do not agree with all of Hart–Rudman's conclusions. But its strongest findings—poor preparation for terrorist attacks, disorganized homeland security functions—were prescient. Six years later, it is high time to get moving.

The military has acknowledged that we need more Special Forces. But, like many entrenched bureaucracies, it has been too slow and timid in effecting its transformation. The Marines have been considering creating their own Special Forces. They should do so immediately. The Army and Navy likewise must move quickly to increase their Special Forces and direct support units.

Within five years, the military should double the number of Special Forces and make it clear to countries that harbor terrorists that we will use our Special Forces to go after those terrorists, even if it means piercing those countries' borders. This will require the creation of a new doctrine, with clear guidelines, which does not entirely fit into conventional diplomatic mores. Too bad—neither do terrorists or those who harbor them.

The expansion of our Special Forces must not happen at the expense of our National Guard and reservists, who are already stretched to the breaking point. Instead, we should pay for it by cleaning out the cold war closet, retiring weapons systems that we will never use and eliminating funding for military projects that have absolutely no merit other than being built in a congressional district that is home to a powerful representative. Too much of the defense budget is simply pork—and both parties feed at the trough.

To former Secretary of Defense Donald Rumsfeld's credit, he saw that modernizing, and cleaning out the closet to pay for it, was critical. Unfortunately, he was unable to get it done. For us to change the system will require a herculean and bipartisan effort. The parties must come together and set reasonable limits for defense appropriations. Republicans and Democrats must pledge to follow our mutually agreed-upon guidelines, even when congressional majorities flip. Though we will cut anachronistic systems and pork, we will not touch the weapons we need to defend our nation.

We cannot depend on relics of the cold war to protect us in the new world. A military with fewer weapons systems designed to destroy the Soviet Union and more Special Forces designed to eliminate terrorists and madmen is the best defense we could have.

Increase "Humint"

To illustrate the value of human intelligence, or "humint," there's a story I like to tell. It may be apocryphal, but it's useful nonetheless.

In late 2001 or early 2002 in an undisclosed location somewhere along the vast border between Afghanistan and Pakistan, in the mountains near Tora Bora, Osama bin Laden turned on his phone. U.S. "sigint" (signals intelligence) analysts had been waiting for this moment—he had stopped regularly using his phone years earlier. They had used sophisticated tracking programs to identify the al

Qaeda leader's satellite phone and hook into his network. All they needed was this one act of carelessness. Within seconds, bin Laden's location was being sent to our commanders in the field.

Plans for a coordinated assault had been drafted weeks earlier. With precision, elite members of our armed forces sprang into action. Their repeated drills paid off. The operation went off without a hitch; our military once again proved that it is the best in the world.

There was only one problem. Bin Laden was not the one that had turned on the phone. He had passed it off to an associate sometime earlier. We don't know when. Osama bin Laden was actually hundreds of miles away, tucked securely in a cave. We had been tricked.

The sigint analysts who so patiently and persistently tracked bin Laden should not be blamed. They had no way of knowing who was holding the phone. They did not know bin Laden's plans. After all, that's not their job. There was no human intelligence on the ground to tell sigint that bin Laden had given his phone to an associate!

Over the last sixty years, we have built the most extensive electronic surveillance system in the world. There is no spot on the surface of the earth that is beyond the reach of our spy satellites. We can intercept virtually every telephone call, e-mail or fax sent by anyone anywhere.

But we now know that this is not enough. Without human beings on the ground, the ability to utilize our electronic capacity is limited. Covert operatives—undercover agents, spies, moles—are what infuse the intelligence into electronic surveillance.

Covert intelligence gathering is dangerous, messy and dirty work. In the 1990s, the intelligence community made the mistake of trying to avoid it. During that decade, the CIA's human capacity shrank by close to 25%. In 1995, the agency implemented guidelines that restricted the gathering of intelligence from "unsavory" sources.

The guidelines were written in response to a single case. A colonel in the Guatemalan military had killed a number of innocent civilians, including at least one American, but had been kept on the

CIA payroll despite the tragedy. That one screwup is why we backed off on human intelligence. It was a tragedy, to be sure, but it alone did not justify giving up on human intelligence gathering.

This is what I call a blame-game victory. If a hundred things go right and one goes wrong, special interests and the media start playing the blame game. It starts with the search for villains and does not end until policies have been changed. Too often, once the blame game starts, no one pushes back. The blame game almost always wins.

It is too bad that Joe and Eileen Bailey don't get a say when the blame game begins. If they did, they might inject a little sanity into the hysteria. As with so much else, they understand reality better than politicians or pundits or reporters. They know that sometimes, when you are trying to achieve a goal, mistakes do happen. They know that no matter which party is in power, no matter what policy is followed, no matter what rhetoric we all use, it will happen. Had Joe and Eileen been in the room after the humint screwup, they would not have indulged in the blame game, gutted the human intelligence program or weakened America. They would have agreed it was a tragic mistake and demanded a constructive response. Then they would have moved on.

Since 2001, the 1995 guidelines have been scrapped. CIA director George Tenet, Senator Jay Rockefeller and others since have tried to rebuild our humint capacity. But the lost years are crucial. In some cases, we threw away decades of work. In others, we have not fully recovered from the mindset of the late 1990s.

Electronic intelligence is necessary, but it is not sufficient. Many of the intelligence failures of the last ten years were not failures of electronic surveillance. They were the inevitable failures of drastically scaled-back human intelligence. Until we get serious about increasing our capacity to gather human intelligence, all the talk of electronic surveillance is a distraction.

The strike forces discussed above depend on top-notch intelligence to be successful. For them to be able to strike quickly and ferociously at a terrorist group hundreds of miles inside a nation's border, they must know where the group is and how capable it is of defending itself. Most important, they must know the how, when and why of any plans the group might have to attack us. Without the best intelligence, often provided by humint, the effectiveness of strike forces is diminished. Strike forces, signals intelligence and human intelligence are necessary; none alone is sufficient.

Therefore, we need to double the number of intelligence agents on foreign soil. The goal should be to infiltrate every terrorist organization or cell in the world within ten years. In cases where American operatives cannot gain access, we need to aggressively cultivate foreign sources—even if they are "unsavory."

We also need to make sure that we have enough translators and analysts to make our intelligence matter. Translators are the pipeline that connects those who gather intelligence, human or electronic, and those who analyze it. When the pipeline gets backed up, it does not matter what we have collected. The data just sit there. If intelligence data is not ingested quickly, it goes bad.

We have to recruit linguists more aggressively. We should beef up our investment in recruitment campaigns in relevant communities across the country. In addition to being a source of linguists, outreach in these communities will go a long way toward proving that our war is with terrorists, not with any religion or nationality.

Finally, we should begin a program for linguists that is similar to the ROTC, the Reserve Officers' Training Corps. Entering college students would be invited to apply to the program. Those accepted would take language classes and spend their summers working at appropriate government agencies. At the end of college, they would be required to serve for three years at an intelligence agency. In exchange, those who participated would receive scholarships and reductions in their loan pay-back amounts.

International Force to Stabilize Hot Spots

Terrorism is born in the twisted minds of power-hungry zealots. But it is incubated in the remote corners of failing nations and rogue states. It is not our duty or in our power to send U.S. troops to police or subdue every international hot spot. Unilateral action by the United States should be limited to immediate threats to national security and rarely used.

However, stabilizing potentially dangerous hot spots is no longer simply a question of moral imperative. In a world tied together ever more closely by transportation and communications, there is a national security imperative as well. In the past, conflicts in East Africa or the South Pacific were unlikely to have a practical effect in the United States, but no more. Today, HIV, Ebola, instability and other crises in the developing world—in addition to terrorism—pose a direct danger to our homeland.

Our interconnectedness has also changed our perspective. Fifty years ago, it was possible to ignore the world on the other side of the oceans. Now, thanks to television and full-color newspapers, world crises are in every home. My daughter Jessica illustrated this point for me. Her senior thesis at Harvard was about the ways that photography has made the world smaller. She told me that the day after Pearl Harbor was bombed, there were no pictures of the event on the cover of the *New York Times*. When the tsunami roared through the Indian Ocean in 2004, images of destruction were on the cover of every newspaper in the country the next morning. And Americans responded with overwhelming compassion.

Today, the Baileys are more aware of national civil wars, hunger and poverty than at any time in history. They understand that terrorists are incubated in the anarchy of Mogadishu. They know that an AIDS epidemic in Africa could affect America within a decade. And when they see suffering kids in Darfur, they want something to be done about it.

World affairs still are not their prime concern. They have too much going on right here at home to focus fully on failing states halfway around the world. They expect America to take care of its own security and prosperity before anyone else's. They oppose sending American sons and daughters into harm's way every time a country fails to take care of itself. They think it is unfair for us to shoulder all the burdens of the world. Still, the pictures pull at their heartstrings. The stories of terrorist havens and emerging diseases in the far corners of the world scare them. They understand that something must be done.

We need to create meaningful international solutions to these problems. As it is currently constituted, the UN cannot do the job. The Arab League neither wants to nor can deal with Hezbollah in

Lebanon; the African Union cannot deal with Somalia and other ad hoc alliances have proven equally insufficient.

Recently, over a great lunch of homemade chicken salad and cold cuts, my good friend Les Gelb shared a thought. For years, Les was a *New York Times* correspondent, columnist and editorial page editor. More recently, he ran the Council on Foreign Relations and sat on the Hart–Rudman commission. When I am looking for creative thinking on international relations, I often call Les.

Based on his nugget of an idea, I believe that we should replace UN peacekeepers with a new international force still under the auspices of the UN and funded by participating countries. The United States would offer training, so this force would have more capability than today's UN peacekeepers. Any country could join the force by agreeing to have a small percentage of its soldiers participate or by offering material support. A critical mass of participating nations (maybe 25%), subject to a veto by the permanent members of the UN Security Council, could vote to deploy the force to stabilize troubled areas. Separate from the veto, a country that did not want its soldiers to participate in any specific mission would not have to send them. Each country could opt in or out of each deployment.

When deployed, this force would have a broad mandate. It would be empowered to go after nations that were aiding and harboring terrorist groups that might pose a danger years in the future (if intelligence found an immediate danger, we would depend on U.S. strike forces). It would be used to prevent the kind of brutality now seen in Darfur, Sudan, which the world seems powerless to halt.

Unlike today's UN force, this international force would be well trained. Best of all, it would be free of much of the bureaucracy and cynicism that has so often paralyzed the UN over the last fifty years.

It is not our job to save all failing nations. It is not within our power to single-handedly take out all rogue states. Much as we'd like to, we alone cannot stop all civil wars and local atrocities. But it is in our interest to save certain failing nations, contain certain rogue states and deal with certain tragic humanitarian crises. This new UN force would accomplish more of our goals, while also keeping thousands of American soldiers out of harm's way.

Improve Homeland Defense

A large part of protecting our country in today's world is eliminating threats before they can get anywhere close to harming us. But there are so many threats from so many places that we need to have a defense too. Offense alone cannot guarantee our security.

Of all the Bush administration's failings, its failure to protect homeland security may be its greatest. This administration gets low grades for its ability to adequately protect our borders and ports; our roads, rails and skies; and our electric, nuclear and cyber networks. I don't have room to detail every failure. That would take its own book. (I recommend the *9/11 Commission Report* and anything Richard Clarke has written.)

There are reasons for the Bush administration's across-the-board failures on homeland security.

The first is a lack of funding. Republicans, when they were in control of Congress, and the administration have constantly underfunded just about every aspect of homeland security. The only thing they agreed to fund somewhat adequately was air security, and that's only because it funds itself, thanks to the September 11th Security Fee, which was proposed immediately after 9/11.

It's not that Congress responded with an absolute no when faced with funding important initiatives. Rather, the Republican leadership put the bare minimum number of dollars into each initiative, just enough that they couldn't be accused of doing nothing, but not nearly enough to do the job. A classic example is nuclear detection devices, which I've been fighting to implement for years. Probably the greatest danger we face from terrorists is, God forbid, a terrorist smuggling a nuclear device into the country and detonating it in a city. Nuclear detection devices at every port that sends us containers and at every border crossing from Mexico or Canada could essentially ensure that a nuclear device can't get in. The cost of doing it is estimated to be about $1 billion. The Bush administration and the Republican leadership, always dyspeptic about spending money, are clever enough not to cut this program entirely. Instead, in 2003 for instance, it appropriated about $5 million to "begin research." (Since then, we have had some success in increasing the number, but not nearly enough.)

Of course, the real reason they severely underfunded just about every homeland security initiative was because of the economic royalists' credo—cut taxes and strangle government above all else—and its stranglehold on their leadership. Even with homeland security, where there is no debate that it's a basic government responsibility, the royalists would prefer more tax cuts for the wealthy to more money to protect us. Department of Homeland Security Secretary Michael Chertoff went so far as to make the bizarre claim that funding homeland security will play into bin Laden's hand by sapping us of our strength.

The second reason the administration and its congressional allies have failed on homeland security is a lack of focus. For whatever reason, they don't seem interested in executing a long-term plan to build homeland security infrastructure. Perhaps it's because, at their core, they are uncomfortable with government of any kind. Creating a robust homeland security apparatus where before there was very little inevitably entails new responsibilities for the government. Many senior Republicans who would rather drown government than improve it are ideologically allergic to the type of sustained focus on governmental structures that improving homeland security would require.

In a most chilling example, in the summer of 2006, just before authorities in London uncovered the plot to use liquid explosives on US-bound flights, the Department of Homeland Security (DHS) tried to significantly cut funding for technology to detect such explosives. Since the plot was uncovered, funding is now back up. But it illustrates their scattershot approach to homeland security—responding temporarily to each incident after it occurs, never finishing the job, and then, when the next incident happens, moving on again.

If the administration had stayed focused on liquid explosives from the start, in all likelihood, detection devices would be on-line by now and each of us could be saved the hassle of culling toiletries into quart-size plastic storage bags and three-ounce plastic bottles.

The DHS, a massive agglomeration of agencies thrown together without enough forethought or planning, contributes to this lack of focus. In retrospect, the creation of DHS may well have been a

mistake; serious thought should be given to breaking it back down. If the Department of Defense is the mother of all pork, then the Homeland Security Department is a fast-growing piglet. DHS's funding formula has as much to do with favored congressional districts and the targeting of purple states as it does with vulnerable terrorist targets. It's not only New York and Washington, D.C., that need antiterrorist funding. Ports, airports, mass transit systems, federal buildings and sensitive facilities all over the country also need it. Regional petting zoos and popcorn museums, however, don't.

These three failures—a lack of funding, a lack of focus and a surfeit of pork politics—permeate every area of homeland security. Here are five key areas, and a couple of priorities in each, that need more funding, more focus and less politics.

PORTS

- Check every container that comes into our country
- Require tamper-proof seals to be put on all containers
- Perform background checks of all port employees here and abroad

AVIATION

- Check all cargo loaded onto passenger planes
- Improve defense against soldier-fired missiles

MASS TRANSIT

- Place detection devices no bigger than smoke alarms—which would detect explosive, biological and chemical materials—in every rail station in the country
- Increase rail security personnel

TRUCKS

- Require a GPS tracking system aboard every truck that carries hazardous materials
- Improve background checks for drivers of hazardous materials transports

Nuclear, Biological and Chemical

- Develop detection devices to prevent dangerous items from entering and being transported within the country
- Improve security at high-risk facilities

Terrorism has become such a popular political football over the last few years that it is sometimes hard to remember its true nature. Because of technology, small groups of bad people today pose an existential threat to our peace and security on a scale that historically has been limited to the world's top superpowers. In this new world, the old rules do not apply. New principles and tactics are needed to meet the threat.

After September 11th, President Bush and the Republican Party were quicker to rally around a new vision for the changed world. Since many in the Democratic Party rejected their vision and we had not yet fully formed our own, Republican strategists created a clever narrative: "Democrats don't get it. They don't think the world has changed."

Democrats were vulnerable to the attack; it was easy enough for Republicans to spin our opposition to the Bush vision into the claim that we opposed any change to the pre-9/11 status quo. Because of the situation in Iraq, Republicans were not able to effectively rile voters again in 2006, though Lord knows they tried. As Iraq fades as a politically potent issue over the next few years, the tough-on-terror argument will come roaring back (especially if John McCain is the Republican candidate for president in 2008). Democrats must be prepared with a satisfying answer that is strong, smart and global.

This section of the book has been an attempt to get beyond the old dynamic. First, we must clearly and with a unified voice communicate that we too believe the world is completely changed and much more dangerous. Second, we must describe our vision of how to protect America in this changed world. And finally, we must propose tactics that will help us accomplish our vision.

We start with some advantages, not the least of which is that the Bush administration's foreign policy failures are becoming increasingly self-explanatory to the Baileys and to the entire country. There is no longer much need to talk about what Bush is doing wrong; instead, it's time to talk about what we would do right.

CONCLUSION

AS I SIT HERE PUTTING THE FINISHING TOUCHES ON THIS BOOK, I feel good. Tomorrow is Thanksgiving (which, this year, is also my fifty-sixth birthday), so I have Iris's sweet potato pie to pick at and tomorrow's feast to look forward to. I have much to thank God for. This is my fourteenth post–election Thanksgiving since I entered politics in 1974; at this moment, I don't recall a year when the sweet potato pie tasted sweeter.

I'm eager for the 110th Congress, the first since 1994 that will be controlled by Democrats, to get started. As part of a Senate team that will be led by Harry Reid and will include the principled and forceful Dick Durbin (my friend and roommate since 1982) and the wise and steady Patty Murray, I am brimming with optimism.

This is an easy moment in which to be optimistic. Two weeks and a day ago we won a close election, our first in years. Our Senate leadership team is as strong as any in memory. There are plenty of promising Democrats who may vie for the presidency in 2008.

Of course, as I write, we have not yet spent an hour in control of Congress. We have not yet sat down with Republican legislators who, after years of control, are ill accustomed to minority status. We have not yet forged compromise with a president who claims to believe in bipartisanship but so far has not shown it. We have not yet (much) suffered the bitter battles of warring factions within our own party. Most important, we have not yet begun to tackle the many pressing issues that are facing our country.

As I write this, in the afterglow of our victory, it is easy to be optimistic. But as you read this, the band could already be playing a different tune.

Whether politicians learn from the message that we've just been sent or devolve into the same old patterns, there's one thing that won't change.

There's a family out there—they work hard, they love each other and they believe in this country. They live near Albany or Atlanta;

Syracuse or St. Paul; Rochester or Richmond; Bakersfield, Buffalo, Boise or Brooklyn. They think life's pretty good—but in the fast-changing world, they could use a hand.

As politicians and elected officials, no matter what party we are affiliated with or what region of the country we come from, our job is reach out to that family. Our job is to make America and its government work a little better for them.

So, this moment—after we Democrats have won, but before we've started—is about opportunity, not celebration. Elections are always the first step, never the goal. Now that we have been elected, the time has come to answer that essential question that almost every Democrat, in every corner of the country, is still asked almost every day: What do Democrats stand for?

If we seize this opportunity over the next twenty-four months, if we finally and unequivocally show the Baileys how much we believe in them and how hard we can work for them, there's one thing I can tell you for sure: On Thanksgiving Day 2008, the sweet potato pie will taste even sweeter than it does today.

Chuck Schumer
Brooklyn, November 2006

ACKNOWLEDGMENTS

FIRST, I WANT to thank my family. Iris, Jessica and Alison have spent a lifetime living with my endless schedule and exhausting energy, both of which were exacerbated by this book. I want to apologize for taking over the den for months on end and to thank them for their limitless patience and support. They each deserve credit: Jessica and Alison as the two greatest joys a father could ask for; Iris, for raising such incredible daughters and, despite her own busy career, being my sounding board and our family's stalwart.

Special and heartfelt thanks, as well, to my brother, Bob, both for his counsel and for serving as my counsel—he's as great a brother as he is a lawyer; to my sister, Fran, who's always keeping me on my toes; to my parents and to the entire Schumer family.

To work with me on this book, I looked for someone with extraordinary energy, eloquence and insight—Daniel Squadron was the perfect choice. Twice I have hired him with high expectations (as a top aide in the Senate and for this project), and twice he has exceeded them. Whatever success this book has, he deserves much credit. Daniel has talent to burn; any path he chooses, political or otherwise, I have no doubt he'll continue to hit home runs.

Jim Kessler is also due a special thank-you for his early work with me on the book, much of which has been incorporated. I never could have recalled and recounted my prior elections nearly as creatively or effectively as he did. And his insights about the state of the Democratic Party are, in a word, invaluable.

Carol Kellermann, my best friend since college, also contributed thoughtful and fascinating material early in the project. Since then, she has read the manuscript more times than I, or she, would like to remember. The book and I share something in common: Without Carol's ideas, insights, intellect and wisdom, we would be much less than we are now.

Special thanks as well to my editor, Leigh Haber, for adapting to the "Schumer method": thriving under tough questioning and tight deadlines yet always keeping her eye on the ball. Incredibly, she got it done. I also deeply appreciate the commitment that Steve Murphy and Liz Perl made from the beginning—even before we took back the Senate. Many thanks, too, to Mary Lengle and Katrina Weidknecht for guiding us through unfamiliar media territory, and to Bob Anderson, Nancy Bailey (for real!), Donna Bellis, Keith Biery, Sara Cox, Nancy Elgin, Chris Gaugler, Brooke Myers, Angela Polidoro, Staci Sander and Sara Vigneri. The combination of the political calendar and publication date created an impossibly ambitious schedule that we only met because of the dedication of the entire Rodale team.

Arthur Klebanoff has been a friend since college and, despite serving as my agent, he continues to be. He is, it turns out, as much a shepherd as an agent—and is equally prodigious as both.

Mike Lynch, Martin Brennan, Mark O'Donoghue, Josh Isay and Hank Morris, five of the smartest people I know, each of whom has been so important in guiding my career, were generous with their sage advice and astute analysis; as always, I owe them much. Martin, my state director, provided thoughtful and incisive edits that unmasked a literary sensibility to match his political instincts; I am sure he was a man of letters in a previous life (and will be in a future one). Mark is a true intellectual and great friend; he discovered much that otherwise would have been missed. I sang the praises of Mike, Josh and Hank in the body of the book—they deserve every compliment and more.

I also want to express my gratitude to Harry Reid, who has been a best friend and a mentor, and who offered insightful comments on this book, and to my Senate colleagues, with whom I talk about these issues all the time and who have, in ways big and small, shaped my thinking and contributed to the ideas included here.

In thinking about this book, I discussed foreign policy with Mike Froman and the Foreign Policy Leadership Council, Ambassador Richard Holbrooke and, particularly, Les Gelb. I want to thank each for their time and their insights (though they may not agree with where I've ended up). Likewise, Chris Cerf critiqued my thoughts about public education and offered up more than a few of his own— he deserves much thanks and credit for both.

When I reflect on my years in elective office, there is nary a memory that does not include one of the incredible individuals who has, over the years, worked for me. I'm sure there are elected officials who are easier to work for than I am, but it is hard to imagine that there are any who are more appreciative. For thirty-two years, I have been blessed with the greatest staff in the world. All the Schumerland alums out there know as well as I do that the accomplishments and ideas in this book (and in my career) are as much theirs as mine. Thank you.

I want to single out the exceptional regional representatives who throughout my first term taught me so much about each corner of the state I love. Jack O'Donnell, Scott Sroka, Joe Hamm, Jill Harvey, Amanda Spellicy, Steve Mann, Jean Bordewich and Chris Hahn are world-class politicos—thank God they love New York State as much as I do.

For offering to sacrifice some of their free time to work independently on this book with me and for adding so much to it, I want to thank my education and health wonk, Heather Langdon, who is wise beyond her years; my finance guru, Jeff Hamond; Cyndi Bauerly, who in her day job is my legislative director from heaven (and Minnesota); and David Hantman, my chief of staff, whose masterly analysis and superb judgment are always crucial and were while writing this book—even when I didn't listen. Risa Heller brought her remarkable combination of moxy, charm, savvy and dedication to this project; among her many virtues, she is an exceptional communications director. Thanks also to the members of my staff who have kept all the balls in the air and have made my complex life and schedule manageable: Sam Schaeffer, Lisa Soto, Nick Kutryb, Bridget Petroczuk, Kim Magee and Ryan Whalen.

I mentioned the four great DSCC leaders—Ruth, Gehrig, DiMaggio and Mantle—earlier in the book and will do so again now. Without J. B. Poersch, Guy Cecil, Julianna Smoot and Phil Singer, as well as Kelly Glynn and the entire DSCC staff, there would have been no victory in 2006 for me to discuss.

Many thanks, as well, to Jane Isay, for the title (and other great suggestions), and to Eric Schultz, Matt Cohen, Josh Kriegman, Matt Kutcher, Rebecca Richards, Bradley Bazzle, Patrick Raden Keefe and others for their generosity and keen advice.

The book owes much to the late Howard Squadron, to Anne Squadron and to the Squadron family (especially Bill, Rich, Diane and Seth). Particular thanks to Liz Weinstein, whose instinctual understanding of the Baileys helped immeasurably (as did her support through six months of losing Daniel on Sunday nights).

As I have traveled around the state and the country, countless people have offered suggestions and ideas. Their contributions are anonymous but invaluable. Whoever and wherever they are, they deserve a large share of credit.

Last, but certainly not least, I want to thank all of my nineteen million constituents—from Appleby, to Bailey, to Zutter—who have offered me their trust, and from whom I have learned so much over the last three decades. They are my driving force and my inspiration.

POLO PUBLIC LIBRARY DISTRICT
302 W. MASON ST.
POLO, IL 61064

Name Index

ABOUT THE AUTHORS

CHUCK SCHUMER was elected to the New York State Assembly at age 23—making him one of the youngest members since Theodore Roosevelt. Six years later he was elected to Congress at the age of 29. In his eighteen-year career in the House of Representatives, he accumulated an impressive slew of accomplishments, from the Brady Bill and assault weapons ban to the Violence Against Women Act and the Freedom of Access to Clinic Entrances Act, from the Omnibus Crime Bill, which is the law that put 100,000 cops on the beat, to credit card and other consumer protection laws.

In 1998, he ran for Senate from New York State, challenging and defeating the three-term incumbent, Alfonse D'Amato. In the Senate, he hit the ground running. His first-term accomplishments included bringing low-cost air service to upstate New York, passing college tuition deductibility for middle-class families, working to expand access to generic drugs, fighting predatory lending, leading the fight to keep extreme judges off the bench and securing $20 billion to rebuild New York following the September 11th terror attacks. In 2004, he was reelected to the Senate with the largest percentage of the vote in New York State history.

For the 2006 election cycle, Chuck was the senator in charge of the Democratic Senate Campaign Committee (DSCC), the organization responsible for electing Democrats to that chamber; he has been widely recognized for crafting the successful strategy to win the majority for the Democratic Party.

In the newly formed 110th Congress, Chuck will again be in charge of the DSCC and, in his new role of vice chairman of the Caucus, is now the third-ranking Democrat in the Senate.

A graduate of Madison High School, Harvard College and Harvard Law School, Chuck was born and raised in Brooklyn, where he still lives with his family. This is his first book.

DANIEL SQUADRON has worked extensively in politics and government, among other pursuits. Raised in the Bronx, he is a graduate of Yale and currently lives in Brooklyn.

WITHDRAWN